The Heroin Users

The Heroin Users

Tam Stewart

An Imprint of HarperCollins*Publishers*

Pandora
An Imprint of HarperCollins*Publishers*
77–85 Fulham Palace Road,
Hammersmith, London W6 8JB

First published by Pandora Press 1987
This revised edition 1996
10 9 8 7 6 5 4 3 2 1

A catalogue record for this book
is available from the British Library

ISBN 0 04 440974 5

Printed in Great Britain by
Caledonian International Book Manufacturing Ltd, Glasgow, G64

ℭ Contents

Acknowledgements

Firstly, I must thank Elizabeth Young, journalist and writer, for her support and encouragement during the preparation of this second edition.

I would like to thank all the heroin users who so generously shared their experiences with me, making this book possible. All the individuals described in the text are real people and their comments are genuine but their names have been changed to protect their privacy.

Friends have helped with the project in all sorts of ways and I owe special thanks to Kevin who encouraged me from the start and supplied constructive criticism as and when required. I am also indebted to Robbie for his advice, optimism, encouragement and helpful comments.

In the professional sector many people were very willing to offer advice and assistance. My special thanks are due to Dr James Willis, former Consultant at the Liverpool Drug Dependency Clinic. I am grateful for assistance given by Dr Brian Wells and Dr David Forshaw from the Drug Dependency Unit at the Maudsley Hospital in London. I am indebted to Dr Susan Boobis, advisor to the National Childbirth Trust, for her advice and speedy response to my request for information.

Dr John Marks helped in many ways, offering useful advice as well as articles and information needed to complete this second edition. Dr R. Newcombe of 3D Research Bureau in Liverpool provided invaluable research material and Gary Sutton of Fairways clinic in London was always willing to confirm important factual details.

Many organisations which deal with drug addicts responded promptly when I asked for advice or information and I would like to thank them all, especially Phoenix House, Alpha House, Inward House, the Blenheim Project, City Roads, Narcotics Anonymous and the Bridge Project. The Institute for the Study of Drug Dependence was also most helpful.

I wish to thank SCODA (Standing Conference on Drug Abuse) for their ongoing advice and assistance during the preparation of the manuscript. The Home Office responded most readily to my enquiries and was very helpful in supplying background information promptly.

I would like to thank Jane Hawksley, my editor, for her continued encouragement and helpful guidance. Special thanks are due to Doris, my mother, for her dedicated effort in typing the manuscript, to Mick for his patience and his faith in me and to Arthur for his support and encouragement. In particular, I am grateful to Gary McDermott for his loving support.

Thanks are due to Westminster Music Ltd for permission to reproduce lyrics from 'Suzanne' by Leonard Cohen; to Pink Floyd Music Publishers Ltd for lyrics from 'Comfortably Numb' by Roger Waters, © 1979 by Pink Floyd Music Publishers Ltd; to Logo Songs Ltd for lyrics from 'The Needle of Death' by Bert Jansch, © 1973 by Heathside Music Ltd; and to RCA Music Ltd for lyrics from 'Heroin' by Lou Reed (Velvet Underground). Lyrics from 'China White', words and music by Lowell George, © Naked Snake, and from 'Precious Angel', words and music by Bob Dylan, © Special Rider Music, are reproduced by kind permission of the British publisher Warner Bros Music Limited.

Glossary

amp	injectable form of drug
bad hit	injection resulting in unpleasant side effects
bird	prison sentence
(in) bulk	in a bad state
busies	police
buzz	good feeling induced by drug
chasing the dragon	smoking heroin
cold turkey	withdrawal symptoms
crank up	inject
cut	adulterate drug with another substance
dope	usually cannabis
draw	cannabis
fix	inject
gear	heroin
get a line	get needle successfully into vein
gun	syringe
habit	state of addiction
hassle	trouble, bother
hit	one dose of drug – usually heroin
juice	methadone
kite	fraudulent use of someone's cheques
linctus	methadone
meth	methadone
nicked	arrested
nod out	doze after taking heroin
OD	overdose
pinned out	refers to shrinking of pupils of eyes after taking heroin
rush	sudden surge of pleasure associated with injection of heroin

scag	heroin
score	buy drugs
script	prescription for controlled drug
shoot up	inject
sick	suffering from withdrawal symptoms
skiddies	underpants
smack	heroin
snort	sniff drug up nose
spike	needle for syringe
stoned	under influence of drug
straight	not drugged, someone who does not take drugs
tick	credit
toot	a snort (usually heroin or cocaine) can also refer to smoking heroin
wimp	weakling, drip
works	syringe

Introduction to New Edition

By way of introduction, let me state what this book is and is not. It is an attempt to describe the sort of life experienced by heroin users, especially those who move on from experimenting with drugs to a state of addiction. It draws on my experience of many years as an addict, both using street drugs and as a client of a Merseyside drug clinic. It is not, however, an autobiography, but includes comments and observations made by many other addicts who shared their insights with me over the years. Their views were recorded and are quoted throughout this book. I have endeavoured to trace the path of addiction from the first acquaintance with heroin to the treatments and cures available. My goal has been to tell the truth as addicts see it, to explode the myths of heroin as a demon drug and junkies as public enemy number one.

Since I completed the book, however, the focus of debate has changed. Whilst the experience of the addict has remained much the same, it is the responses of society and, in particular, the type of treatment available to addicts that are uppermost in the minds of observers and participants alike. From politicians and policemen to the man in the street, everyone has a viewpoint on what should be done about addiction and how society should respond to both heroin users and their suppliers. Indeed, the debate has moved beyond heroin. It has become apparent that drug use in general touches the majority of young people today. New drugs abound. Ice, white, ecstasy are three names that spring to mind: drug abuse rather than addiction to any particular drug has become the issue.

Doctors, politicians and those working in the drugs' field are acknowledging the obvious trends they see before them. Keith Hellawell, West Yorkshire Chief Constable and drugs spokesman for the Association of Chief Police Officers, recently stated that 'within a decade, nine out of ten of our 16-year-olds could be drug dealers or drug takers.'(1) He points out that we can expect a similar increase in drug related crime and violence – at present 50 to 60 per cent of all property crime is narcotics related, and some observers suggest the figure is even higher, at 85 per cent of all crime. Education, arresting dealers and seizing more drugs appear to be Hellawell's answer to the problem, but none of these things has been seen to work so far. Even he accepts that despite increased police activity and success, 'we are on a downward spiral into a drug culture'(2).

Recognising this fact, other senior law enforcers and politicians are suggesting that we should radically alter our approach. Cdr John Grieve of Scotland Yard asks that we might consider 'controlled legalisation'(3) and Raymond Kendall, Secretary General of Interpol favours 'decriminalisation for the user'(3). It is becoming impossible to enforce drug laws and politicians are starting to recognise the fact: critics of current policy include four out of five senior police officers and 70 per cent of GPs (4). The war on drugs is still raging. The public have endured over ten years of brainwashing by the media. They have been led to believe that 'there is no better reason for building a prison than filling it with drug traffickers' (5). The law makers and politicians have put themselves in a Catch-22 situation; some would like to change the drug laws but few dare to risk the wrath of a public they themselves have worked hard to inflame.

In the present climate, what can most heroin users expect? Health problems, unemployment, arrest and imprisonment – and little in terms of realistic or helpful treatment from drug clinics or doctors. Why? Because the American model of treatment for heroin addiction has for some time been adopted by the majority of clinics and doctors here. The goal of such treatment is abstinence. Methods of achieving this happy state vary, but methadone is usually offered as an alternative to in-patient hospital detoxification. Most addicts want neither. What they want is a prescription for legally obtained pure heroin which they hope to continue to receive until they wish to stop taking drugs. And they may not want to stop taking drugs for some years to come. In fact, it has been demonstrated that 'the addictive mental set is impervious to external agency and that abstinence is achieved spontaneously at a rate of about 3% per annum'(6) – in other words, addicts only stop when they want to and no outside factors (other than inability to obtain the drugs) will influence their behaviour. As the drug remains available on the black market, in the absence of a legal supply, that is where they will continue to go. Why then do doctors here continue to copy the American response to drug users when it has been seen to fail? Perhaps because they share an intrinsic puritanism that lies at the root of such policies: their aim is prohibition. They believe that we can stamp out drug abuse. Accordingly, those studies that suggest decriminalisation or applaud the benefits of offering realistic prescriptions of controlled drugs via clinics are dismissed as unproved or based on faulty logic – or seen as special pleading. Furthermore, during the 'Thatcher Era' our 'special relationship' with America meant that the success of any system totally opposed to the American model could have been a source of severe embarrassment to those in power. Indeed, it is interesting to note that, early in this decade, a storm blew up in Washington 'when the major in-depth US television news report *Sixty Minutes* broadcast a favourable report' on the work of Dr John Marks, Consultant Psychiatrist at the Widnes and Warrington drug clinics on Merseyside, 'just as President George Bush was whipping up support for a global military offensive against drugs'(7).

These Merseyside clinics were pioneering a return to the former British System of treating addicts by maintaining them on legally prescribed heroin – and achieving dramatic success. Studies among clients there showed over 90 per cent reduction in acquisitive crime and zero infection from HIV. In an editorial applauding this success *The British Journal of Hospital Medicine* (1994) remarked, 'the reluctance of British doctors to reinstate the British System more widely seems to be due to the past 30 years of touting the American system, especially in London'. The same article reminds us that 'it would be difficult to create a more unhealthy, more dangerous, more criminalising, more socially destructive, more expensive, more efficient way of making heroin available than we do now under prohibition'(8). Herein lies the paradox. Most treatment available to heroin users in this country aims to separate the addict from heroin immediately. As there is no legal way of obtaining the drug without a doctor's prescription, treatment is, for the most part, another means of enforcing prohibition, ignoring the fact that 'coercion is not a treatment option'(9). It is not, therefore, surprising that many addicts are reluctant to seek treatment at all. When they do, it is often as a means of pacifying the courts.

If, however, they had been lucky enough to attend the Widnes Clinic, addicts could have received a prescription for heroin and been effectively maintained on clean, pure, legal drugs until they eventually felt ready to come off drugs altogether. At most other clinics, however, they would be offered either a brief detoxification using methadone, a short stay in hospital to come off, or a long term maintenance prescription for methadone. Methadone is a heroin substitute, synthesised during the Second World War by the Nazis to replace the supplies of opiates that were unavailable at the time. Research has shown that it is 19 times more toxic than heroin(10), and responsible for a far greater number of deaths per annum(11). On the whole, addicts prefer heroin but often accept methadone as a currency they can trade or sell to buy black market heroin. Doctors who refuse to prescribe heroin either for ethical or political reasons, allow themselves to believe that they have cured the heroin problem among their clients because they have sent them away with a prescription for methadone. Their patients know better, and so do the major criminals who benefit from the heroin trade.

Home Office sources revealed that the number of people receiving prescriptions for heroin each year in the UK is below 200 – 'somewhere between 150 and 200 (addicts) receive prescriptions for diamorphine each year', adding that such cases fall into a 'highly specialised and very tiny niche in treatment policies'. While the law allows for the prescribing of diamorphine, 'the preponderate view of the medical profession is that such prescribing is very specialised and justified only in very particular cases'(12).

Clearly, in the present climate of medical (and political) opinion, Dr Marks' success became a thorn in the side of confirmed prohibitionists and those who see methadone as the only appropriate treatment response to those individuals not yet able or willing to come off heroin. It follows that, early in 1995, the purchasers of local health care were replaced by individuals whose attitudes reflected government preferences in treatment policies. These new health care purchasers took the decision to cease using the services of Dr Marks – without consulting the 62 per cent of his clients known to be opposed to a methadone-only regime of treatment. Officials in the Health Service appeared to see Dr Marks as a renegade rather than the mastermind of a unique experiment and sole hope of many addicts in the Mersey region. Now they have succeeded in marginalising him so that addicts from Liverpool and surrounding areas who previously benefited from his daring stand against reactionary policies are being deprived of his help. Already the effects of his loss are being felt among his former patients as they begin to drift back to the black market and, in desperation, some turn to prostitution or other forms of crime.

It has long been understood that a country can only be policed by consent. Similarly, addicts can only be treated by consent. If they are not happy with the treatment on offer they will find ways around it. How can a treatment be successful when it swaps an addiction to a drug that takes two weeks to come off (heroin) for addiction to another (methadone) that can take up to six months to come off? When that treatment does not take addicts out of the black market but leaves them facing many of the problems they hoped to escape from by going to a clinic in the first place?

The crucial factor in terms of treatment for addicts is flexibility. Indeed, 'it has been found that a variety of treatment needs to be offered, and that different users respond to different approaches and even the same user may respond to different approaches at different stages in their addiction'(13). If this is so, then surely the greater the number of treatment options, the greater the number of addicts presenting themselves at clinics will be. Why should heroin maintenance be arbitrarily viewed as unacceptable? Even a spokesman at the Home Office stated that it was 'undeniably true' that addicts can remain well and productive for 20 years or more when maintained on diamorphine.

Professionals dealing with addicts who have seen the benefits of heroin maintenance, and likewise observed the anguish suffered by those trying to survive on the black market, are beginning to suggest that the State has declared war on its citizens – that in fact, what we are seeing is a kind of civil war; the war on drugs is a war on those who take them as well as those who supply them. These people are citizens. Surely our own citizens cannot constitute 'the greatest peacetime threat to our national well-being'(14)? What about nuclear testing, the hole in the ozone layer? Unemployment? Heart disease? Pollution? Famine? We encourage youngsters to learn to swim but if we looked at the figures, we would find that 448 people drown each year. We bring back duty-free cigarettes from our holidays and hand them out to friends without pointing out that 100,000 smokers will be dead by the end of the year(15). And what about the thousands killed on our roads annually? Home Office figures for sporting deaths in England and Wales show that, in 1982, 15 people died playing ball games, 19 died in horse riding accidents,

4 while cycling and 9 mountaineering or climbing. In short, just being alive is a risk. The death rates from illegal drugs are often far lower than those from many 'acceptable' leisure activities; all lawful pursuits. In a ten year period, the Widnes clinic reported no drug related deaths among its clients. They were far safer taking heroin than going swimming. Surely, it is time to look beyond the hysteria generated by the very word 'heroin' and start taking an honest look at the real facts. Drugs are here to stay whether we like it or not. There are an estimated 150,000 heroin users in this country at the present time. A very small number of these people can obtain the drugs on which they have become dependent without breaking the law. A high percentage of them must repeatedly commit crimes to raise the vast sums needed to finance their habits. A return to the British System pioneered by Dr Marks in Widnes would produce a dramatic improvement in the lives of heroin users. With realistic prescriptions for the drugs they need – or even under some other method of supply such as controlled legalisation/decriminalisation – heroin addicts could carry on with their lives in peace. For pity's sake, if for no other reason, the smug reactionary prohibitionists in London and elsewhere must review their punitive policies and the law makers must think again. They must find the courage to address the realities of drug abuse rather than continue hiding behind the myth that the war on drugs can be won.

There have been many twists and turns in the progress of drug treatment and policies since this book was first completed but it seems that 'the end of all our journeying has been to arrive back where we started from'. We have reached a watershed. Does prohibition limp towards 'an inevitable collapse'(16), as people realise that 'the constant harping on prohibition is not only unrealistic but irresponsible'(16), or are we about to see an escalation of violence as the gangsters and the police 'shoot it out'? The last couplet from Shakespeare's *The Tempest* seems an appropriate final word from the point of view of the drug user, who would be trapped in the inevitable cross fire:

As you from crimes would pardoned be,
Let your indulgence set me free.

Notes

1 & 2 '90% of Kids will be Druggies in Ten Years' *The Sun*, 2 November 1995.

3 'Methadone and Madness' Liz Young. *Guardian*, 20 August 1995.
4 BMA Survey, April 1994.
   ACPO conference, May 1994
  (Also both quoted in John Marks' article, 'Who Killed the British System?', *Lancet*)
5 David Mellor, Conservative Party Conference, 1985.
6 Stimson G. & Oppenheimer E., *Heroin addiction*, Tavistock, London, 1982. This quotation taken from 'Reply to Task Force', correspondence between Halton NHS Trust and Department of Health.
7 Henman A. *Harm Reduction on Merseyside: The rise and fall of a radical paradigm of health care for illicit drug users*, (Paper presented at the Conference 'Drug Policy in the 90's: the Changing Climate' – Liverpool John Moore's University, 29/30 June 1995.)
8 'Drug Misuse and Social Cost', *British Journal of Hospital Medicine*, 1994.
9 A. Palombella, 'Philosophy Widnes Drug Dependency Unit', 1991 (revised 1994).
10 John Marks, *The Lancet*, vol 343, 16 April 1994.
11 Dr R. Newcombe, *Methadone Mortality*, 3D Research Bureau, Liverpool, June 1995. Discussion paper for Conference, 'Drug Policy on the 90's: the Changing Climate' held at John Moore's University, Liverpool.
12 Telephone conversation between myself and member of Home Office staff who wished to be quoted only as 'Home Office Sources'. Similar information/views are expressed elsewhere in HMSO publications.
13 As 9 above.
14 Wagstaff A., Maynard A.K., *Economic Aspects of the Illicit Drug Market and Drug Enforcement Policies in the United Kingdom*, Office Research Study Number 95, H.M.S.O., London, 1988. *Interestingly, this statement is also quoted as the opening remark of a section entitled 'Services for Drug Dependency' in the Annual Report of the Director of Public Health for North Cheshire Health District, 1993.
15 Polly Toynbee, 'Ecstasy and the Agony', *The Independent*, November 1995.
16 A. Henman as in 7 above.

Introduction

I have been in and around the heroin scene in Liverpool for many years. Last summer I kicked my heroin habit. I did not really decide to stop. The decision was forced upon me. Things had been hotting up for a while: the bank was on my back; I had nothing left to sell; there was no direction, no creativity, no hope. Sanity was being sucked up the tube. I became marginally paranoid. People were following me. Trips to score caused panic, paranoia, actually something close to terror. I ditched my car for someone else's. They would not know the number. They would not be able to get me. At night I slept with 'It' a hand's reach away – but would I wake in time? Every dawn the door was kicked in by a phantom drug squad and I held my breath listening for their footsteps. I slept with the curtains parted so I would wake at first light to pre-empt their beastly plans.

In this month, July, I rowed and raged, I fell out with people. I cried a lot. And I slumbered on, blissful much of the time, in rash, brittle oblivion, numbed and Lethe-lulled on a pillow of never, never, never. Relationships became erratic, but Bobby and I united in mutual need. We got a system going. We were never without. And we were scared, very scared, we might have to be. The money was always found. Food went by the board. We went nowhere except to score. Or to visit other devotees on similar errands. I lost weight. One particular Sunday the paranoia peaked.

We went down around lunchtime to our usual place. The weather was hot. Very hot. There was a party spirit on the streets. Loud music wailed. Rastas hung out of windows in Warwick Street, bare-chested and celebratory, but the scorched grass at the roadside reeked of dog shit and discontent buzzed through the ghetto with the flies. I waited. He was out. Come back in three-quarters of an hour. We did. Sorry. Come at 3 o'clock. Try later. By now there was a queue. A rag-taggle bunch of desperate people who did not care who saw them or who knew what they wanted – so long as they got it. And got it fast. They argued about who would be first when something turned up. The lunacy continued. In cars, in taxis, on motor bikes they set off in convoy to another part of the city. I waited. They had no luck. The madness went on. I went home. I gave up. I would just get sick.

Bobby turned up at teatime. Everything was all right again. Our eyes and noses were dry once more. We had spent six hours of the day and a lot of anxiety just for that. To say nothing of the £60. Self-disgust was swelling like an over-ripe boil. I had almost had enough. I resolved to get the hell out while I was still sane. I resolved to stop. There were no more mountains to climb this side of September; no job, no tasks, no nothing. I phoned a friend in London. I could stay there.

Tuesday was the last of it. At the station I panicked. £20 had been despatched at the last moment. But Bobby did not make it back with the supplies and I left on the train, beside myself, nearly stepping off to wait, after all, for as long as it took. In the toilet, before we even passed Edgehill, I whacked off the last of what I had. The journey passed in seconds, the few when I had my eyes open. Getting my bags to the taxi was quite hard.

I came off in London. It was not easy. I spent August in Wales, looking to the green countryside for a sense of renewal and well-being. In the autumn I began this book.

PART ONE

Initiation Rites

CHAPTER I

ℭ *Into the jaws of the dragon*

Who are the drug takers?

Let's start at the beginning. Two questions spring to mind immediately. Who takes junk and why? Who is easy. You probably already know at least one junkie. No? Think again. They are in all walks of life, in all sorts of jobs. Your first meeting with a drug addict may have been with your doctor or teacher. Perhaps that friendly pharmacist is one, or maybe your son's probation officer. There are lawyers, singers, actors and artists who take junk. Your local butcher, the taxi driver who drove you home yesterday, the ice-cream man, any of them could be strung out. I have met heroin addicts who work in all these jobs. Heroin respects no barriers of class, race, religion or profession. There are junkies of 14 and 40. Just because you want to sample smack you do not have to be instantly recognizable as a weirdo or a freak. You might be a kid of 16, anxious to prove yourself to the big lads: you can take your drugs with the worst of them. You might be a social worker of 25, a bit bored and secretly sympathetic to the users. Really, you could be absolutely anyone. Even detectives in the drug squad have been known to get around to trying it in the end. There are junkies who are talented, beautiful and intelligent. Some are honest and hard-working, others are schemers and thieves. There are drug users who are clean and smart and some who are tatty and smelly. There are wives and mothers, husbands and fathers – and never forget that every addict is somebody's child.

The large numbers of young unemployed people using heroin are perhaps the saddest. For the jobless, smack is a major tranquilliser to blank out the pain of daily rejection by a society that simply has no role for them to fill. For them, and for many others, smack is a kind of inner city homeopathy, the ultimate self-medication, the final antidote to stress, violence and ambition.

This brings me to the question of why people take drugs. That is the million dollar question and the reasons differ. One answer, however, is a lot simpler than many psychologists, doctors, social workers, parents and newspapers would have it. At first, at least, we do it because we like it and we like it because it is nice. It starts out that way, at any rate. You do not feel as if you are corresponding to a page in a sociology textbook by falling prey to the problems of inner city decay. I am not, of course, suggesting that drugs are good for us and I am not advocating their use. What I am doing is setting the record straight. Most drug users, in order to get help, have to pretend that they hate taking drugs and are compelled to do so by bodily need alone. They put on the sackcloth and ashes expected by the doctors and others whose help they ultimately seek. In this way, society takes its pound of flesh and the truth is obscured. Taking heroin may be foolhardy and ill-advised, but, initially, users do have credible motives. We are not all deranged lunatics who enjoy living in squalor facing daily disasters ranging from getting arrested to dying.

Most people first experiment with heroin because they are curious. Heroin has always had its own mystique. The property of musicians, pop stars, writers and wicked, faceless men whose souls are lost, it attracts publicity and publicity creates glamour. Glamour sells. It sells cigarettes, alcohol, cars, consumer goods and it sells heroin. Quite what we bought I am not sure. Rebellion, danger, excitement, talent, a wild reputation, some strange distinction as a bad lot – the 'Billy the Kid Syndrome' – but we wanted something and we got it.

Day-to-day life is fairly humdrum and mundane for most of us, so there is a gap that needs to be filled. Heroin can be the ultimate filler of gaps. It can substitute for career, religion, romance, virtually anything, and if heroin gets there first, everything else takes second place and finally goes by the board. It has often been compared to a lover and if we continue that metaphor, you could say that involvement with drugs is, for many people, like a relationship. Attracted, fascinated, at first you seek out the object of your desire and blunder on into involvement. Only later do things start to go wrong. Ditto with drugs. Only when it is too late does the light at the end of the tunnel go out.

Why is it that would-be junkies do not heed the papers, their teachers, the warnings? Because they look to their own friends, their own peers. They see them surviving, coping, appearing to be having a good time, and they follow, as anyone would, the evidence of their own eyes and ears rather than the dramatized, sensational-ized, patronizing newspaper account written by a hard-pressed journalist hungry for news. And anyway, the human spirit is not so easily crushed by fear. Motor-racing, mountain climbing, skiing and horse riding all carry a death warrant. We are not put off. On the contrary, the danger adds to the value we place on the skills involved. So it is with drugs. The secrecy, the dangers of arrest or disease add to the excitement. If it carries such penalties and risks it must be good. If it is so good, let's try it. Quick.

Of course, there must be deeper reasons. There must be reasons that the average drug taker does not even want to consider. Perhaps the most honest answer to the question 'Why do we do it?' is that nobody really knows. If we did then maybe the disease could be treat-ed, the epidemic halted in its tracks. The trouble is that nobody has ever really isolated the junk bug or understood it. This means that no truly effective vaccine is readily available. People who take heroin have, on the whole, simply been thought to possess deviant personali-ties. Society has always frowned upon self-inflicted wounds. Grudg-ingly, the stomach pump is fetched out for the patient who has attempted suicide.

Time wasted here could be spent on more deserving victims, who have been struck down through no fault of their own. Thus, heroin addicts have been seen with a degree of disapproval and contempt, not least because to get into their situation in the first place, they have had to break the law, not once, but many times. Even if they commit no other crime the act of consuming or even handling the drug puts the user outside the law. Despite the suspicions of society, however, junkies are not suicidal. On the contrary, it is the search for kicks, the longing for new and more intense experiences that leads them on to the dangers of disease and death.

Admittedly, the fact that many people first take heroin for kicks implies a somewhat frivolous grasp on life. It denotes a certain lack of drive and direction. One regular drug user who is a university graduate suggested that I should mention the fact that addicts often have 'a low sense of self-esteem'. Perhaps he was trying to locate his own motives when he continued, 'They may feel that their job is below par; they may be underachievers – lab technicians who are not doctors, doctors who are not consultants or teachers who are not heads of department'. In his view, a belief that they are not living up to their own expectations or those of their friends and relations could be significant. These feelings may not be out in the open but it is possible that such disappointments could, for some people, lie at the root of a drug problem. They may not make someone seek out heroin in the first place, but once they have discovered it, such feelings may be part of the reason why they continue to flirt with it until it becomes a problem in itself.

Drug takers usually start young. You may meet 40-year-old junkies but they are generally old hands. Anyone old enough to dare and young enough to want to is a potential user. Each generation seems to have its drug of choice. Today, young people are keener to try ecstasy than heroin. The availability of drugs in general lies at the root of the problem. They do not seem to discriminate between glue and smack. Heroin has no more mystique for them than a trip to the swimming baths. It is just something else to do when they are bored. Either way, 14 or 24, the young are more foolhardy. They do not value their health and well-being, but take them for granted. Certainly when I started out I was young and fit. It did not enter my head to consider the effect taking heroin might have on my body.

Once heroin does take over, it damages people. It changes them. It makes them want to go on taking it even though they thought they were strong enough to hold out against it. It is, literally, an unknown quantity. By the time you get to know it, it has got you hooked. This is because the craving takes over and becomes a compulsion. Ultimately, it appears to be the action of the drug itself that is the problem rather than the personality of the user. You take it despite yourself, even though there may be times when you do not want to be stoned. This is summed up in the words of one addict I spoke to: 'I don't know why I take it. I don't even like the fucking stuff. I don't even want it. I just do it.' Thus, the motive for taking heroin can finally decline to the level of a conditioned response. Long-term exposure to the drug reduces any personality to its lowest common denominator of desire and need.

If we drop a certain acid onto metal it will burn a hole. This is a simple law, the reaction of one chemical on another. At its simplest level, the human body is only a collection of chemicals. If we drip heroin onto human tissues for long enough it, too, metaphorically speaking, will burn a hole. That hole can only be filled by more heroin. Without it there is pain and anguish. Often, therefore, a person continues to take heroin to avoid a negative experience rather than to achieve a positive one. Thus, the reason why someone takes heroin may change as time goes on. What started out as a pleasurable and exciting adventure can end as a boring and monotonous daily necessity. You think that you will never be 'normal' again without it. This is when you are really stumped to find a way forward.

Of course, most junkies, with a few ultra-masochistic exceptions, do not set out to become addicts. They often do not even set out to take heroin at all. The first rule of the drug culture is that if you are anywhere within reach, heroin will come to you, because even being on the scene where you can get it at all implies an attitude of mind or a set of circumstances that lay you wide open for drug culture devotees to invade, damage and occupy.

You may know someone for years. You could have grown up with them, gone to school or college with them. They could be an older brother or sister, a boyfriend, a lover, a member of a band you play in, someone you see in the pub. You like them, respect them, even look up to them. One day you find out. They take drugs. They might be open and enthusiastic, encouraging you to try it, or they might be secretive and dismissive, saying that it is just something they do and that if you have not tried it before you should not bother. These are the real junkies. They are well-meaning but insidious. You think they are keeping their secrets from you and you even more desperately want in. Like parents who smoke, they will tell you the evils of their habit, but 'Do as I say, not as I do' does not even keep kids off the Embassy Regal. It certainly cannot restrain a potential heroin user. You will soon be asking them to turn you on. They will not refuse. How can they? You have your rights – and you would only get it somewhere else. Before you know it your place on the bandwagon is reserved.

'I'm going to try for the kingdom if I can.'
'Heroin' by the Velvet Underground.

My place on the bandwagon was reserved a long while before I ever took smack. At 18 I went to college. I fell in with the bad crowd as quickly as I could. As I was studying science my contemporaries were largely male. An overweight tomboy with no dress sense,

I had not yet blossomed. I, therefore, became one of the lads. I acquired a tin of Golden Virginia and learnt to roll cigarettes. The lads grew their hair. Those who could grew beards. We were into music and we followed our heroes closely. We favoured the irreverent and anarchic: the Stones, Dylan, Janis Joplin, the Grateful Dead, Jimi Hendrix and the tortured Leonard Cohen. They were the outspoken heroes of our generation. They took risks and they took drugs. The glamour and power of the erupting volcano of rock and pop spewed out a deluge of fine narcotic dust that threatened to cover us all.

I heard 'Heroin' by the Velvet Underground for the first time. I was impressed. An 11-plus success, I was straight out of a single-sex grammar school and playing Hunt the Identity. I wanted to try heroin but I was scared. Some of the friends of the lads I knew were experimenting with it. A classmate was an addict. He was older than the rest of us and we looked up to him. When we gave him a lift in the car, we felt we had a celebrity with us. We watched, intrigued, on the days when he picked up his script. He would come into class and nod out. The teacher told us about him and said it was sad. I felt there must be a deep secret behind his pinned-out, dead eyes. He was silent and smug, sitting quietly, like a downtown Buddha. He had to know something.

What he knew, I chose not to find out for a long time. After much deliberation. I steered clear of smack. My mother's anxious pep talks had gone home. I was ambitious to get to university and smack would not have helped. There is no doubt, however, that the seeds had been sown. By the time I went to university at the end of the year I was a regular dope smoker. I graduated to LSD in my first year but when smack sidled in, I opted out again. I did not risk the heroin experience until years later when I had left university and started work. It presented itself suddenly and unexpectedly. By then, I had no goals to aim for. Life was reduced to a repetitive, disappointing, everyday grind. The rainbow petered out in a dusty classroom. There seemed no reason not to try it and fulfil all those early fantasies. Perhaps what people need is a reason not to take heroin. I felt I had nothing to lose and I took it because it was there.

It was there because I had been going out for several months with a boyfriend who was regularly injecting himself with it. In the early days of our relationship he had carefully hidden his habit from me. As time went on, he revealed the truth bit by bit until the full facts became acceptable to me. He remained the person I cared for. Taking drugs was something he did and it met with my disapproval. For women, being initiated into drug use by a boyfriend or husband is not uncommon. Suzie, who agreed to participate in my efforts to research this book, described the events leading up to her first injection of physeptone, a heroin substitute, in the following way:

> It was 1975. I started out on physeptone via a boyfriend. The first thing I had was half an amp cranked up. I was persuaded to try it. It took two months of watching people every day to get around to that stage. I was terrified. It was like being in hospital and having an injection. I couldn't look.

It was only after I had observed drug abuse at close quarters that I, too, lost a lot of my fear and actually developed a serious urge to find out at last what it was like. I am 99 per cent certain that, had I not been exposed to heroin by someone I respected so much, I would never have tried it. I would, along with millions of others, have looked on aghast while the habit swept the country. At the time when I first tried it, I was doing nothing more dangerous than having a few drinks once or twice a week.

The first hit

> Blow away, blow away
> This cruel reality
> And keep me from its storm.
> from 'China White' by Little Feat

The first hit is nearly always free. This is not because aspiring young Mafiosi set out to advertise their wares, but because you are usually turned on by a friend or lover. Whatever they say, deep, deep down junkies want you to be like them, to share their experiences, to join them, to prove they are not weird outsiders after all. Against their better judgment, they want your acceptance, involvement and approval. Your consent is enough to salve an uneasy conscience. To a new recruit, therefore, drugs which would otherwise be haggled over or sold are freely and generously given. This is no great sacrifice as the amount needed to get a non-user stoned is fair-ly small. The newly converted also bring in a fresh supply of cash and become a new source of drugs for their friends. In the revealing words of one woman: 'When you give someone heroin you know he will have to come back to you for his supply. You will, of course, take your cut before handing over his. He, in turn, will assume you have not done so and will give you more. You are doing all right.'

The first time people try heroin they are obviously quite excited. They have finally plucked up the nerve and cannot wait for the buzz. So what is it actually like? Funnily enough, that is a question I cannot really answer because the heroin hit is probably not exactly the same for any two people. Heroin is the all-purpose drug. It can be all things to all people. This, in my opinion, is partly the secret of its popularity. It does not live up to your preconceptions or expecta-tions. On the contrary, it is far more subtle. It gives you whatever feeling you think you want – oblivion, talent, confidence, peace of mind, energy or stimulation, but only if you persevere. This last fact can constitute a challenge to a bizarre contest: you against the drug. For some men their macho image is on the line. The more they can take and still stand up, the better and braver they are.

There is, of course, much mythology about the experience being like the ultimate orgasm but better. People have described it as totally euphoric, ecstatic, the best and nicest thing that has ever happened to them. In actual fact, the first hit probably comes nowhere near any of these descriptions. It may well even be a com-plete disappointment. Mine was. Along with a lot of other people I have spoken to, I was left feeling disappointed, throwing up and wondering why on earth this was supposed to be the ultimate, the *crème de la crème* of drug experiences.

The way you respond to the drug will, of course, depend on the way in which you choose to take it. Initially, you wlll ponder over this choice. Latterly, you will not care how you get it into your body as long as you do. You will smoke it, snort it, inject it in what-ever quantities you can get. You will take liquids, tablets, powders, cocktails. You will not even consider the question of your health. Your body is merely a barrier between you and it that must be over-come. Need is total. The first time, however, you are cautious.

My first opiate experience was actually with morphine. A little nervous, I turned down the chance of being injected and chose to snort it. Snorting, in drug talk, means sniffing something up your nose as opposed to blowing something down it. In American movies the wealthy snort cocaine with fine silver tubes specially designed for the purpose. In Liverpool bedsits a rolled up bank note is often the order of the day. A dope dealer I knew used to show off by using £20 notes. Most people settle for lesser ones. In time, they might rip bits of paper off anything lying around – an envelope, the corner of the telephone book, an advertising circular. My house used to be full of magazines with rectangular bits torn off the corners of the pages. Whatever is used, it is simply rolled up tightly to form a tube. After the tube is prepared, the gear is put onto a smooth surface and spread into a thin line. Some people keep a tile or mirror for this purpose, others use the back of a library book or a record sleeve, virtually anything which is to hand. The tube is then placed into the least blocked up nostril (Liverpool is the home of catarrh) and the gear is sniffed up through it. People have to take care to hold their breath at this crucial stage. Early on in a drug user's career there can be disasters where an accidental gust of breath sends the gear flying onto the floor. If this happens, people tend to end up on their hands and knees studying the carpet and sniffing hopefully.

The gear goes up and the user sits back to wait for something to happen. When I first tried it I waited in vain for this supposed wonder drug to take effect. Ten minutes or so passed. I complained that nothing had happened. I was told to give it a chance. I waited. I felt let down and complained again. The sceptical old hand who was turning me on eyed me wearily as if he knew what would happen next. He offered me more and I accepted. Five minutes or so elapsed. Suddenly I began to feel odd, very heavy and woozy, slightly giddy. I did not quite feel at ease with the sensations. He studied me. He asked if anything had happened yet. I said that I thought it had, but that it was not much. I was still waiting for the great moment of enlightenment, the great rush. I began to feel sick. I imparted the news and headed for the bathroom. I was stoned and spewing up.

Being sick after taking opiates is not quite like vomiting under any other circumstances. You feel detached. You do not retch violently. You are sick very suddenly in one great, powerful, irrepressible spurt. The feeling is nothing like as unpleasant as when you are drunk or ill. One addict I spoke to actually claimed to enjoy being sick on smack. He told me, 'You could explain it all night, but I used to get a buzz off being sick. You get a euphoric rush as you spew. It's pure relief and I love doing that spew.' I still do not share his feelings. Morphine, I am told, is even more strongly emetic than smack, and on that first occasion I had taken far too much. I was very, very sick.

All new sailors are seasick. All new junkie recruits throw up. Like sailors they ride out their initiation willingly, longing for their sealegs to come. I lay on my friend's settee for two days, dozing and vomiting in turns. It was a weekend and on Monday morning I was still too ill to go to work. Much of the time I was on the nod, which is not unpleasant but is hardly something to sell your all for. Being on the nod is a term used to describe a semi-waking state induced by taking opiates. You appear to doze, your head nodding forward onto your chest. You snatch awake suddenly, jerking your head up, struggling to take in your surroundings. You loll off into a dream again. Relaxed. And you do sometimes dream. In this state reality and dreams merge. You get confused between them. You doze and twitch awake, doze and twitch awake, until maybe two hours have passed. Just as suddenly as you nodded out you will be ultra-alert, hyperactive, up and buzzing, ready to run around and take on the world. Somewhere deep down in your centre there's a glow, a throb, a tingle. A golden thread runs up your spine and out through the top of your head. A happy smack puppet, warm and comfortable, your body dangles around this taut, buzzing chord. You are stoned.

For what it is worth, that, for me, is the heroin high. Along with most people, I find it very difficult to describe. It is too personal and too private. Generally, a sense of well-being and a feeling that problems are lessened or solved are mentioned by other users as important aspects of their high. Here is Jimmy's account:

> You talk a lot and have a feeling of well-being. It's a relaxation. The speedy effect turns into a deeper feeling later. When I'm on it I feel totally relaxed and I feel nice. My problems all go away till I've got no gear again. It's like being sedated but still being able to do things easily. It's not a hassle. It's a dead nice buzz.

Suzie described her first experience as follows:

> I felt very talkative and felt as if I was being far more interest-
> ing than I usually was. I felt generally on top of the world.
> I did really enjoy that. I'll never forget it. It was a Saturday
> afternoon. I felt very extrovert and unlike me. I startled the
> ladies in the corner shop. I went in and started talking and
> talking. I bought a bottle of lemonade – in fact, I think that's
> what made me throw up.

Clearly she felt that smack gave her a new confidence which she
normally lacked. She also highlighted the idea that smack makes
problems fade away: 'I didn't feel as if I had many problems at the
time anyway but if I'd had any they would have all disappeared.'
Tony reported the same feeling: 'I don't feel my problems completely disappear, but I do feel they're less of a problem. They don't seem
to matter so much.' He described his high as follows:

> It changes my personality, elevates my mood. It makes me
> more gregarious. It makes me more enthusiastic about things.
> Not much happens, but you feel enthusiastic. It's Jekyll and
> Hyde. I can feel my mood changing within minutes.

Back in the 1960s and 1970s popular music of the day, as I have
already suggested, offered several versions of the heroin buzz. The
Velvet Underground share the sense of being numbed to pain and
stress in these lines: 'When the heroin's in my blood/And the blood
is in my head/I thank God that I'm not aware/I thank God that I
just don't care.' The folk song 'Needle of Death' provides a different angle on the same idea: 'In peace your mind withdraws/Your
death so near/Your soul can feel no pain.'

The references are many and varied, but the experiences recorded do, in fact, share a surprising number of similarities.

The unpleasant aspects of heroin use, such as nausea and vomiting, may be a point where the person who is temperamentally and
psychologically suited to becoming a drug addict and the rest of
humanity diverge. Most of the junkies I have spoken to have confessed to being sick the first time. For many people that would have
been enough but junkies try again. I did. On that first occasion I
was not high, I was merely very sick, but as soon as I was over that

first disastrous attempt I listened to the reassurances that, if you persevered, you could go through the sickness and finally get the buzz and I was ready to repeat the horrible experience only a few days later.

Becoming addicted to heroin can be hard work but there is a self-destructive element in some of us that will be satisfied. You will find that many long-term junkies also drink and use other drugs. The problem seems to be linked with a desire to alter your own consciousness, to change your basic state of mind before you even begin to interact. I recall an interview with a famous Celtic actor where he was pressed about his alcoholism and self-destructiveness. 'It's not me, it's my race,' he replied wearily, passing the buck, placing the responsibility at a point beyond his control. While there is no doubt in my mind that heroin works on people creating new needs and altering their motivation, it does seem to be likely that there is a significant lack, or an additional 'X' factor, in potential users' personalities that drives them over that hurdle of nausea and vomiting and on into addiction.

You will be aware that I am, to some extent, vacillating between two positions, one that junkies are 'normal' people who fall prey to circumstances, the other that they belong to a particular personality type which renders them vulnerable in the first place. Perhaps both these things are true. I have been unable to make a certain conclusion either way. I leave that to the reader, who can, perhaps, understand more by observing at a distance than I can see at close hand. To continue the exploration of the experience of drug taking is, in the end, far simpler than to comprehend the reasons for it.

The drugs

You may have seen heroin before, even if it is only on television documentaries. You will have gathered that there is nothing unusual or spectacular about it. On the streets today it usually comes as a fine powder. The quality will vary but much of what is readily available is not very strong.

Addicts always disagree as to which type of gear is strongest and best. For a long time, so-called Chinese heroin was thought to be the most desirable opiate. Hence the cynical remarks made by one disillusioned addict: 'It's harder to kill yourself now as you can't get Chi-

nese or Dike, so there are fewer deaths and you have to suffer longer.'
He agreed that some people used to favour good old British BP scag
which very occasionally appears on the streets after someone has
done a chemist, but he added, 'You can't get that either-these days.
The chemists round here have all been ripped off already.'

Pharmaceutical heroin can come in different forms such as
tablets or white crystalline powder, but what people prefer and
what they can get often differ. Street smack comes in all the shades
from white through to dark brown. Much of it tends to be a non-
descript fawn or beige colour. It has virtually no smell but tastes bitter and a little unpleasant. Mostly from Iran or Pakistan, it does not
tend to meet with much enthusiasm from long-term users who want
to inject it. One addict commented, 'I hate Paki gear – that shitty
brown stuff. You feel like you're having half of Pakistan every time
you have a fucking hit.'

When you buy heroin you have no way of knowing what else has
been mixed with it, or whether it has even been completely converted from morphine. Morphine is very similar to smack in every
respect. When there is no smack it will do just as well to straighten
up an addict who snorts or injects it. At one time, some so-called
smack was indeed probably morphine. The fashion for smoking
heroin has probably altered the situation. If you try to smoke morphine it turns red, tastes odd and does not get you stoned. Morphine is, therefore, rarely seen on the streets these days. When you
come across white smack it is often more dodgy than all the other
colours. It may contain crushed up codeine tablets or palfium, making it totally unsuitable for smoking and more dangerous to inject
than the rest.

Assuming that you have acquired some smack of an acceptable
quality, you have a choice of ways of taking it. In the early days,
you may experiment with all the different methods. A few people
find that snorting it suits them and, for a while, they go no further.
At the present time, however, smoking or chasing the dragon, as it
is colloquially known, is the easiest and most popular route to
addiction. It requires no special equipment and there is not quite
the same problem of gauging the dose that you have to face with
injecting. You smoke until you feel you have had enough and then
you stop. It is still possible to overdo it, however, and the injudicious new user can chase the dragon right into its lair and be hopelessly mauled before realising the danger.

There is another danger in smoking smack. Smoking is a social activity. Since American Indians first smoked the pipe of peace, people have sat down together to smoke as a sign of shared interests and mutual affection. A refusal to join in is a rejection. A crowd of people who stumble across smack can egg each other on quite easily. Together, they can learn to enjoy new skills that will lead to far more than they bargained for and will, one day, have to be unlearnt.

In order to smoke smack, you need a tube, a strip of tin foil about five inches long by two inches wide, and a taper. Users often joke about the fact that the manufacturers and retailers of foil must have noticed a sudden rise in sales. When the craze first took off, all the corner shops in my district of Liverpool were frequently sold out. Now market traders offer foil at four rolls for fifty pence. The landlord of a local pub also recognised the need of smack users for a steady supply of foil. He began to sell strips of it over the bar at 2 pence each.

Toilet roll is the traditional raw material of the smack taper. Addicts who will put up with using newspaper in their toilets want the best bog roll for tapers. A whole roll of toilet paper can be used pretty rapidly by a group of people smoking scag. It seems likely, therefore, that, despite the fact that using heroin leads to chronic constipation, toilet roll has been successfully redeployed. In the absence of an abiding interest in world affairs addicts will titter about these things.

The technique is to place the smack onto a strip of foil and heat it from below with a slow-burning taper. The smack melts and, as the foil is tilted, runs along leaving its trail of fine smoke. The user keeps a tube made of foil and reinforced with paper in his mouth. With this, he hovers over the foil, sucking in the sacred smoke as he heats the smack from below. The whole operation requires minimal skills of co-ordination and nothing more. As with cranking gear, the ritual preparations can have their attractions for the user. Tapers are made by taking a length of toilet roll about three or four feet in length and rolling it along your thigh. Most smokers find this activity compulsively satisfying. Some have a worn patch on their jeans as a result. Heavy users can cause a nasty bruise by constantly rolling these tapers, but the scag stops it hurting.

Tubes and foil are sometimes passed from user to user in the way that joints used to be passed around by hippies. Everyone gets in on the act and feels they are having a good time. Smoking, however, is just as likely to lead to addiction and all its problems as any other method of consuming the drug. It must be said that smoking smack is totally compulsive. As one friend explained, 'You would do it all day if you could. Your tolerance builds very quickly and you can reach the stage where there are not enough waking hours for you to consume the smack you want.'

At this stage, users who can afford their habit rarely go to bed, but nod out for most of the night in a cosy chair, taking more smack whenever they wake. If you go through a lot of scag you will probably sport a blackened front tooth where thick deposits of smack have settled. People usually forget to scrape it off and, if they lie about the size of their habit, their friends will catch them out because their tooth will give them away. I can only assume that smoking heroin like this must be bad for the chest, but heroin suppresses coughs and kills pain. When you smoke it you feel that you are breathing mountain air. Despite the illusion, smack heads can succumb to some terrible coughs as soon as the drug starts to wear off.

Chasing the dragon is traditionally a noble activity in England, undertaken by brave and chivalrous knights. It does seem an inappropriate name for something so unromantic and mundane as sucking up noxious fumes. It is a great pity that no higher adventure presents itself to so many young people. There are no sailing ships to carry them on voyages of discovery to far off lands, no hidden territories to explore. They settle for an inner city Odyssey where self-destruction is the Golden Fleece.

Once they are committed to drug use, most people do end up trying all the ways of taking their poison. Smokers discover cranking when their supplies run low or the money runs out. Shooting up requires far smaller amounts than smoking to get you straight. The effects last for much longer and the rush is more intense than it is with smoking. Thus even today, when injecting yourself is no longer a prerequisite of heroin addiction, people are still learning to do it and still risking the dangers, such as overdose, septicaemia, hepatitis and endocarditis, to name a few. Once the bond between smack and the user has been thoroughly formed, no risk will keep her from experimenting, pushing experience and her body to the limits. Despite the craze for smoking smack, I know of few really long-term, serious junk abusers who do not either inject themselves or get someone else to do it for them. For my part, I was anxious to learn the skill. I thought it daring, romantic and outrageous. I was eager to shock by performing it. I learnt quickly and easily after having decided to do so. I even made sure I could use both my left and right hands. I no longer wanted to wait around at other people's pleasure. I did not want to suffer their bungled attempts to inject me when they could barely stand up.

Shooting up

Cranking is the most exciting, enjoyable and dangerous way to take heroin. It feeds the human capacity and need for ritual. The dangers are many and varied. At first you may worry about things like getting sterile water to be safe, and then someone reminds you that the gear itself may well have spent some time in a set of smelly underpants or down a dirty sock. It will have been heaped up and shovelled about on dirty floors; packed and shipped in dirty conditions; chopped up and mauled around on countless tables and tiles; spilt on the carpet and scraped up. We are told it may have been cut with anything from lactose to lavatory cleaner. In seconds, you could be lying about 'gaga' with a bleached brain.

Your paltry little bit of gear finally gets to you wrapped up in a small square of paper, ranging from an unidentifiable portion of someone's anatomy from a *Penthouse* centrefold to a piece of one of the dealer's kids' school exercise books. Out it comes onto your own personal surface where it is pushed around to make it look as much as possible with a far from sterile penknife. There it sits while you mull over the facts. At least, that is how it is the first time.

However you disguise the fact, you are usually a bit nervous the first time. After all, you will have read the papers too. Nonetheless, your mates are abundantly confident. They assure you all is well. They insist their hepatitis is not active this month. You will be OK. If you OD, which you will not do because they know what they are doing, they will, of course, provide mouth-to-mouth resuscitation ... or, if they are too stoned themselves, they may just nod out while you breathe your last. Never mind. It will all be all right in the morning. On the other hand, you could get the best whack of your life, the ultimate orgasm, the all-consuming high, the greatest experience known to man. Typically, your mates, uninterested in hanging around for you, will shoot up and loll around in various states of semi-consciousness, depending on how lucky they have been. Gradually, you overcome your fears. You must find out what it is like. You are ready and you are looking for a vein.

The syringe was always a problem. Unless you were registered yourself, or in a medical profession, clean syringes with sharp needles were hard to come by. Even if you did get one, you would probably hang onto it and use it so long and so often that the spike would be ready to be sharpened on a match box and the plunger would need greasing with butter to make it slide down the barrel. So compelling is the urge to hit up once the habit is formed that these practices are quite commonplace. Even though they horrify you at first, these activities can quickly become acceptable to even a bacteriologist. I know one who has had a needle habit for years. It is usually those with a little learning who set dangerous precedents for the rest.

Among student users, a first year undergraduate might make pronouncements to all her friends regarding reliable safety precautions, hedged bets or minimal risks, only to discover when she moves into the second year course that her assumptions have been dismantled. The damage remains done. I recall one biology student telling everybody that crushing up and injecting Diconal tablets was comparatively safe because they were composed of biodegradable chalk that would easily be broken down in the body. Years later, the news broke that injecting any crushed up tablets was about as safe as injecting crushed glass. Years too late for some.

For heroin users, the rule of thumb tends to be that if someone else has done it and they are still alive, you will *probably* make it too. The risks, too many, too varied and too much of a drag, are best forgotten. I remember once complaining because a friend started cooking up our gear in a room which had just been sprayed with a woodworm treatment. There was a sign on the door saying that pets, food and people should be kept out for several days. He just lost his temper. I can still picture him muttering bitterly as he decamped, plus spoon, to the bathroom which had also been sprayed that day, 'I don't know why some fucking people do this at all. If you can't stand the heat, stay out of the kitchen.' I shut up and shot up.

Some people are deterred by fear from shooting up while others are attracted by the sheer excitement of something so risky.

Whatever your attitude, the first hit is usually taken with a works still warm and wet after someone else has used it. They may or may not have bothered to wash out the traces of their own blood. If they have done, it will have been to avoid the blood clotting and blocking the needle rather than to spare you from an invasion of their blood proteins. Junkies are ever practical in these matters. They are all far more concerned with the hit than with hygiene. At first, you may think that the steps they take are to protect themselves. Soon you will realise that everything is done to protect and ensure the hit. You cannot shoot up through a blocked spike, so you wash it out immediately after you have used it. Unless you crush them carefully, semi-soluble tablets will not pass through the needle. Junkies worry about how to get drugs into their bodies, not about the damaging side effects that might ensue. Bacteria are another matter. They will not inhibit the high and so they are disregarded for most of the time. A very conscientious person might occasionally buy a can of sterilising spray. He might have rules about using a fresh needle for every hit. He might buy sterile water if he can do so easily and without arousing suspicion. Whatever he does, he will know that the gear itself, the magic 'X' factor, the reason for it all, is thoroughly non-sterile. His precautions are, therefore, comparatively futile. To other users, they can appear quaint, even ridiculous. Gradually, they will be abandoned and the addict will tote his half-worn-out works around in an inside pocket, wrapped up in a Boots bag. The Urban Cowboy must be ready to shoot whenever the chance or the need arises. He may be armed with a variety of semi-blunt spikes to be used and re-used in rotation. He will never bother to swab the chosen site for injection. Later on, when he has lost a few veins, he might need to try half a dozen new sites at one sitting before he gets a line. Sterilising his body piecemeal while fretting about his hit would be a nuisance and a bore.

A few real zealots will dare to administer their own first injection, but most people get someone else to do it for them. This can be a bigger favour than it sounds. When an unpredictable substance like Diconal is being injected or the strength of the gear has not been tested, there is a serious risk of overdose and death. On the drug scene there is always somebody who has to live with the knowledge that a friend might be alive today but for his naive willingness to shoot him up with the fatal hit.

It is quite an unbelievable feeling sitting staring at your first syringe full of smack. That clear, faintly discoloured, yellowish liquid can change your life forever, even end it. Yet the experience of the needle is compelling. The fact that you can feel one way one minute and be totally different the next is fascinating. You are tampering with your own being, confronting the life force itself. In a bizarre, mad conflict, conquering death by embracing it. When I crank up, I do not connect what I am doing with myself. I am doing something to an arm in order that I can feel good. Somehow, the medical microbiological horror show is completely blanked out. You lie to yourself. It will be OK. You create myths about the magical powers of your white cells. Like an army of cartoon warriors, they are fierce and efficient. Watchful intravenous guards, they will arrest, impound and beat to death any invading germs. They will wrap them up and bundle them back out through the sweat glands. When they catch a whole band of them they can make a boil and push them all out at once. And anyway, if you want to get stoned you simply do not worry about germs.

Most of the risks are actually worsened by attempts to control intravenous drug abuse. Years ago syringes could be bought locally in ones and twos from medical suppliers. It was quite hard to come by them and the stories that junkies told to con them out of chemists could be very inventive. They might, despite a dishevelled appearance, have a go at promoting themselves to medical status. The chemist could just believe them, or he simply might not care that they did. Alternatively, they may have a nest of hungry baby budgies/hamsters to drip feed. An eye-dropper was definitely not suitable for this task. Only a syringe would do. Another good tale used to be that of the ailing diabetic uncle who had come to visit and left his syringe at home. That could be good for a pack of diabetic disposables or even a re-usable glass number. Disposable diabetic syringes are not actually ideal as they do not hold much and the modern ones do not usually have separate needles. The needles are also too short to inject in any but a very obliging surface vein. Even so, in dire straits they can be used. Glass syringes are simply a drag. Most people, therefore, used to come by their works via registered addicts. Otherwise, they would steal them from hospitals or doctors' surgeries. I recall one addict who used to take used syringes from hospital waste bins, considering them quite a good find as they had only been used once. This may seem an extreme measure, but even asking for a works at the counter can be difficult. Many a user leaves the chemist clutching unwanted aspirin or laxative because they cannot bring themselves to ask for a syringe.

For my part, I remember a day when I drove all the way across Liverpool to borrow a worn-out works from an addict who had recently had syphilis. If you get a needle habit, you will try to take your heroin that way whatever the difficulties. Even if you are an addict you will try to get a works and endure being mildly ill for lack of smack before you will capitulate and snort or smoke it. Some people are more addicted to the act of injecting themselves than they are to heroin.

A local man who has been using smack for over twenty years and has collapsed nearly all the veins he can reach still persists in taking heroin by injection rather than any other way. I think that, at one time or another, all of his blood has been through a syringe, because when he injects himself he flushes the blood in and out of it repeatedly, concentrating intensely. I believe he would inject water alone if there was nothing else. Heroin has nothing to do with his needle habit.

Serum hepatitis is a scourge among junkies, yet most junkies, when offered the use of a works by someone who has got hepatitis, or just had it, will hesitate for a moment and then use it. Perhaps it is even the action of smack itself that removes what would seem to be a normal sane and healthy desire to avoid this kind of risk. In the end, most junkies worry about what they have done to themselves. Needle freaks have got most to worry about.

Acquired Immune Deficiency Syndrome, commonly known as AIDS, has now been added to the list of dangers facing intravenous drug abusers. AIDS is primarily a sexually transmitted disease, but contact with infected blood can also be a means of acquiring the virus. The practice of sharing needles and syringes has meant that junkies have made themselves vulnerable to this potentially fatal illness and some have already become victims of it.

Their obsession with needles makes some addicts unwitting accomplices in the spread of the virus. The compulsion to inject usually overcomes common sense, making the spread of the disease among a local addict community almost inevitable once one member of their group has become infected. That is why sensible doctors may prefer to make clean syringes readily available to addicts in an attempt to minimise such risks. In Britain doctors who did so were sometimes heavily criticised by observers who felt that providing syringes was tantamount to encouraging intravenous drug abuse.

It used to be such a problem to get hold of syringes because established thinking was based on moral opposition and the belief that making it difficult to come by the necessary equipment would discourage, even halt, the spread of injecting. This strategy did not take into account the determination and resourcefulness of drug users. Nor did it foresee the appalling health consequences in terms of the ease with which hepatitis B and C and, worse HIV infection would be spread as addicts developed the practice of sharing the few syringes available to them. Places where they met to share syringes and inject drugs soon became known as 'shooting galleries' and in Edinburgh during the 1980s, a horrifyingly high incidence of HIV infection among injecting addicts resulted from their habit of shooting up together, passing a used syringe from one person to the next. Some studies suggested that the number of users infected in this way in the Edinburgh area might be as high as 90 per cent. Following this shocking discovery, syringe exchanges which gave out free needles and syringes to drug users were set up throughout the country.

By 1984, the first British needle exchange had started in Hope Street, Liverpool, while addicts in Edinburgh were finding it almost impossible to obtain clean supplies of syringes and needles. The tragic consequences to addicts north of the border were avoided in Liverpool, where the incidence of HIV is still only 8 per million of the total population. All major centres of population are now, according to the Home Office, covered by syringe exchange services, backed up by similar services offered at certain chemists. Over 4 million needles and syringes are supplied annually in this way.

One place, however, where syringes are not readily available to users is inside prison. Yet it is widely known that drug taking occurs on a large scale in gaols. It follows that the few syringes smuggled into prison are shared by as many as 20 or more inmates at a time. Debate regarding the supply of both syringes and condoms inside prison to avoid the spread of HIV among the prison population has come to nothing, presumably because it would be unthinkable for those in power to publicly acknowledge what they know to be the truth. They should remember that the majority of prisoners are serving relatively short sentences at the end of which they will return to the community, constituting a threat to us all.

Surely it would be better to protect them from infection inside prison than to pretend the problem does not exist. Injecting carries many dangers but society can easily minimize the risks.

On the first occasion when I risked the perils of intravenous drug use, AIDS was virtually unknown to local addicts and I had not even heard of its existence. I progressed very rapidly onto the needle, partly because I had long harboured an urge to try it and partly because that was the way everyone I knew took smack when I started out. I had, so far, only snorted smack, but had a minor tolerance. I was ready for the hit.

Everything about it seemed exciting. I was told to find something to use as a tourniquet to make the chosen vein stand up. I collected the dressing gown cord from the bedroom and returned triumphantly to the kitchen to sit down again. Beside me were the spoon and the glass with the syringe balanced across the top of it, waiting for me to finally decide. My willing accomplice was edgy and keen to hurry me up. An addict himself, the business was routine to him. From his angle, my reservations and excitement were both equally burdensome. He had delayed his hit to be sure of doing mine properly. I, on the other hand, was taking a big step. Although I had made the decision, I was nervous. My stomach was churning, my pulse fast. He was kneeling at my feet now for ease of access to my veins. Seizing my hand in his, he pushed up my sleeve and started to finger my arm, running his practised hands along the faint blue channels where the veins lay. Pressing or jabbing upwards to see if they rose willingly, he announced, satisfied with what he saw, 'Women can be difficult: their veins can be really small.'

He examined the other arm and chose the spot. The right brachial seemed to be favourite. I drew my arm back a little as he reached for the cord. I had insisted on doing this thing properly and wanted to make it as safe as possible, but now I had doubts. 'What about blood poisoning?' I declared, as matter-of-factly as I could. 'Is it actually possible to get it doing this?' He sighed, his mouth tight at the corners. Tensing visibly, he left his efforts and snapped, 'Look, I'm no fucking doctor. It's up to you. I've told you. If I were you, I wouldn't bother. I'll take it myself if you like.' He picked up the syringe and started sizing up his own arm. 'No. No. I just meant was it safe, that's all,' I said, battling to maintain my cool and keep my hit. 'It's not fucking safe. None of it's fucking safe. I've told you,' he replied in a taut, low voice, struggling to keep calm himself, perspiration on his forehead. He was fighting his own mixed emotions as he waited impatiently for his turn. After all, it is a great gesture for a junkie to shoot you up before he fixes himself. 'Look. I'll do mine and you can think about it,' he said. I was not prepared to give up. I knew that, being in the habit of taking large hits, he might not even be able to stand up straight for half an hour after cranking himself up. I did not want to be left wondering and let down.

I took the cord and amateurishly tried to apply it above the bend of the relevant arm. Now I was shaping up. He was there again; correcting, adjusting, demonstrating. I held the cord in my left hand and pulled it tight. He had the needle up to my arm already. A cotton wool swab dabbed cold against me. He slapped at the vein gently and stroked firmly upwards to make it stand out.

'Won't you have to wipe it again now?' I asked, worried that he had touched the relevant spot with his unwashed fingers. He groaned and irritably dabbed again for my benefit alone.

'The smack's not fucking sterile, you know,' he snapped. 'It's probably been up a Paki's arse on the way here.'

'Don't be revolting,' I replied.

'Well, where do you think it came from, Boots?'

We were almost enjoying ourselves now. Amused in our collusion to offend against sanity, decency and the law. The atmosphere relaxed again.

'Come on,' I encouraged, 'I'm ready.'

The needle slid into my arm gently, firmly, easily, uneventfully. I watched, intrigued, waiting for something to happen. He pulled it back slightly and drew out the plunger a little. Blood shot eagerly into the barrel like a little tongue of flame and quickly dispersed into a small mushroom. I have, ever since, thought of getting that line as exploding a personal atomic bomb.

'OK. Loosen that tie. Quick!' he urged.

I fumbled at the cord and it loosened. Confidently, he pushed the plunger in. Quite fast, his eyes flicking quickly from my face to the job in hand. I watched, holding my breath, as the contents of the barrel, with its dark red core, disappeared miraculously into my body.

'You have to put it in fairly fast,' he said, 'so you get a good hit.' He was pulling back on the plunger again. Fresh blood was flowing into the syringe.

'What are you doing?' I asked, in the seconds before the smack hit.

'Just flushing,' he replied. 'You don't want to lose any.' The blood was disappearing back into my arm for the second time when I began to feel something. The needle slipped out cleanly. 'Bend your arm,' my friend ordered, placing a bit of tissue over the tiny pin hole where a blob of blood was forming. I obeyed. 'Are you OK?' He peered at me momentarily, quite hard, as he deftly began to wash out the works ready for his own use.

I murmured a wordless response as the smack came on. The rush is so hard to describe. It's like waiting for a distant thunderstorm to move overhead. A strange foreboding. A bizarre, awesome calm. It's in your blood, moving towards your brain, relentlessly; unstoppable, inevitable. A feeling starts to grow like a rumble from the horizon. The feeling swells, surging, soaring, crashing, screaming to a devastating crescendo. The gear smashes against the top of your skull with the power of an uncapped oil well. You won't be able to bear the intense ecstasy. It is all too much. Your body may fall apart. The rock that is your head shatters harmlessly into a million sparkling, tinkling smithereens. They tumble at a thousand miles an hour straight back down over your body, warming, insulating, tingling, denying all pain, fear and sadness. You are stoned, you are high. You are above and below reality and law.

'Are you OK?' he asked again.

My chin was on my chest, my eyes closed, I suppose.

'I'm just great,' I murmured. 'I'm fine. It's fantastic. It's wonderful. I want to do this forever ...'

A smile on my lips, I nodded quietly while he shot himself up, aware of a strange, metallic taste in the roof of my mouth: a taste I later came to recognise as the taste of shooting smack.

Anyone reading this who has had the experience will ruefully recall the days of their own wild enthusiasm for cranking, when they believed that the hit was worth it all. Many other people who have marvelled over that hit will not be able to read this. Dead people do not read books. Friends and relatives of casualties may be angry, feeling that I am advertising a deadly pursuit. That is not my intention. I hope to record the experience. Heroin addiction cannot be understood or fought against unless people accept that it has attractions. Surely, nobody believes that all drug abuse is a squalid, mindless activity that affords no pleasure. Without the pleasure, nobody would end up with the pain.

What those of us who know must get across to the others is the massive imbalance between the apparent advantages and the very real disadvantages of taking smack. Trying heroin just once could mean death. Becoming a junkie has no advantages. As one friend put it, 'There is no free smack.' Every hit you enjoy will have to be paid for with your health, your peace of mind and, one day, if you give in to it, every single thing you own. Every hit you take is another step down a treacherous stairway. It is always twice as hard to climb back up stairs as it is to go down them. The same flight that will see you running down easily will have you puffing, wheezing and crawling your way back up. At the bottom of that stairway, there is nothing but despair. On each step you leave something for the gremlins to take away for the dragon. It may be money, your car or your looks. It may be your lover or your friends. It may be your talent or your belief. By the time you reach the bottom stair, you will have nothing left to leave. In that place, the only reality is smack and more smack. You plan your life around supplying your own medication, and waste no time on anything else. There is nothing to do there but die, slowly or quickly. That is the one choice you have left. Smack is completely anti-life. It blocks out all other needs and desires but itself. No short-term thrill is worth the loss of your life.

At first, getting stoned is great fun, and an experience you are keen to repeat, but in due course the question of 'how stoned is stoned?' comes in. You are never stoned enough and when you are, you are unconscious. The exciting hit or buzz eludes you. You begin to feel less and less, to worry more and more. Without smack, you are ill. With it, you are a new kind of numb-normal. This journey from high to low can be made by so many different paths that some people who can be seen by those at the bottom to be, clearly, on their way down to join them actually believe they are walking on the hill. We have all been there. We have all believed that it would not happen to us. We have all felt free to dabble in smack, taking the highs and evading the lows. I do not know anyone who has stayed up there on that hill. In the end, however high you go, you will always have to come down.

CHAPTER 2

☙ *More pieces of the heroin jigsaw*

Getting in on the scene

What seems most incomprehensible to an outsider is that those who are not yet too involved can, and do, continue heading down that slippery slope. It is, however, quite easy to work out the riddle of their conduct. It is the same everyday cockiness needed to succeed or survive that blinds people to the ongoing process of osmosis by which they are sucked into the scene.

Because users are often not as stereotyped as may be thought, almost anybody can find themselves rubbing shoulders with someone who has access to heroin. Most of us have different groups of friends that we see at different times. We may identify totally with none of them. It is, therefore, likely that when a person discovers that she is on the periphery of a scene where smack is available she will consider herself detached and aloof from the dangers. Even if she can see quite plainly the risks the others are running, she will delude herself into the belief that she is above their problems. If your self-image and confidence are even in average shape, it will not occur to you that any big changes are likely to take place just because you want to experiment with a certain drug. You may look at the others and fret about the state they are in but still imagine yourself to be immune. As one user put it, 'I never used to realise I was in bulk. Now I look at my mates and think, God, I must be like that!' What people fail to see when they set out is that even those at the edge of the scene are still a part of it. Someone who is standing in the road gawping at an accident victim does not see the bus as it knocks him down.

Usually, potential junkies are still leading ordinary, normal lives and do not envisage having to change anything. They can smoke a cigarette, take a drink or get through hundreds of joints unscathed.

Why should smack get to them? Even junkies themselves can seem quite normal to the uninitiated. If you did not know them before they had a problem, you will not realise how they may have changed. No one enjoys admitting to their own incompetence, so junkies will probably try to conceal their unhappiness from anyone who does not share their situation. Even if they admit to their troubles, their obscure references to 'holes in their heads' or 'doing turkey tomorrow' have little real meaning for anyone who has not experienced these things.

At a distance, even the threat of cold turkey seems romantic and preferable to boredom. It looks like a trial of strength, a primitive test of manhood, a measure of courage. (Of course, not all users are men. Approximately one-third are women. Girls crave adventure, too. Many are not afraid of a challenge. Some set out to emulate the boys. Others embark for their own reasons.) Nobody worries too much about mythical symptoms. Four days? It can't be that bad! Some recruits are even anxious to find out what it is like. No one is aware that cold turkey will be the least of their problems. As the song says, 'Fools rush in ...' There are, however, various routes to addiction. I travelled more slowly, but my destination was the same.

Whether you dabble for years or whether you do 'rush in', when familiarity finally allays your fears you will become an apprentice junkie. One minute you will be outside the smack bubble, the next you will be in there learning the skills. There seems to be so much to discover. Friends and associates lead each other on while the old hands inform, instruct, demonstrate and, occasionally, issue pertinent warnings.

After the disappointment of my first experience with morphine, I was left feeling determined that I would crack the code and get the buzz in the end. Laying good sense aside, I strove for an insight into smack. At the time, I was fertile ground for a heroin habit. Scag was a perfect antidote to disenchantment, a friend indeed. A sense of purpose and direction was lacking in my life and smack could take away the need for them and lessen the tension between what I wanted and what I had. Experimenting with it became an end in itself. It was a new, exciting project that had been endorsed by heroes and intellectuals from Coleridge to Crowley. I did not want to miss out. An eager disciple, I embarked on a career of sporadic dabbling and, in due course, the buzz began to dawn on me. I knew that the nice feelings I was beginning to discover were a dangerous misrepresentation of the power of opiates but I took no evasive action.

Smack carves its way into your life with a double-edged blade. On one hand, it comforts and warms, on the other, it thrills and stimulates. Perhaps that is why it is so lethally compelling. Like Salome, dancing for your delight, smack will have your head on a plate before the dance is done. Starved of romance, you may be willing to embrace the 'demon lover'. I was already mesmerised by its power and I took it whenever the chance arose. I became a regular dabbler, usually at weekends, when I could nod out or throw up in peace.

This is the way that most people get into smack. If heroin is available to you and you are tempted to indulge, sooner or later you will begin to enjoy it. The amounts you take get larger. You become more enthusiastic and more daring. You still do not have a problem. It is not true that sampling smack once or twice, even a dozen times, turns you into a junkie. It may take that long just to learn to enjoy it. But, once you do discover that you like it, you will probably carry on until you are in trouble. You sit around, glowing and gleeful, while your addicted friends issue quiet warnings, then score for you and rip you off, taking half of the drugs you have paid for themselves. After all, their need is greater than yours. They will mutter darkly and jealously about your drug virginity and tell you how lucky you are to be able to get so high. They will not really pay you much attention. You are not actually yet one of them and they do not take you very seriously. Left to your own devices, you can quietly build up your tolerance and increase the frequency of your indulgences. You will start looking forward to getting smack. You may start asking for it.

In the early days your hit will lay you out while your addicted friends will become hyperactive and loud. Gradually, things will start to change and you will find yourself running around with them. Your body chemistry is obligingly moving along towards a tolerance that will allow you to really get off on the smack experience. You now have the best of both worlds. When it is not available, you may be grumpy and disappointed, but you will not be ill. You will still feel that you are in control. A friend who is at the dabbler stage spoke about his position as follows: 'I suppose I'm psychologically dependent on it to get things done. I want it to make my day, to do jobs or anything difficult.' We have all warned him that he should stop taking heroin before his troubles really start. He is not deterred. Few people are.

Part-time users believe that their credit is good. A day without drugs on which they have not degenerated into a twitching wreck gives them *carte blanche* to carry on. This is the Fools' Paradise. Sometimes a whole group of friends shares it together. Later they will share the problems it brings. I dabbled on in this limbo land for months, mostly snorting small amounts, before I came anywhere near having a problem of even minor physical dependence.

This is not everyone's experience. Some people discover smack and like it so much that they never want to stop taking it. They simply supply themselves with as much of it as they can get, as often as they can get it, for as long as they can. Jimmy explained this 'monkey see, monkey do' approach as follows:

> I knew heroin was supposed to be dangerous. People had warned me to stay away from it, but as I began to take it continuously and continued to feel fine I ceased to worry about it. I could not understand what all the fuss was about. I felt great.

He was, without realising it, slipping slowly and painlessly into addiction. It is usually this naive concentration on taking the moment and letting the future fend for itself that leads to addiction. Obvious prerequisites are the time and the freedom to indulge. If your job is not taxing and your commitments are easy to cope with, you will be in a position to carry on. If you are unemployed, the circumstances are perfect. Before you have a habit, even your dole money is enough to send you on a spree. There is not enough to pay for a holiday or a new coat and saving seems impossible but for £20 or £30 you can get yourself a bag of scag that will take you right out of it for two or three days.

Not surprisingly, young people on the dole can be attracted by short-term solutions. Some are ready to take them. For the older, long-term unemployed in their twenties and thirties heroin can be just as appealing. People can throw themselves wholeheartedly into chemically induced euphoria without considering the drawbacks. Jimmy, who is quoted above, enjoyed the initial experience but, in only a matter of months, he had plunged right into the centre of a holocaust of pain and loss. He describes the pattern like this:

I took heroin for six months without a break, spending all my savings on it. I also began to inject it in an effort to make my supply last longer. Finally, my money ran out and only then did I realise that I had a habit I could not support; a habit of spending £40 a day for a bit of powder.

Jimmy ended up in hospitals because of the severity of his withdrawal symptoms. After that, he succeeded in stopping for a while, but two years after recognising the disadvantages, Jimmy is still an addict. Like most addicts, he wishes he had never taken smack and yet he can find no alternative. Once a smack habit has been formed it is very hard to break.

Another addict I spoke to was acutely aware that heroin abuse is a bad thing. She highlighted the fact that users become increasingly dependent on heroin very gradually, believing that they are not in any danger because they still find it fairly easy to stop. She explained it this way: 'At some point along the path there comes a time where the memory confuses and you find it's been a long time since you've had more than a week or two straight. Then the point comes where you're in too deep to get out.' She went on to describe the way that heroin can take over and wreck your life, but she finished with a rueful comment on her own inability to stop using it when she said, '... and the trouble is, it's all so fucking nice.'

When you are well it is hard to imagine being sick. That is why most people setting out on the slippery slope ignore the warnings and the woes of others. They convince themselves that they are smarter, and safer, than the rest and more in control. Tickled with their new toy, they push on relentlessly. They believe in the wild good times. The bait tastes really good and they cannot see the hook. As one man put it, 'Like a lobster in his pot, you don't worry till you want to get out.'

Clearly, just like the lobster, some people desperately want to get in. If that applies, you will experiment keenly with the drugs and the methods of taking them. If you have any qualms about the fact that heroin is actually an illegal substance you will begin to lose your reservations and lower your defences. While you will be aware that buying heroin always involves a risk, you will have discovered that the emphasis of the risk shifts somewhat depending on how much you are buying and where you are. Initially, the risk is small, but it goes up rapidly in direct proportion to the length of time you are involved with the drug and how much you need. If you are a new user you will probably score at the lowest level of the junk pyramid, buying small bits now and again from a personal friend. He will be unlikely to be well known to the police because he is not, in any formal sense, a regular dealer. In this case, you are unlikely to come up against problems. You will still be on the edge of the scene and buffered from its ills. Wherever you are, in the unlikely event that the police do call, it will not be you they are looking for. Safe and secure, surrounded by knowledgeable companions, you can single-mindedly pursue disaster as rapidly as you wish.

There are, of course, as many different scenes as there are addicts and only some of the rules are alike. Firstly, the type of drugs you can afford and what you must do to get them will differ considerably depending on who you are and where you start out. While all junkies will eventually learn the same lessons, the circles in which they move and the rules for interaction will also vary. Social standing and the size of your bank balance will, naturally, be particularly significant factors in determining your daily reality. Certain common features will remain. Whether you live in a tower block or a stately home, your own little scene fosters and feeds your habit. This scene might include anything from ten to a hundred interdependent users who form a secret network where people can mix and mingle, with the underlying aim of buying, selling and consuming drugs. When you are still a newcomer, you do not identify with other heroin users. You see yourself in a different light. One addict reflected as follows on this self-defeating pride, 'When I first started, I had no time for junkies ... Kenny used to offer me morphine and I used to refuse.' Once, he thought junkies were pathetic and weak. He believed that he could take smack or leave it. Twenty-three years later, he is still taking it. As I have already pointed out, this initial arrogance is common and helps to deceive and defeat even the strong.

Once you do enter the junk scene in earnest, you are always in danger from overdose, bad hits, rip-offs and bum gear. Although you aim for maximum high and minimum hassle, there is a daily chance that you will end up puking or unconscious. In time, there is a daily likelihood that you will end up sick and sneezing. There is some chance that you will end up nicked. Most of the good times are at the beginning when your body is well and your mind is free from fear. Once you have acquired your first decent-sized habit, the best times are usually over. By then, any plusses will start to be cancelled out or diminished by the bad times. As we have seen, to reach this stage can take you months of really concerted effort or years of part-time attempts. Either way, you have a ticket that could take you to rock bottom and there are no fast round trips. The mysterious and glamorous world of the heroin users will begin to reveal itself as a shabby merry-go-round peopled by seedy punters, riding their nightmare horses. After you buy a ticket, it is anybody's guess when the ride will end. And you may never get off again. The machinery is controlled by sharp operators who turn up the music, refuse to switch off and constantly demand more money from those who are screaming for them to stop.

Despite everything, addicts are still individuals. They may share a liking for drugs, but their attitudes, reasons, activities, talents, intelligence and output will differ. Even when they are committed to smack, you cannot make rules about how long they will stay alive, how much gear they will use, how quickly they will decline, or whether, even when you see them at your idea of their most disgusting, there is hope for them to claw a path back. They may be shut off from you, but they have not forgotten you are out there.

The cannabis connection

I cannot leave the question of how people come to embark on a career of heroin abuse without considering that old chestnut, the claim that smoking cannabis plays a big part in leading on to the use of hard drugs. My observations lead me to query this assumption.

The direct link with heroin addiction has never been proved, and yet a lot of circumstantial evidence is erroneously and, perhaps, unfairly used against cannabis. Society has attempted to trace the path of the heroin user back to the point where he 'went wrong'. Somewhere along that path, the careful observer will probably find a joint. He assumes, therefore, that the heroin user has built up his daring and his confidence with lesser drugs before moving on to smack. The path has been painstakingly tracked in the wrong direction: backwards. Most dope smokers have never tried smack. On the other hand, most people who take heroin will try anything. Most of them have, therefore, smoked dope. This is where the confusion arises.

If we were to locate the thousands of young dope smokers of the 1960s and 1970s and trace their steps forward to the present day, we would find that most have never gone beyond dope. Many will have abandoned even that. As they lose touch with the scene, and their suppliers, they begin to fear detection, loss of jobs, and loss of social standing, or they simply tire of dope altogether. Some give up cigarettes too, take up jogging and start eating health foods.

Thus, I do not believe that cannabis plays a part in forming a heroin habit. There must, for example, be millions of cigarette smokers who have never discovered cannabis. The progression from the use of one drug to another is not inevitable. Of course, smoking cannabis may possibly enable those who use it to come into contact with people who use heroin. This is not a foregone conclusion. The dope and smack scenes are usually quite separate. Some junkies like a draw now and again, but many more do not bother. The dealers who operate at street level do not usually sell dope as well as smack. They are too busy coping with their heroin supply to bother worrying about something else. Even if someone does come into contact with one drug via another, the rest is their choice. It is only in films that people hold you down and make you take heroin. When the chance to try smack presents itself, most dope smokers choose to ignore it.

The current situation seems to imply that there is no direct correlation between cannabis and heroin use. Most young people who form the tragic new wave of heroin takers have had little or no experience of cannabis. For many kids, heroin has been their first indulgence. Indeed, during attempts to quit heroin, users will sometimes seek out cannabis as a crutch to help them through. It can actually lead you away from hard drugs rather than towards them.

A word about your sex life

> It's my wife and it's my life.
> It's killing me.
>
> 'Heroin', Velvet Underground

I discuss sex here in this section on why people take drugs because, in some cases, a belief that heroin will improve their sex life sets people off on the slippery slope. In all my comments I refer to heterosexual activities so as not to complicate gender references. Furthermore, I do not feel qualified to discuss the gay scene.

When I was a student and sex was much on everyone's mind, I remember being advised to cop off with a junkie because they, reputedly, made the best lovers. Dangerous and mysterious on the one hand, when it came down to basics, they could go on all night! For some men, especially those who are anxious about their sexual performance, heroin does, therefore, seem to be a glorious discovery. If they are afraid of coming too soon and looking foolish, smack presents a welcome combination of stud spray and aphrodisiac. Although, on a bad day, he might be finished in a few minutes, with the aid of a hit of heroin, a man can easily carry on for a couple of hours: smack can spare his blushes every time. It can be an enormous boost to his ego and his popularity. Women will be impressed. Well satisfied, they will stick around for more. And they may tell their friends. If she knows a man is using gear, a certain type of woman will be compelled to look after him. Smack can add spice to a dull image overnight. Our romantic hero will be pampered, petted and fed regular meals.

It must be said at this point that dope, speed and cocaine are all much better than opiates if you are looking for drugs that enhance the quality of sexual encounters. Nonetheless, heroin can make its contribution, and once a man has crashed through the puke barrier into the realms of drug use he can take advantage of this handy side effect of delayed ejaculation. It is, literally, quite true that under heroin's influence people can make love more or less all night.

Entirely contrary to what outsiders may assume, however, most drug users are actually a fairly conservative lot so that, although on a one-to-one basis sex may be pretty hot, they are still quite likely to be faithful to one partner and avoid media-invented nasties like group sex and random promiscuity. Most junkies could not be bothered to get either of these together. Much is also said about junkies selling sex to buy drugs. It does go on but it happens on the very bottom line of the junk pyramid. Many users would never even consider turning to prostitution, but it is true that a high percentage of prostitutes working the streets do take heroin. Junkies are often quite ordinary married couples. True, they may engage in crime, usually drug dealing or cheque frauds and occasionally burglary, but a lot of junkies I know would be utterly horrified at the thought of prostituting themselves. These are not people who have merely a passing acquaintance with smack. They have mostly been involved for years and still have not resorted to prostitution. Even junkies can maintain a vestige of self-respect.

If you take junk you will be something of a hedonist who will try most things in pursuit of pleasure, so many junkies probably have reasonably exciting sex lives before they even begin to take opiates. Heroin does not improve your sex life, it changes it. At first, you have some good times stoked up on smack. When you are stoned you cannot sleep. You may go to bed wide awake, buzzing and randy. Smack gives you the energy to go a bit crazy and do things that, otherwise, you might not consider: you will not need to take stock of the bruises and accidental injuries until tomorrow. In a spirit of drug-addled abandon one woman I know embarked on her first attempt at anal sex. It seemed like a good idea at the time but smack tends to dry up bodily secretions. Owing to lack of fore-thought and the size of the man's penis the attempt had to be aban-doned and the woman ended up with an anal tear that bled for weeks. That's the sort of thing people do on smack. You get a bit irresponsible because you do not think ahead. You do not think much at all. You sprain joints and pull muscles because you cannot feel the pain until later. You end up in funny positions, in funny places, wondering how you got there.

When you are stoned you can do the same thing for hours and not get bored. The fuzzy, backward telescope concentration of the smack high allows your lover to devote his attention hour after hour to your big toe if you want him to – and sometimes when you do not. Repetition is irrelevant as only the moment counts. Thus you never tire of sex, even though you are sometimes oddly detached, as if you were watching yourself from the next room. Things seem to happen more slowly and sensations are often more exotic, more ecstatic. It appears to last longer; your cunt seems to squeeze tighter, more rapidly, more determinedly. You hold your breath; a new spasm may lead to unwelcome peaks. At other times orgasm is pecu-liarly gentle and prolonged. Just as the process should be slowing and ceasing it begins to intensify and repeat. At all times your body seems more alive, lighter, freer, your senses keener than ever. You have that 'good to be 18' feeling when you are over 30.

But, along with the increased physical sensations, the intensifica-tion of emotion and the sudden changes of mood that are charac-teristic of the smack experience can cause you to fight mercilessly with your lover, even about who gets up to make the tea. Over-reaction can be such that tears, recriminations, anguish, misery and devastation can follow an argument the cause of which cannot be remembered five minutes later.

As he gets more involved with heroin our would-be Don Juan may find complications setting in. If, for instance, he takes too much he simply cannot come at all, however hard he tries. His glorious two-hour rutting sessions may decline into desperate bouts of violent, fruitless thrusting. His partner, by now will be polite but bored. He could be left wakeful, breathless and sweating while she drifts off to sleep. While she sleeps he will leave her warm bed to take another hit. In the morning his cock will be sore.

Of course, not all junkies are Casanovas to begin with. Plenty are shy, even isolated, but however you started out, as you get more involved you become less available, less communicative, less able to form relationships and less willing to do so. In the end, sex, like eating, loses its attraction for junkies. They simply run out of libido. Other factors may coincide to curtail their activities. Firstly, junkies often neglect their personal appearance, making themselves less desirable to all but their nearest and dearest. More importantly, for men, women do not enjoy competing with smack. Who wants to play second fiddle to a chemical? Women can, at the end of the day, handle the threat of another woman better. At least they are fighting on equal terms. When junk comes into a man's life in a big way there are two things a woman can do: join in or get out. If she is very stubborn, she can grit her teeth and get set for a long hard fight that might last years, and which, in the end, she may lose. If she does join in, things will seem great for a while, but in due course the lies, fights, tears and tantrums will drive them apart, perhaps permanently. Few relationships can survive a triangle situation when the third party is heroin. In time junkies forsake sex for drugs. They would choose a hit before a fuck every time. Instead of improving your sex life junk will finally end it.

My last word must be that I have had as good a time sexually without heroin as I have had with it. The physical and emotional drawbacks are not worth the trouble.

PART TWO

Living With Addiction

CHAPTER 3

ℭ *The lifestyle*

In Wordsworth's poem *The Prelude,* a group of people set out to walk to Italy along a path that leads across the Alps. Engrossed in their climb and excited by the knowledge that they must soon reach the highest point, they meet a traveller who explains that they have, in fact, already crossed the Alps. The moment they had all waited for and toiled towards had passed unnoticed. For junkies, too, the most significant moment of their journey often passes unnoticed. They travel onwards believing themselves to be still a long way from addiction when they are very close. A potential junkie will find himself using heroin not just every few days but every day while still thinking that the choice is being made by his mind rather than his body. It comes as a shock to him to find that he not only wants smack but also needs it. Pete described this moment of recognition: 'You find yourself right in the middle of a hole you've dug and you say, "I'm sure I didn't dig it this deep."'

There are, of course, degrees of addiction. Early on it is much easier to pull out than it is after a year or two. It is possible to become physically addicted to quite small amounts of heroin after a period of only a few weeks, but unless you are determined to make an issue of it, the physical symptoms in this case will amount to very little: a restless night or two, a slight cold. If you have not been warned in advance what to expect on the day when the drugs do not turn up you may not even realise that you are suffering from mild withdrawal symptoms. Once an addict does know what to expect if he runs out of drugs there is a tendency for panic and self-dramatisation.

For this reason people are best off in a state of ignorance. They can dabble on unaware of the impending problem and perhaps pull out in time. As time goes on, however, and dabbles turn into two-, three- or six-month sessions of daily use, things get harder.

Physical symptoms of withdrawal become more unpleasant and psychological dependence increases. Even so, half a dozen valium and a few drinks can get you through. It is after two, three, six years without stopping that the really serious problems begin. All that time the habit will be increasing. People find themselves dealing, stealing, pleading for more drugs wherever they go. The drug culture will become their life. Even if they stop using heroin and go through withdrawal they find it hard to adjust to life without drugs.

What is it like being addicted to heroin?

The first thing you notice is that you wake up in the morning late, aching all over from sleeping too heavily and too long in one position. Your eyes will be watering. You feel rotten, just rotten. You can barely be bothered to get out of bed, no matter what. Then you remember. Realisation dawns. You need and you want drugs. Soon. Immediately. Later you will try to keep in a supply for the morning, but in the early days you may not bother, thinking you will be able to do without, thinking you can hold on until later. Before long your first waking thought is always heroin and your first act to smoke, snort or inject the amount needed to get straight, often without even getting out of bed if you can manage it.

Once you have had a hit you can function. Things look brighter, better, how much so depending on the dose you have had. Your thoughts can then turn to other matters – like scoring again as soon as possible. If the money is a problem, you will set about getting it by whatever means possible. Somehow the money is nearly always found, and, as soon as it is in your hand, you are away to find the man with the scag. The major priority in your life has now become ensuring your supply. Nothing takes precedence over that.

For most people, the worst thing about the whole business is finding the money. Without it they cannot buy the drugs to keep them feeling well enough to lead their normal lives. That is what addiction means. Without heroin, a regular user will become ill, listless and depressed, and will be unable to carry on his or her usual, everyday activities, not least of which might be earning a living. Carol, a married woman with children, summed up the situation when she said, 'I take it just to be normal; to do the washing;

cook the tea; do the housework; go to Tesco's, just to be my normal bloody self.' The addict experiences a crushing sense of being hopelessly trapped. All his actions are manipulated by bodily need. Drug addiction is recognised by many as a kind of illness, and Dougie echoed that view when he said, 'I'm tired of living like a fucking diabetic.' He was referring to his need for daily injections, registering the frustration of knowing that his life revolves around a drug. In the case of the diabetic, however, everyone is at pains to ensure his supply, smooth his path, make life easy and convenient for him. Indeed no one would wish it otherwise. I merely compare the situation of two sick men. In the case of the junkie, the customs, police, screws, government, doctors, social workers, his family and friends, the neighbours and even other junkies conspire to come between him and his supply. Tough. Yes, it is tough being a junkie and most addicts will recognise themselves in Pete's remark when he says, 'I've had a good go at the old self-pity business. I've given it the full bash ...'

Whatever else, drug addiction is not a static condition. Even for dependent users there are degrees of addiction. Users may try to keep their habit down to a minimum level but to experience the same feeling of being stoned they will need to continue to increase the amounts they use taking larger and larger doses. The fact that a person's tolerance continues to grow, and grow indefinitely, is probably the origin of the belief that, in time, junkies cease to enjoy taking heroin. What actually happens is that, once tolerance has developed, the majority of users cannot afford to buy the amounts of junk needed for them to get really stoned. If they are lucky, they will be able to get themselves straight. Often they are on the edge of withdrawal, not because the drug no longer works on them but because the dose they need is prohibitively costly. Life becomes a battle to be normal, to be well enough to carry on. Naturally, junkies usually develop a love-hate relationship with their drug. They love being stoned but they hate the problems they have to endure to achieve their goals. Obviously, money worries begin early on. Then there are the fears of arrest and conviction and, of course, the ever-present threat of unpleasant withdrawal. Would anyone give their unconditional devotion to a drug that exposed them to these threats?

The demon drug: a junkie's eye view of smack

This probably goes some way towards explaining where the notion of smack as a 'devil drug', 'a scourge', 'a terrible evil' comes from. Junkies themselves award it these titles in their darkest moments of despair and fear. Rather than blaming yourself for your situation, it is easier to feel that an evil outside force has invaded and taken you over. A lot of junkies talk in these terms. They transfer the contempt they sometimes feel for themselves onto the drug. Like a wronged lover who attacks the other party, a junkie transfers anger onto the drug. Heroin becomes a dangerous, larger-than-life adversary, possessed of supernatural, demonic powers. This is the way junkies explain their helplessness and inability to fight against it. Carol told me, 'It's an evil drug. It really is. I used to wear a cross around my neck and one night it dropped off.' When I asked another friend how he felt about heroin he said that he saw it as evil: 'The worst thing is the insidiousness of it. There's nothing particularly good-vibed about heroin. It grabs you. It's got an icy fucking grip that just shuts on you. It's the nearest thing to the devil ...' Dougie's response was a little less dramatic, but just as anti-smack: 'It's obvious,' he said, 'Who wants to be slave to an indifferent master?'

Other users try to cope with their addiction by minimising the seriousness of their situation. In answer to the question, 'What is the worst thing about heroin addiction?' addicts have responded with quips like, 'You can never get enough,' 'Your mum tells you off,' and 'It gives you spots.' Despite listing the disadvantages of drug use, when asked what advice he would give to somebody just starting out another man replied, 'Any time they want to know how to do it just tell them to bring the gear round and I'll show them what to do.' I have heard friends joke that they are looking forward to being old so that they will no longer feel guilty about wasting their lives taking heroin. Ray revealed the extent of his allegiance to smack when he quipped, 'I can't wait to be 60 so I can do it and not feel guilty.'

The drug scene abounds with flippancy, wry humour and contradictory opinions, even from the same person. The life of a junkie is very much a life of highs and lows, a series of great swings between states of optimism and despair, between pleasure and pain. The paradoxical nature of the heroin experience is such that it must be hard for a complete outsider to come to terms with the contradictory reports of its devotees. Those who denigrate and condemn the drug for which they have lost their livelihoods, their liberty or their reputation will also go to inordinate lengths and repeat impossible risks just to carry on taking it. Thus there is a double standard; knowing that they enjoy junk but aware of the consequences of using it, most junkies will say that smack is a bad thing yet continue to seek it out.

Despite everything, junkies are truly in love with heroin. They will endure any indignity and difficulty to be united with the object of their desire. Indeed junkies spend a good deal of time daydreaming about what life would be like if they had enough smack to last forever. They imagine putting out lines as thick as a man's wrist, as thick as gutter pipes. They joke about winning the pools and buying not mansions and private planes, but kilos and kilos of smack. They see themselves moving to Pakistan and camping out next to hills of heroin. Last year when she came off heroin one local user sat writing in her diary to kill the urge to go out and buy smack. What she wrote expresses the intense longing, the passion with which all junkies come to crave heroin:

> I feel as if I want to give everything to the dragon. My possessions; everything in the house; the furniture; the stereo; the TV; sell the rented video; organise a burglary; sell the house; go on the game; set up as a dealer. Every nerve, muscle, sinew and thought are craving, straining towards getting more. Getting so much smack I never need worry again. A box full, a suitcase full, a wardrobe overflowing. I want to buy myself a mattress filled with smack, slash it end to end and wallow face downwards in it forever. I have no other needs now: not success, status, ambition, family, friends, jobs. I am like a monk or nun. Poverty and obedience could be mine. Even chastity. For smack can fill that place, too. Seal me off completely. Me and my smacko, cruisin' down the lanes of life ... It's not love, but smack, I need ... 'All you need is smack ... smack is all you need ...'

In the words of another friend, 'Everybody really wants a kilo. Then they can take it till the last gramme and save that for an overdose.' He was, of course, joking, but the underlying idea is clearly that no junkie would want to go on living once the smack ran out.

This was reiterated by other addicts. Carol for instance, lamented, 'If I thought I couldn't score I think I really could kill myself. I just don't think I could face it.' Most people have no intention of carrying out these threats. They are merely expressing the intensity of their fear of being without drugs. Junkies gear their whole lives to avoiding that fate. The twin needs, to take smack and to be free of it, battle constantly, laying waste the poor junkie in the middle. Surveying this inner battle ground one addict hung his head and muttered, 'My head is fucking cabbaged.' When your head is 'cabbaged' a good hit can wipe out all the arguments. If you are stoned, the war will not seem to matter. Exhausted by the row between their two selves, junkies usually take another hit and give up trying to resolve it.

Smack and the inner life

It is obvious that the effects of heroin are not merely physical. There are profound effects on the user's emotions and personality. Every aspect of his inner life falls under a shadow. Junkies take smack in order to feel 'normal' but it is a new kind of numb-normal. This is what junkies finally want. Junk insulates the user from the trials of the outside world. Junk wraps him up and keeps him warm, protecting the raw sensibilities from the onslaught of painful reality. Junk kills the taste of the bitter fruit of the Tree of Knowledge. It may not fling open the gates of Eden but, even as long ago as 1821, De Quincey asserted that opium held 'the Keys of Paradise' and brought 'an assuaging balm' to the hearts of 'rich and poor alike'. Religion was once called the 'opium of the people'. The people have lost their religion: they want their opium back.

> The child is grown
> The dream is gone
> And I have become
> Comfortably numb.
>
> Roger Waters, Pink Floyd

Everybody wants to be comfortable. So far so good. But who wants to be numb? There is the catch. Heroin dulls emotional pain. It forms an effective barrier between the addict and the inevitable disappointments of life, smoothing the spiky corners of experience. Heroin provides a tremendous sense of well-being, even when all is clearly not well: it opens up the door that leads back to that happy childhood state where 'all's right with the world'. It generates a sense of being safe, of being tucked in on Christmas Eve, knowing that your stocking will be full in the morning. Problems shrink away to nothing. Everything seems possible and, more importantly, worthwhile. Enthusiasm abounds. Once they have glimpsed it, junkies want to stay in this 'never never land' forever.

Smack not only diminishes the ability to feel pain and unhappiness, it completely shifts the user's whole focus on life, changing his response to everything around him. Small things can start to matter terribly. Important events can seem insignificant. Life's normal demons become powerless and impotent. This is why junkies can allow themselves to be defeated; they do not notice the enemy approach. When you are stoned, hurt and distress are seen in soft focus. Your mind is fully aware of events but you do not experience them with the same intensity that you otherwise would. Heroin has a strange ability to minimise or render unreal the true nature of a situation. This effect possibly accounts for a lot of things, such as why junkies who inject themselves and face the accompanying serious health risks fail to respond to warnings from doctors, or threats that they will die if they do not change their lifestyle.

It could explain why dealers who know that the law is onto them sit back and allow themselves to be arrested rather than shutting up shop and avoiding the inevitable. Junk makes threats and danger seem distant and unreal, it takes away their impact. Junkies can allow very real and serious problems to linger on, not taking evasive action until it is just too late. They become like people standing mesmerised in front of an approaching train. Like Doctor Spock, the junkie takes only a scientific interest in the momentum of the machine. Unless jolted by others he could easily leave moving out of its path until it was simply too late. Junkies do not want to die, but some forget to move out of the way.

Thus, although junkies take drugs in order to feel 'normal' and carry on their everyday lives, their personalities and responses to life undergo subtle changes. In time, junk erodes your judgment, ability and desire to see what is going on around you. The protection junk provides not only locks pain out, it locks you in. You are cocooned as surely and painlessly as an Egyptian mummy, as hopeless and motionless as an embalmed corpse. Relationships start to suffer as you slip away behind a haze of your own indifference, unaware that your attitudes have changed and you are becoming a stranger to those who love you. Of her husband, a heavy user, one woman remarked in anguish, 'Christ, I even have to tell him his own fucking name, now.' While you may be able to lead a reasonably ordinary life, ambition and drive are sapped, progress tends to be slow, and you are likely to achieve far less than you would otherwise have done. All those hours spent quietly nodding out in front of the television might otherwise have been put to constructive use. Addicts will recognise the sense of frustration expressed in this remark: 'It's not the physical effects that worry me, but it's held me at first base for the last ten years and stopped me doing anything.'

Smack means that you live a diminished, retracted existence, participating less and less in former pursuits, narrowing horizons, eliminating acquaintances, decreasing your circle of associates until it almost exclusively includes only people involved with heroin. The longer you allow heroin to be a part of your life the more damage it will do. If it stays around too long, then it becomes very difficult to return to anything like the life you had before smack came into it. The longer you stay around, the more you will lose. No wonder junkies call it a devil and a dragon. It greedily eats away at all areas of your life and you are mesmerised, hypnotised, unable to take a grip, pull yourself up and change the situation. Even the strongest, most forceful people can go under if they have a weakness for smack. Those who let themselves get arrested must come to in a state of shock in a cell somewhere, quite unable to comprehend how it has all happened to them.

The junkie look

Taking junk does not do much for anyone's appearance, and the more you take, the worse you look, but the popular picture of a junkie as a dirty, down-at-heel, greasy-haired youth is no longer accurate. It is quite untrue that the majority of junkies can be spotted at a glance as they walk down the street. Only those who are very stoned or those who have completely given up stand out from the crowd. For a year or two, at least, the rest look much like everyone else. It is only their close friends and associates who might notice a change in them. If you meet someone who is using heroin regularly and controlling his habit you will probably never notice anything unusual about him. This is because most people stay at home to enjoy their hit in private. The strikingly noticeable after-effects of taking heroin wear off in an hour or two at the most, and, by the time the user presents himself to the world, he is looking fairly normal again. Whether he wears a suit or a pair of jeans, a junkie will not stand out from other people dressed in a similar fashion. What is noticeable is that any user's appearance will begin to deteriorate in time. It is, therefore, his own close friends who will notice the change rather than strangers who did not know him before he took to using smack.

People who are off their heads on scag do not generally cut much of a dash. They may be a little unsteady on their feet, almost appearing to be drunk. Standing up is not, however, an activity in which they are likely to indulge by choice. They are more typically to be found slumped in a chair, legs stretched out, head lolling onto the chest with a half smoked cigarette just beginning to burn its way through their trousers and into a comparatively unfeeling and, therefore, uncomplaining leg. This cosy condition, known as 'being on the nod', is usually accompanied by half-closed eyelids, a drooping, half-open mouth, gormless expression and a sudden jerking awake when the message from the singeing leg finally gets through. The complexion usually becomes pale and waxy and the breathing shallow. A film of perspiration beads the forehead, and the face is always drawn. Smack, like a peevish adversary who is bigger and more powerful than you, seizes your face in one hand, pushing in the cheeks and pulling down the corners of the mouth. Smack-heads always look down in the mouth, however good they feel. The better they feel, the worse they look.

Smack also has a very specific telltale effect on the pupils of the eyes. After a hit the pupils shrink in direct proportion to the amount of gear taken, or, should I say, its effect on the user. If the user is very stoned, the pupils will be no more than tiny black pin-holes. He will, therefore, be said to be pinned out. Really pinned out eyes give the user a very peculiar expression. In people with dark eyes this is not so noticeable but when the eyes are blue, especially pale blue, the user ends up looking like the Incredible Hulk after he has just taken one of his turns. For the most part, however, users are often not as stoned as they would wish to be so that their eyes may well appear to be fairly normal. Only someone studying them carefully would notice anything unusual. As the drug wears off the pupils begin to widen again. In the early stages of withdrawal they become unnaturally enlarged. Users anxiously hunting a hit which is well overdue tend to appear rather wild-eyed. When the user starts to withdraw, his eyes and nose will run and he will sometimes have fits of uncontrollable sneezing. Users confess to more 'colds' than anyone else. It is the only way they can explain their symptoms to a puzzled observer. No one seems to question the fact that these 'colds' fail to develop and seem to disappear as suddenly and mysteriously as they came. In certain pubs or betting shops in Liverpool an innocent sneeze can cause a whole room full of people to turn in unison and gaze in recognition.

Dirty and down at heel

Rumour has it that junkies are dirty, degenerate and smelly. It is, of course, true that some can take to wearing the same clothes day in day out without noticing that they have become stained or started to smell. It just seems so much more convenient to pull on yesterday's outfit than to look for something new. When you are really involved with junk, the only routine you establish is the one that supplies the drugs. Things like going to the launderette become terrible chores that cannot be faced and which must be put off indefinitely. Of course, not every junkie is oblivious to his public image. It tends to be people who are quite heavily involved with heroin who start to let their appearance go. One addict who has got his habit under control looked back on his life as a heavy user and told me, 'You generally do tend to get smelly and hairy and wear the same things day in and day out. Jimmy wore his shoes till they turned black and you could have peeled them off his feet.' Junkies who are not well off and who have to hustle for their gear tend to be so absorbed in the problems of getting the money that they forget their appearance. He continued, 'I never shaved. I grew a beard. I didn't get my hair cut. I didn't go to the dentist. I wore the same clothes and developed a general hatred of having baths.' This hatred of having baths or 'hydrophobia', as friends jokingly call it, is something they commonly referred to. That is not to suggest that some junkies do not wash, just that they do not enjoy it, especially when they are short of drugs and feeling ill. A lot of things seem to be just too much trouble when you are strung out and having baths is one of them.

Junkies who hold down a professional job are, however, often very concerned about making sure that their image is up to scratch and go to great lengths to be certain that they do not smell or attract attention in any way. Dougie explained it like this:

> Junkies worry about deodorant. You lose your sense of smell and, therefore, you think you must stink. You know you can't but you go over the top and start putting tons of Mum every-where. You're so paranoid you even spray it on your neck. I think I've got a Right Guard habit.

Dougie is able to laugh at himself and the situation but underneath there is a genuine fear of letting himself down and drawing any attention that could make his colleagues suspicious. He went on, 'Drugs can alter your olfactory perception. Your nose doesn't func-tion properly so it's just going to realise its own imagined fears. If you know your nose isn't working then you reckon your feet must stink in public ...'

Most junkies try very hard to keep up appearances and avoid let-ting the side down. When their appearance does suffer it is mainly because they cannot afford to buy clothes, pay hairdressers or go to the launderette. When you are spending every spare minute looking for gear you finally tend to give up on your appearance. Nevertheless, there are probably far more well-scrubbed, neatly turned out, anx-ious heroin users keen to keep their habit secret than there are scruffy, dirty, dishevelled ones. Drug users hail from all sorts of social back-grounds and there are bound to be many for whom the path to a new wardrobe is quite smooth. In the end, the only thing that users cannot disguise is the crumpled, grey face of long-term addiction.

A portrait of despair

The face of the long-term addict probably speaks most eloquently about his lifestyle and situation. In the end junkies come to look gaunt and haggard. Their skin takes on a dead, grey, dry appear-ance. I remember visiting a friend in London who had used heroin for a number of years. I had not seen her for a while but had always thought her to be quite an attractive person. In the eyes of the world she would have looked all right. There are plenty of fine upstanding citizens who look worse than the average junkie. To me, however, the change was shocking. Her skin had the look of deep, bloodless rubber, a ghastly, uninteresting shade, too dark for magnolia, too light for warm beige. It was the sort of colour that would have looked dull on a ceiling. She had become so terribly thin that her features, even her mouth, seemed vulgar and abnormally pronounced. They looked as if they did not belong together in the same face and the big beautiful eyes were glassy and distant. Five years before, she had been very pretty, just like the proverbial china doll with light blonde hair, bright cornflower blue eyes and that traditionally smooth, white skin with a glow of pink to the cheeks. She had been confident and outgoing. People had called her beautiful. Smack had changed all that. Now there was a sweaty look to her face, her hair had grown out to reveal its natural mouse colour. It was greasy and uncared-for. Even for female junkies, paying hairdressers is out of the question when the money could be spent on smack. Her voice was quiet and gruff, affected by the amount of gear she was using. I came away speculating on whether my friend would ever recover her looks if she decided to stop taking drugs. For most young people a full recovery is possible but the older you get, the longer it takes and I suspect that there comes a point where you fail to bounce back, or even crawl back, at all.

It requires a fairly long-term, concerted effort to really start looking wrecked but quite a few people manage it. In fact longtermers look even worse when they try stopping. I remember seeing John, one of Bobby's friends, walking along with his little boy. From a distance, I thought the child was with his grandfather. John looked so stooped and haggard and grey that, for weeks, Bobby and I were making 'sick' jokes about our 'grandad'. Every time we saw an old man hobbling along we would say, 'Look! ... There goes John,' and dissolve into hysterical laughter. It was our defence mechanism, our way of coping with the realisation of where we were heading. That kind of shock is enough to make you think about stopping. You have to face the fact that your friends are not the only ones who are 'messed up, hassled and worn'. Bobby himself was the unwitting inspiration for one occasional user to pull out in time. The man met Bobby on the way to score. After seeing the state he was in he changed his mind and went home. When Bobby heard the story he laughed but he was not really amused.

Food for thought?

If you are not well off and you start using smack you will find that you have to abandon all thoughts of eating normal meals straight away. Shopping and cooking take up too much time and energy, but more to the point, they cost money. Even a small habit costs £20 a day to finance although the purity of street heroin has become so low that one person could easily spend £100 just to stay well. When money is tight, buying a bag comes before getting food. Users frequently have to make do and sometimes do without. Food will soon become a luxury they simply cannot afford. Moreover, junk diminishes the desire to eat normal meals and substitutes a craving for sweets, cakes and chocolate. The evening meal for a junkie in Liverpool might comprise two chocolate eclairs and a packet of biscuits. For afters he might select a bag of some old-fashioned juvenile treat like cinder toffee or dolly mixtures. When you arrive on the scene you are as incredulous at the sight of grown men fishing in various pockets for bags of penny sweets as you are at the prospect of people injecting tap water. Soon, you will be down at the sweet shop with the rest. Buying fruit gums in bulk is a sure sign. Bobby, laughing about his fondness for sweets, quipped, 'You can always spot the junkie in the off-licence. He's the one who doesn't buy any ale and spends a fiver on sweets.'

It is not, of course, entirely true that junkies never drink alcohol. Some do, but, on the whole, alcohol is not really compatible with heroin. Users who have a large habit would probably be sick if they had more than one or two drinks. Nevertheless, well-established junkies sometimes enjoy a drink. A few have problems with alcohol; some replace heroin with drink during periods when they are fighting against drug addiction. Needless to say, that only compounds their problems.

If you are dependent on smack you cannot depend on much else and although junkies usually manage to keep in a supply of basic necessities, there is always the day when the shops have shut or the money has run out. On these days, it is cereal with water, dry toast and black tea. Meals degenerate into dishes like chips with ketchup or pasta with puree. Heroin addicts are renowned for simplifying their diets down to the bare necessities. Cornflakes are a popular choice. Junkies seem to discover them simultaneously and quite independently. When she is stoned and does not fancy eating, it is easy for the user to toss a few cornflakes into a bowl, add some dried fruit and a splash of milk. I have known users for whom cornflakes made up a big part of their diet. Two men who shared a flat used to have a big white bowl which they filled up with cornflakes. Each took a spoon and dug in. People who share a syringe do not baulk at sharing a dish. Obviously, weight loss follows these deprivations and some addicts are badly undernourished. Clearly, it is starvation rather than the direct effects of the drug that accounts for this. Until the money to buy cornflakes runs out, however, junkies are not too concerned. Those who worry about their health buy vitamin pills when they can afford to.

Stoned behaviour

People who are very stoned are basically only semi-conscious and so they tend to make rather dull companions. A group of junkies enjoying a hit together can make a tragi-comic scene as they stumble and mumble their way through snatches of broken conversation, lapsing into silence and confusion just when communication seems possible. On another occasion they might become loud, volatile and garrulous. As Jimmy explained,

> Part of the symptoms of being stoned are that people talk a lot. You talk fast. You talk ahead of yourself, even when you're trying to control it. I've been in a group where everyone's talking at once and you have to start shouting to get your point over. It really annoys me the way you get six people all talking at once.

It never occurs to any of them to shut up and such a scene can easily degenerate into a series of irrational, hysterical shouting matches. These confrontations rarely lead anywhere and the reason for the row is often forgotten before a compromise is reached. Junkies impress neither the outside world nor one another when they are in this condition. When they look in the mirror they stare at a blank person who looks puffy, tired and accusing. They lose the gleam of stoned enthusiasm and are simply left with the drawn face of addiction.

In regular users, a hit can generate a good deal of activity. Even the most mundane task can be eagerly carried out. The more junk people have, the cleaner their houses. One woman remarked on this saying,

> Sometimes when you are high you can clean the whole house from top to bottom without even bothering to stop for a break. When the gear wears off you feel wrecked and too tired to take your clothes off to go to bed. You don't want to do anything until you get more gear.

This energy, however, is not always put to good use because, when people are stoned, it is easy for them to get side-tracked. This means that they might achieve far less than they would have done without drugs. Say, for example, a user decided to take some cuttings from a potted plant. She might go to the cupboard for a pot and start looking. She does not find the one she wants. Three hours later she is still there, surrounded by every dish in every cupboard. She has taken them all out and they are now piled all over the floor. She is cleaning them, polishing them, sorting them into piles: by shape, by size, by colour. She is making a catalogue of them all to stick on the cupboard door. Then she will do the knives and the forks, the pots and pans, the ornaments, perhaps all her books. The cuttings have been forgotten. This is what happens to the washing. It is not uncommon to find the bath or the sink full of it. It was placed there with good intentions but the gear wore off. Junkies try to plan their activities around the next hit. Unpleasant tasks are saved up until the gear arrives and yet, quite often, the plan misfires and nothing gets done. Carol summed it up when she said, 'Without smack all I want to do is stare at the wall. With it I don't want to do much more but, at least, I think I want to.'

Scoring: keeping up the supply of drugs

Anyone reading this book who has not had experience of the heroin scene, but who is hoping to gain an insight into the lives of heroin users, must already be starting to build up a fairly unpleasant picture. It must be made clear, however, before I go any further, that there are many different scenes scattered across the country where the daily reality and the rules of conduct differ. Most of my experiences have occurred on the lower rungs of the heroin ladder, and I can claim little knowledge of the lives of wealthy or titled drug users. Even so, one common factor that unites all junkies whatever their advantages, or lack of them, is the need for a daily supply of heroin.

Because heroin is a controlled drug everyone who uses it will face similar problems. Heroin is a great leveller. Everyone who uses it will also be part of the same undercover network. On the drug scene no man – or woman – is an island. The more users and dealers you know, the better your chance of keeping yourself supplied. Remaining aloof means trouble; it means not knowing where else to go when your regular dealer hits a bad patch or gets arrested. In every small group of interdependent users, there is always someone with a foot in another camp. In that camp there will be others with contacts elsewhere. In times of drought, I have known heavy users or desperate dealers leap into fast cars and hurtle up and down the motorways from one major city to another on the say-so of someone who knows someone who knows someone who knows someone else who can supply heroin. There are pockets of users all over the country and they are not confined to the big cities. There is always someone with junkie friends in a little Welsh village or a little Yorkshire town. The different heroin scenes are not as separate as an outsider might think. Distance is no barrier; wherever you go, you can never outrun smack. Nor is class the barrier it might be in other circumstances. Upper-class users mingle with the middle classes, the middle classes get in on the working-class scene. Ultimately users are not divided by their accents and backgrounds: they are united by their heroin habit.

Day-to-day life for all addicts revolves around scoring (most people are aware that this is the popular term for buying drugs). It might seem sensible to buy in quantity like someone doing their weekly shopping at a supermarket. Most junkies, however, do not operate like that. Availability of the drug and its high price are not the only reasons for this apparent lack of foresight. Junkies live from day to day. The more junk they have, the more they take. If you have enough heroin you are likely to go on a massive binge, building up your habit to a point where it is out of control and you cannot afford to keep up your supply. Drug taking, like drinking, tends not to be a solitary pursuit. Anyone with enough junk will probably discover a gaggle of mates who will hang around for the rake-off of their friend's stoned goodwill. This, too, means that the junk will disappear faster than intended. Some will be given away, some will be sold as the result of pressure from those who need it, or in an attempt to recoup funds. Either way, it will be gone much faster than the user planned.

Drug busts happen in any area at any time. All users live close to the loo in hopes of dropping the junk down it if the worst should occur. The more junk you have, the bigger the worry. Anyone who buys in more than a gramme knows there is a very real risk of being charged with dealing if the police should call. It is hard to explain away a quarter ounce as being simply your own supply, even if that is the truth. Despite these considerations, however, the main reasons why junkies need to score daily are still their own inability to resist the drugs once they have them and the struggle to find the money to score. Obviously, the nature of this struggle depends on who and where you are.

In London, for instance, there are glamorous scenes that swing and there are pathetic clusters of down-and-outs. There are junkies who pack themselves off to private clinics to be cured and those who overdose in mouldy basements. Some junkies sell shares to finance their habit while others flog the furniture. It is obvious which of these sacrifices is easier to make. The papers show us that rich and titled junkies do suffer. They are not above the law nor the personal problems that heroin brings. It is possible to spend huge sums of money buying smack. Even rich junkies can become poor in time. Nevertheless it is those who start out poor who suffer most.

CHAPTER 4

ℭ The price of feeding the dragon: getting the money

Empty pockets: the first sign of trouble

Obviously, the kind of trouble addiction brings will be of a different order for people from different strata of society but money will be a problem for most people who live on a fixed income. As money begins to flow in one direction it ceases to matter whether you earn £50,000 a year or live on the dole. There is never enough cash to finance a heroin habit because one day the money will run out. Whatever your circumstances, you will probably be living up to your income already. When you find yourself dependent on heroin money will, therefore, have to be recalled from other directions. This can involve painful decisions. If you had a comfortable middle-class life you will begin to look for ways to economise. You will drink less, socialise less, eat fewer meals in restaurants and stop buying clothes. You will cancel winter holidays, weekends away and give up expensive sports or hobbies for which you no longer have the energy. At the other end of the scale you might fiddle the electric meter, sell what few belongings you have and start ripping off the people you do not like. You will leave robbing your friends until you are really desperate. Drug addicts have to plan their lives around heroin and being a junkie can be hard work. Dougie hit the nail on the head:

> You've got to be fairly intelligent to last more than a year or two on the smack scene. You've got to have a good act to convince everybody that you've still got credibility rating. You can only pay for so many funerals on overdraft. I've buried my grandad three times.

Those of us who have received a good education, who are articulate, capable, plausible, employed, have comfortable lifestyles and supportive, similarly well-heeled associates can survive on the smack scene without too much aggravation for quite a long time. Those who lead jobless, hopeless lives more rapidly end up registered, nicked or both. The rest of us can cover our tracks better. We are less likely to be under suspicion and we can keep our noses clean by getting others to do our dirty work like scoring in 'hot' houses where the police may be about. As we have more collateral to begin with, it takes us longer to sell off our belongings, lose our jobs and finally join the rest in bedsitter land. When our backs are against the wall we can borrow from liberal, sympathetic acquaintances who will be too concerned and too embarrassed to press us for the return of their cash. We need not risk the perils of petty pilfering, shoplifting, cheque fraud, or getting our heads kicked in over a tenner. For a long time we can manage to support a heroin habit unobserved, unharried and without too much to worry about. Even so, for every addict who fails to respond to the warning signals and bail out there comes a time when the money and luck runs out.

When someone who is employed starts taking heroin he views it as a leisure activity. Instead of going out to the pub, he and his friends stay in and get stoned together. This will not cost very much. I have known new recruits make a bag of smack costing £10 or £20 last them for two or three days. At this stage using heroin is actually cheaper than a night on the ale. Heroin will be a weekend activity for these people, and £10 a week can easily be found from what a working person might see as his entertainment budget. For those who move on to addiction, however, Monday morning starts to be a time when work can only be faced if enough gear for a hit has been saved. If not, absenteeism and the buying in of extra supplies to face the rest of the week may begin. Once this happens expenditure on heroin rises rapidly. £10 to £20 a day is a typical initial outlay. £100 a week might be going on smack. More scag will very soon be required to achieve the same feelings of euphoria and relaxation. Expenditure can rise rapidly to £200 a week or more; some people spend over £60 a day. Realising that he has walked into a trap, the sensible user will plan to stop at the first convenient moment. Weekends, holiday periods like Christmas and Easter or half-term holidays for teachers will become times when withdrawal must be faced. The strong take their punishment and climb out, managing to keep paying the mortgage and the bills.

After a few weeks free from the chaos of watching his money flowing out faster than it comes in, the user will feel confident again. He has got out unscathed. All is well. He can afford to have a little treat. Back he goes to the smack shop. Now he faces a new dilemma; he likes being stoned but he knows he cannot afford it. He casts around for ways to finance his habit. This is when, like alcoholics, heroin users start to borrow from banks or run up large bills on Access cards. As one local man said to me, 'You're all right. You've got the plastic.' Up to a point the remark is true, but the plastic does not last indefinitely. When things get hot the plastic melts away like snow in the rain.

Before this happens, quickly thought-up tales about new kitchens, carpets, window frames or cars that are urgently needed will have the unsuspecting bank manager authorising loans of up to £2,000 or £3,000. The smack user is delighted. What a binge he can have! He and his friends wallow on. They can have all the smack they want – for a while. At the rate of at least £20–£60 a day, it is much easier than the user imagined to spend a £1,000. People can smoke two or three grammes a day, each one costing £70 or more. Accustomed to thinking of a £1,000 as a lot of money, the addict will be shocked when he realises that the money and his credit can run out in only a matter of months. No more loans. What next?

Shocked by his own predicament, he may try to pull out but, often, circumstances make this impossible. Pressure of work, family commitments, fear of seeking medical help can mean that the user simply cannot find the time and peace of mind to get off heroin. He is right in it up to his neck and he starts looking for a way out. Overdrafts begin to appear at this stage, followed rapidly by concerned letters from the puzzled bank manager. In time, the friendly manager will begin to smell a rat. He will assume reckless behaviour of one sort or another and his letters will become less forbearing until they end up being downright aggressive. Cheque cards will be recalled. Relations will be soured and the user will remain desperate to keep himself afloat. To quote Dougie again:

You all pay the same. Either dealing out of the letter box fighting the forces of law and order and ending up in the nick, or getting sued by the bank and ending up the same way. There's no way of being clever about it unless you're the Marquis of Arsehole.

Onto the slippery slope: loans, losses and pawn tickets

Soon, the user has to start making the painful decision to sell things that he would dearly like to keep. The car is the first thing to go. That money is not used to repay loans. Some might go to stop the gas being cut off, but the rest will be spent on smack. He has bought himself a little respite. Relieved, he sits back to enjoy it. Weeks later something else will have to go. All this time the user spends no money on clothes and little on food. By now he is on the way down. His finances are shaky, his credibility slipping. There comes a point where he only sees his possessions in terms of how much smack he can get by selling or trading them. All sorts of loved and valued belongings are sold for only a small percentage of their value. A much-loved guitar might be relinquished for a quarter of its real worth. When the smack runs out and the body calls, desperate and speedy measures are needed.

Humour can sustain the drug-hungry addict on a search: many can still laugh at themselves. Dougie has that gift. He quipped, 'It's a good job you can't sell bits of yourself at the body bank or I'd be down there to find out what you could get for a pair of "Princess Margarets".' The term 'Princess Margarets' denoted the lungs of a heavy smoker. A black joke I admit, but when you hit Skid Row, the only choice left is laughter or tears. In Liverpool, even among junkies, laughter is far from dead.

Once the supply of belongings is getting depleted, finding the money comes down to scams. Scams are schemes, ploys or activities by which money can be acquired, often through some shady deal. The insurance job is popular. This means shipping all your remaining possessions off to a 'safe' place of hiding and letting everyone know you are going away for a few days. On return, if the door has not already been kicked in, you kick it in yourself and apply for a claims form immediately. On that you list all sorts of exotic and expensive items. In due course, you can expect a nice fat cheque that will keep you going for a while. Most people only pull this trick once. Some try it two or three times until no company will insure them. One local person was rumoured to have made three successful attempts and even to have moved all his original belongings back to his place after he had made his claim. Of course, it is not uncommon in Liverpool for the real burglars to call and when they do, if the victim has got himself to a stage where he is uninsured he will be left feeling pretty sick. This, too, is reputed to have happened. One man was said to have robbed himself three times and then been left flabbergasted when burglars picked the place clean while he was away. The poetic justice amused all his so-called friends. Indeed, on the junk scene there are plenty of 'friends' who would call back to help themselves to what you have left if they knew you were going away.

If you are in the know, another scam is the stolen car scam. For a small fee it is possible to have your car crushed. If it is fairly new, and insured for a good sum of money, but needs work that you cannot afford before it can be sold, this is a good ploy. When it is crushed and has disappeared from the roads forever, you report it stolen with a tear in your eye and a tremor in your voice. After that you sit back waiting to be reimbursed by your long-suffering insurers.

I am not suggesting that all junkies resort to these measures, and plenty of people who are not strung out will also try them, but sometimes a user who owes money will be encouraged by his creditors, or by other junkies who egg him on, to take one of these apparently easy routes out of his problems. Many more addicts will struggle on, actually too proud to admit defeat in this way, too scared to take a risk, or too wary of risking their self-respect.

Anyone trying to pay their way on wages will be hard put to manage. After the car has gone, users will trudge around selling treasured bits and pieces to so-called antique shops, getting ripped off themselves by the fine upstanding members of the community who run these reputable businesses. I remember one friend taking a set of old pictures to a shop which offered her £15 for them. Not because she knew any better, but because the sum involved was not more than the magic £20 to buy a bag, she moved on, lugging the pictures around to other shops. It was a cold, rainy day. On such occasions, trying to sell things can be soul-destroying. You are faced with the sadness of losing your favourite things and the unpalatable knowledge that you are letting yourself down. You are also faced with the disappointment of moving from shop to shop without finding a buyer and the growing nausea and fear as withdrawal begins.

By the time you have visited three or four shops your nose and eyes are running uncontrollably, making you look like a flu victim to be avoided even by potential buyers of the goods you have to sell. You could be seized by a major attack of sneezing just as you set out to haggle over a price. These things make matters worse.

You begin to feel that the first person to offer you £20 can have everything. You wish you had brought the better things you left at home after all. Surely somebody could have bought something by now. You worry because you do not have even your bus fare back. Your arms are dropping off with the weight of the bags you are carrying. Then, success. At the last shop, just when you were giving up, somebody wants to buy your clock, or your old oil painting. Somebody believes they have found a fool to rip off. And they have. You exchange goods and money fast, explaining that it must be cash as you have no bank account. You are safe again. On that rainy day, by trying another shop my friend made more than an extra £65 for herself. She sold her pictures for £70, several times the amount she was offered in shop number one. That day she was lucky beyond her hopes. Sometimes you tote your wares all over town and slink home identifying self-pityingly with the little match girl to dream up another plan before you become too ill to carry on.

Once you have sold something, provided there is cash to spare, it is straight into a taxi and off to score, sneezing all the way. Taxi drivers often get to know where dealers live or, at least, they have a good idea simply because they take so many people there. Sometimes a driver makes snide remarks like, 'What is this, the local supermarket?' You are not deterred. Ignoring his sarcasm, you ask him to wait. You rush in, hoping it will be there. You will die if there is no gear. Everything is OK. Back into the taxi and off home for relief. You sit back, gritting your teeth. 'It won't be long now ...' Until next time. Some taxi drivers use gear themselves. Once a mischievous driver told a friend, 'If I'd known you were going to score, I'd have picked you up sooner. I've just been here to score myself.' There are junkies everywhere now and they have an infallible nose for finding one another.

Once users start selling their possessions they are on the slippery slope. I have known people sell everything and finally lose their homes altogether. A junkie who fails to pull out in time can literally end up on the streets with nothing but the clothes he stands up in. It is actually possible to go from being a typical middle-class professional with your own home, car and comfortable lifestyle to being a tramp on the streets in a matter of a couple of years. Junkies can take the path that was worn long ago by alcoholics. The majority of winos on bomb-sites had homes and families once. The struggle to find money is relentless and the bigger your habit the harder you have to work at it. Brian, who is unemployed, summed it up like this: 'You crash out, go to bed and it might only be for three hours. Then the first thing you think of when you wake up is where you've got to go to get smack.'

Most junkies have huge debts. At first when things start to get out of control and the bank has given up on them, junkies borrow from friends. Initially, making excuses about unexpected bills, then brazenly admitting the truth, begging for clemency, understanding, and more to the point, help. Junkies can develop a good streak of cynicism, especially about their own promises. They ask to borrow money in the persona their friends knew: they accept it under a new guise. The 'old you' would have paid it back promptly, the 'new you' might never do so. As one friend said, 'The road to addiction is paved with good intentions.' Small debts are usually paid, but the big ones can hang over you forever. At the very moment you are making promises you disregard the notion of paying back. It must be OK. You are honest, decent, fair. You know you are. You will pay, somehow, someday. You will. Either way you must have £2000. You must. Friends cough up, disappointed in you, guilty that they cannot help. Giving money is the easy part. Putting up with you is more difficult. Some of these debts are paid, in part at least, others are simply put on ice or written off. Like a sword of Damocles they hang between you and your friends. Any time the sword could fall and the friendship finish. Marriages break up because of rows about gear; tormented families cut off their black sheep.

For many users, though, it is their families who suffer and who help the most. Relatives, mothers and fathers driven by total love give more than they can safely afford, go without themselves, worry and wonder. A junkie with a caring family always has a safety net and a reason to come off. A loner does not. Unburdening yourself to your family, however, is not always the best policy, as you may lose their respect and be constantly under suspicion. Brian explained, 'I told my parents. They were really good and helpful but now I've only got to have bags under my eyes or twitch or anything and they're asking if I'm all right.' Pete, who has used junk for many years, has never confessed to his family. He gave the reason for this as an attempt to protect them, 'It's not guilt,' he said. 'I just don't want to hurt them.'

While you still have something to sell you are comparatively high up in the junk hierarchy. Away below lies rock bottom and, in time, most junkies will glimpse its granite floor. High above rock bottom, on a grassy slope, stands the ignoble pawn shop, and many a worried junkie passes through its narrow door. Making a solemn pledge that you are prepared to forfeit a few baubles may seem easy, but it is not. There is a degree of embarrassment and humiliation involved for most people. There is a notice on the wall of my local pawn shop that reads, 'No pledge is insured while on these premises.' When I first took my turn at the counter I cast a bloodshot eye upon it and promptly imagined a robbery. I saw my trinkets carried off by another desperate junkie to pay for heroin. I allowed myself a wry smile and considered how I would explain the loss at home. This was not an honourable poverty.

Until I started this book I did not talk much with other heroin users about the lengths they went to in order to get the money, but now I know that most of my female friends who are addicts have pawned or sold their jewellery. A couple have sold their wedding rings. Junkies cannot afford the luxury of sentiment. It is little wonder that, when faced with the choice of daily humiliations, some people prefer to start dealing in smack to finance their habit. Living with the fear of the police could not be worse than facing an all-day struggle every day just to get enough money to buy enough heroin to make you feel normal. Everyone involved has his own theory as to when and why a junkie will decide to come off heroin. Much is talked about the dreaded rock bottom and how a junkie will only stop when he reaches it but, for every individual, rock bottom might be different. It might be losing his job and selling his house or living abroad selling his blood, but wherever it is, when he feels he can take no more hassle, he is reputed to give in and get out. It is clearly true that many people stop when they reach a point where they feel they no longer have the energy, the resources or the wit to keep themselves supplied. Even so, the rock bottom theory is an over-simplified platitude not true in every case. Some people never reach it while others grub around there for years quite undeterred.

The battle to stay hooked: time to pull out?

All junkies know they will have to stop one day. When you are in your twenties it is hard to believe that you will succeed in keeping up an uninterrupted supply of heroin until death do you part. Death seems a very long way off. Most junkies simply refuse to consider the possibility of a premature death. Everyone 'has it sussed.' Everyone will manage to be smarter and safer than the casualties who fell along the way. Most junkies hit some very hard times but they do not necessarily reach their own rock bottom before they stop. Many lead an on-off life, stopping using heroin for periods of weeks or months when the going gets rough, then sliding back in when life fails to come up with any new answers or when they feel safe to indulge without getting strung out again. There must be many more junkies who stop on their own without help than there are in hospital being assisted by doctors. Often they stop simply because there is a drought or they are held in police custody or there is a period where they have no money to score. Some stop simply because they are sick and tired of the whole business and need a break.

Once you have made up your mind to stop, you can take the pain and fight the craving. Not everyone can face making that choice. One man commented, 'I've met a few high society types and they're the least likely to stop because they've got no backbone. No balls!' Whether or not his observation was true, no one stops willingly, whoever they are, unless they feel ready to do so. If circumstances conspire to force you to come off when you are not ready, you will fight for all you are worth to avoid giving up heroin. You will do whatever is necessary to get more. Sometimes people go through two or three nightmare days, after which the worst of the extreme symptoms of withdrawal will be over, and rush straight out to get heroin as soon as the opportunity exists, putting themselves back to square one.

Obviously, any junkie is one of a group and that makes it harder to stop, or at least harder to stay stopped. Once the going gets rough, few junkies can afford to give away gear, so it is not very likely that someone will offer to come round and turn you on if you have decided to turkey. The pressure comes after you have gone through withdrawal. Even if you avoid old haunts for a while, during your first week or two without gear there are always friends or acquaintances who will ring or call asking if you can go halves on a bag if they are having a bad day or pressing you to score for them if you know somebody to whose house they cannot call. For most users the internal pressure to relapse is relentless. Dougie articulated the intensity of the yearning: 'Every time I walk into my kitchen I see the spoon jutting out over the edge of the table and my

stomach starts churning and my heart pounds.' This sort of longing
can be sparked off by even the sight of someone with whom you
have used gear in the past. Psychologists must have terms to explain
the process that is then set in motion. Often the trigger is days
ahead of the action. A user can allow the longing for gear to fester
and grow for a week or two, having refused to indulge on a particular occasion. All the time he will know that, when the moment
comes and it gets too much to bear, he will crack. The decision is
often made long before the action is taken. Then he will bargain
with himself. He will plan to have one hit and leave it alone again.
That almost never happens. Soon the user will accept that he is
becoming addicted again yet be unable to pull out before it is too
late. He blunders on each day, always planning to stop tomorrow.

If you are serious about coming off, friends who know you want
to stop are usually supportive. They encourage you, talk about
their own plans to come off and offer to stay away while you are
'making the effort'. Privately, they view your attempt with cynicism. Your effort is an inconvenience. It means there is one less person on the scene to tap for a hit when they are desperate, one less
place to score. If you manage to make it, they are shocked. They
congratulate you, wish they were in your shoes, plan their own
campaigns and watch you with eyes like cats, just waiting for you
to slip up. That is not because they do not want you to succeed. On
the contrary, when someone pulls out, it gives hope to the rest. It is
simply because they do not believe in your success.

If you remain drug-free for a few months you will be starting to
turn your attention to other matters. You might take up new hobbies, and work at getting fit. Now the others will watch with awe
and envy. As you jog past them, suntanned in your new shorts, they
will talk with amazement of your achievement. They may start setting you up, privately, as an example to follow. Alas, you will meet
them one day on your way to score. You will chuckle together,
knowingly. Their attitude is ambivalent. They will be partly relieved that you have rejoined the ranks, partly disappointed. Your
failure is a mirror of their own. You will listen keenly for details of
who has been busted, and who has the best gear. You will hurry off,
a little embarrassed, perhaps disquieted, having told yourself, and
your friends, that you are just having a 'little toot'. They will know
better. In your heart, so will you. The whole mess is rearing up
around you again. The wheels are in motion, the wagon is moving

and you are in your seat. A snippet of conversation sums up the situation quite well:

Ray: 'Every time I stop something crops up to set me back.'

Dougie: 'Like the morning!'

As Pete said, 'You reach the stage where everyone thinks you're on when you're off so you don't bother to mention it.'

Sometimes junkies who are using gear will kid themselves that they, too, can be fit. It is possible to see someone who has just had a decent hit and is filled with illusory health and well-being running round the park, looking pale and peaky but feeling great. Everyone has a good laugh when this happens, recognising the ridiculous irony of the situation. In due course, the runner will revert to exercising the dog by driving slowly round the park in a beat-up old car with the dog trotting along behind.

Truly reformed junkies can be a bit of a pain, like ex-cigarette smokers, who start opening windows and emptying ashtrays. They can sometimes minimise their own former problem, perhaps shutting it out to start afresh. I have met long-term ex-junkies who are more critical of people using heroin and less sympathetic than their more liberal counterparts who have never used drugs. They have had to be hard on themselves; some can be hard on others. There is nothing more irritating than a do-goody 'barrack-room' psychiatrist playing upsetting games with your head in a misguided attempt to increase your self-knowledge.

Despite all the problems, many people keep up the battle to remain strung out. If they hang on in there, their troubles will continue to multiply like flies on a hot day. They will meet the police at some stage, and they will continue to lose in every way; financially, physically, in their relationships with others, and in terms of their attitude to themselves. Carol commented ruefully, 'I would give five years of my life to go back to a time when I had never used heroin.' This demonstrated the intensity of her dissatisfaction with her present way of life.

Seeing yourself change: poor man, beggar man, thief ...

Dougie pointed out one of the changes to expect if you take junk: 'It makes everybody similar, you learn to lie; lies, deceit and acting, that's all you become clever at.' Lies are an essential part of junkiedom, at first, to protect yourself from the obvious consequences of heroin, later, to avoid having to share your drugs with someone else. Junkies become suspicious of one another and they are sharp-eyed. It is hard to hang on to your gear when someone else is sick, and little networks of people who share and help each other out will spring up. In these situations there can be a good deal of camaraderie and trust. The rule tends to be, if someone helps you when you are in need, you help them back. If they are mean to you, you do not forget. All sorts of petty spite and grudges abound. A junkie who had been turned away by someone he knows will wait until that person is sick and go round just to chase gear in front of him. Some people remain proud against all odds. Others blubber and wheedle. I have seen men crying because someone has refused to give them drugs on credit. Knowing someone else has gear is much harder to bear than facing a drought.

The scene is riddled with gossip and hearsay. Junk-think has a lot in common with the rest of the criminal underworld. You have put yourself on the wrong side of the law and your original framework for interaction becomes shaky. You find that people you know are stealing, kiting cheques, or doing insurance jobs. In other respects they are likeable people. The process of osmosis into this world is slow and gradual. By the time you realise what is going on, you have ceased to be shocked. You erect new rules. You listen to people making remarks like, 'Oh, I'm waiting for him to pay me back. He'll go out and steal something in a day or two and then he'll see me all right!' and shrug your shoulders. You will get your money back too, when the robbery takes place. This mentality and junk walk the same streets. Junk comes to you through the hands of some of these people. You learn to accept a new code. You do not kiss and tell. If you are middle-class and comparatively sheltered you begin to really understand what the now unfashionable sociologists were getting at when they coined the old joke, 'It's a fair cop but society's to blame.' When you are deprived, it is much easier to go out and take what you need by whatever means available. The weak cheat their friends; the strong find other means.

This underworld polices itself. There are strict rules and those who transgress are dealt with. In the hunt for money to buy drugs, for instance, one young man stole some jewellery belonging to Linda, his friend's wife. He pawned it and then sold the ticket to someone else who, in turn, redeemed the pledge, recognised the goods and returned them to Linda. When Linda's husband learnt how close she had come to losing these much treasured trinkets he went out and battered the thief. Justice had been done. Had the goods come from outside his circle, Linda's husband probably would have been happy to buy them.

I must emphasise that, contrary to popular opinion, many junkies never resort to crime of any kind to finance their habits. They sell up, borrow, beg and finally get registered or simply call it quits and go off somewhere for a cure. Those who do commit crime often do so under extreme duress, feel very ashamed of themselves and try to struggle back into their own good books again by changing their ways. The few who make a career of thieving are usually caught in the end. Most junkies who steal will say that they had not done so before they had a heroin habit and would never have done so unless driven by desperation. The crimes are usually petty and only involve getting enough money to score. There is never any left over for anything else. Many junkies seek help from doctors because they are simply not prepared to steal to buy drugs. Others are comparatively unrepentant, but very few are violent. I do not seek to judge or to condone their actions, merely to provide an insight into what becomes a way of life for some people.

Cheque fraud is a common method of obtaining money for drugs. It involves stealing a book and card, then getting out as soon as possible to buy goods by impersonating the owner. These are then sold or swapped for gear. One acquaintance told me he had kited (fraudulently used up) over forty books to buy gear, so many, in fact, that he could not remember them all. He said that after coming to Liverpool as a student he had met some local people who were doing this and he thought it a clever way to get the money he was beginning to need. In his own words he was 'chuffed to meet some real villains'. He commented,

If I didn't have smack in me I wouldn't have had the nerve to do it. I can't look back and say that if I hadn't wanted smack I would have lots of money in the bank. I wouldn't because if I hadn't wanted smack I wouldn't have done it. It's an art really, playing the game. No single person loses money. I wouldn't be able to steal off someone. I wouldn't have the bottle. It never seemed a great crime to me as no individual was suffering a loss. That goes some way towards salving whatever conscience I have left.

He refused to lay the blame for his predicament totally on heroin: 'Smack was the motivation but I don't blame smack 100%. You can't blame it totally for anything.' He now has a criminal record as a result of activities geared towards buying heroin. I asked him if he was sorry he had started taking it and he replied,

> I'm sorry for what smack has brought me to but I'm not sorry for taking smack because I've enjoyed it and if I was truly sorry I'd stop taking it now. Yet I don't think I've ever refused an offer of heroin. I've never felt it was time to say no.

He made it clear that he had not tried other ways of getting money: 'I don't think I've been the classic case of someone so desperate he runs out, bashes someone and grabs their money.'

From talking to people I get the impression that there are fewer of these 'classic cases' than the media implies. It only takes one person to turn to mugging full-time for quite a lot of damage to be done. The only one I know of mugs other junkies for their gear. He waits outside dealers' houses and takes the gear away from anyone who has just scored. He has been known to kick in front doors threatening violence if the drugs are not handed over. The public has far less to fear from him than other drug users do.

Shoplifting is another method by which some people make money for gear. Others try burglary, although they are far more likely to steal from someone they know than go out raiding the homes of strangers who are an unknown quantity. Paul used heroin for two years before he risked burglary. He recalled his time as a junkie and his struggle to find the money he needed:

> I spent my dole on it. Then I got a lot off my wife. I fiddled some, I stole some, I just got it by hook or by crook. I've begged, I've stolen, I've borrowed and I've mugged. I didn't hurt anybody though. One of them got a bump on the head, but, that's all. Then burglary. Joey and me burgled this pad ...

He went on to tell me a tale of incompetence and bungling that can only be described as comical, rather than shocking.

With a friend he called on a dealer who was out. Desperate for gear, they decided to break in and look for drugs to steal. The kitchen window seemed the ideal point of entry but, on the way in, Joey got stuck, wriggled through awkwardly and fell into the sink smashing all the dishes. On searching the flat, all they came up with was half an ounce of cannabis and so they took that to trade for heroin. On the way out, Joey again got stuck in the window. Paul ran off leaving him there and only Joey's stricken yelling brought Paul back to pull on his arms until he flew through the gap like a cork and the two of them fell in a heap on the ground. Their activities hardly amounted to major crime. The two sped off to swap their haul for scag and gain a few hours' respite from withdrawal. According to Paul, 'The money just kept on coming. We got a load of giros and that kept us going for a few days. We went through literally hundreds of pounds. The money just kept on coming.' He shamed himself into taking a stand. He is now off heroin and looks back on these times with regret. He added. 'Things are better now, but then I had lost all self-respect. I just didn't care about anything or anyone. Everything was geared towards getting smack.'

The lengths to which people will go to get heroin depend on two things. One is the size and seriousness of their habit and the other is their self-image. These two things are juggled constantly, the habit hungrily calling to be fed, the image pleading to be preserved. All junkies compromise. How far they go is a very personal choice. One man who admitted to having stolen thousands of pounds in cheque frauds still felt that the worst compromise he had made to buy heroin was to steal his son's money box. He told me, 'I've borrowed money with no way of knowing how I would pay it back. I fully intended to, but I knew I couldn't. I've stolen from my kids. I've taken money off a 7-year-old to buy smack.' He went on, 'I draw the line at mugging old ladies and stuff like that. Anything violent I draw the line there. There's no way I'm going to go out and mug somebody just to get smack.'

Money worries are endemic among junkies but everyone draws a line somewhere that he will not cross to get drugs. Junkies may take steps that some people would not, but only a very few lose all restraint. I asked Eddie what he considered to be rock bottom and he replied, 'Rock bottom is pure animal. It's giving people valium to render them unconscious then going through their pockets for their gear.' Rock bottom has a lot of layers.

I must admit that I have not drawn a very flattering portrait of some of the people who find their backs against the wall because of their involvement with drugs. They seem, perhaps, to stand condemned out of their own mouths. Some readers may be sympathetic, others will feel they have been reading remarks made by amoral, self-centred, selfish morons who show comparatively little remorse for what they have done and only small concern for their victims. It is true that there is a great deal of selfishness among drug users. After all, a heroin habit begins as self-indulgence, but junkies do find themselves in a position of total need. Total need makes most people selfish, even those who have never seen heroin. Up until recently, there has been little help available and admitting to being a junkie still means taking on a yoke that you may have to carry throughout life. At the very least you could find yourself being asked to find a new doctor but there are other, far greater, inconveniences. If discovered, junkies face the prospect of being turned down for employment or losing the jobs they already have. They may be refused a visa to travel to some foreign countries. With increasing computerisation of all sorts of personal information, who would be keen to have the fact that they are a heroin addict made known?

As it happens, many do face up to these pitfalls. Some prefer to seek medical help rather than steal. Others turn to crime, are finally arrested and have to face life with a record. It is not my intention to judge or justify the role played by them or all the others who have carried out similar crimes. What must be said is that junkies themselves are usually the greatest losers and they are left with a craving for heroin which could last many years and which could still destroy them. No one's life can ever be quite the same once heroin has become a part of it.

Unemployed young kids who get into junk to assuage the boredom of their hopeless, futureless lives have the worst of the drug world. They start out on the bottom rung and go down. Many experience all the horrors that junkiedom has to offer in a very short space of time. Pilfering from mum's purse, selling your parents' possessions and filching their pain killers cannot go on for long. There are quite a few very young dealers who have chosen to sell drugs as a way out of their troubles. Older addicts are shocked when they find themselves buying gear from young lads who could be their children.

An honest day's work? Keeping up the pretence

Working people who buy their way into a heroin habit soon face problems holding down their jobs. Students flunk their courses and drop out. Paul was a student when he started taking drugs. He had smoked cannabis for years but when heroin came into his life, everything crumbled and he found he could not concentrate on his studies. He left college and worked full-time at the hunt for heroin. He admitted that he could not have coped with employment: 'I couldn't have held a job down. That's the way I am. You can't do a job when you're thinking about where the next bag's coming from.'

Anxiety about the next bag can certainly interfere with your working life, although buying heroin is often quite straightforward. You can come in from work, pop out to see a dealer and be back in half an hour to have your hit and eat your tea. Obviously, if you work you will make sure you buy enough heroin the night before to see you through the next day. So far so good, but despite claims by the press that heroin can be bought on any street corner, that is simply not the case for any individual junkie. There could be a dealer in the next street whom you have never met. You, therefore, remain ignorant of his presence. You could not call at his house even if you knew him, because his suspicion of you would probably lead to your going away empty-handed.

Most junkies visit a maximum of three or four dealers regularly. Some only know one or two. If your dealer has run out of luck or simply run out of drugs to sell, you may be stumped. It is not uncommon to be told to call back in an hour. That hour can stretch to two or three hours. It can turn into days. Your body cannot wait that long. Alternative supplies will have to be discovered. Fast. The hunt for drugs can go on all evening and have you ringing round everyone you know and perhaps travelling out to unfamiliar parts of the city. On a really bad day, at the end of all your efforts, you might still have failed to score. When this happens you can sometimes persuade a friend to sell you something to tide you over till the next day. If not, going to work will have to be written off. The hunt must go on. Thus heroin addiction, like alcohol abuse, can lead to the loss of working hours.

It is possible to carry on with your job, however, and I know junkies who have remained employed in the same jobs over periods of ten years and more. What the public does not understand or, perhaps, prefers not to acknowledge is the fact that heroin addicts are at their most comfortable and efficient when they have a steady supply of the drugs that keep them 'normal'. In that respect the comparison with diabetes rings true. A remark attributed to London Stipendiary Magistrate Mr Crowther by the *Liverpool Daily Post* (16 April 1985) bears out the fact that even the judiciary can fail to comprehend the real situation of the heroin user. When sentencing a man convicted of possessing heroin he told him, 'How disturbing it is to know that heroin was in the car you intended to drive that night.' The misguided magistrate must have been equating heroin with alcohol. In reality, the thought of an addict trying to drive when he had *not* taken heroin is far more disturbing. The onset of withdrawal can render the user clumsy and careless beyond belief. At this stage you can bump into things, drop things, or convey your coffee cup straight to the middle of your chin rather than up to your mouth. Driving is positively hazardous. You are 'all fingers and thumbs', crashing gears, and failing to notice red lights or respond to emergencies. Spatial judgement deserts you. Your nerves are shot to pieces and your eyes watering so badly that you can hardly see the way ahead. If possible, therefore, junkies will make sure of their supply of drugs before planning any sort of activity. Not only does heroin give confidence; in regular users, it is essential to competence.

What misleads observers is the junkie who gets stoned when she should only be straight. If the addict takes a measured dose, she will be 'normal' and function effectively. If she takes more and gets stoned, she can, for practical purposes, be equated with a drunk. The user is always fighting the temptation to over-indulge. The use of an excessive dose of heroin will make a person drowsy and addled. The second problem for the working junkie is, therefore, gauging the dose that will give optimum efficiency without causing her to 'nod off'. The experienced addict nearly always manages to get it right, but no one is infallible.

One friend reported that, in five years of work, she remembered twice failing to 'hit the mark'. Someone with a heavy habit must take doses of heroin throughout the day to keep going. Morning and evening are not enough. At regular, four-hourly intervals the addict will slip away to the toilets, lock herself in the loo and separate the necessary amount from her day's supply. On one occasion, having heard some bad news, my friend slipped away and took all of her day's ration at once in an effort to comfort herself. In minutes, she knew that she had overdone it. She was forced to spend the rest of the day hiding in the rest room, afraid that her colleagues would notice her drooping eyelids and wobbling knees. Her work load was light that day and she was able to make up for lost time later. In some jobs, that would not have been possible. When stoned, it is easy for users to fall asleep in the chair and miss appointments or fail to meet their commitments. They wake up shocked, realising what has happened, and feeling very embarrassed by the untimely lapse.

I know of one long-term user who drives an ambulance for a living. I called to visit his wife one day at around 2 p.m. in time to see the ambulance pull up outside. He staggered out, barely able to stand, and told me, in slurred speech, that a social worker friend had turned him on, leaving him too stoned to drive. He had somehow managed to get home and had written off work for the rest of the day, leaving the ambulance where it stood, right outside his house. I could not resist a smile at the insane anarchy of a social worker and an ambulance driver in collusion that way: the blind leading the blind. Those with eyes open must be aware that much of life is not what it seems. In the junk world, chaos rules. These occurrences are comparatively rare among working junkies but it is not surprising that employers who discover a junkie on their staff are keen to jettison him at the earliest convenient moment. Even junkies despair of other junkies at times.

When you take junk, your working life is characterised by sporadic bouts of intense, genuinely effective effort, followed by others of extreme fatigue. If your job involves keeping to regular hours and dealing with people it can be hard to cope with your moods and tiredness. Junkies have very bad problems with sleep. If scoring is delayed and a hit is taken late at night it can keep you awake for hours. You can lose time at work through sheer exhaustion. Sometimes you just cannot make the physical effort required to move. You are likely to doze off at dawn. Extreme fatigue leads to oversleeping. It can mean erosion of health and well-being, causing a string of minor illnesses. Sometimes you simply cannot go to work because you have not scored and you are too sick. This is not cowardice, it is fear of detection. If you start sneezing and vomiting at work people might want to know why. A virus infection that crops up too regularly can have your work mates boring you with well-intended advice about doctors, specialists and antibiotics. Sometimes the embarrassment gets too much and the secrecy becomes an intolerable burden. You feel like blurting out the truth, telling everyone that you are a heroin addict and you will be just fine when you get some smack. You fantasise that, one day, you will. Needless to say, you never do. It is true that junkies talk a lot and, perhaps, say more than they intended when they are high, but they rarely lose control in the way that alcoholics do. They never blab the truth to a dumbfounded, po-faced audience. They simply clam up and suffer in silence, giving strange excuses for their behaviour. Others think they are unfriendly or eccentric, while, in fact, they are making supreme efforts to fulfil their obligations and live up to the demands made on them.

Those in the professions have a better chance of remaining undetected as they are more able to pace themselves to the rhythm of their habit. Drug addicts working in manual jobs such as bar work or waitressing are caught out in time, however hard they work. They have less leeway, are more open to scrutiny, or are condemned by the tittle-tattle of their co-workers. I know of several women who were sacked from jobs in pubs and wine bars when their employers discovered the truth about them. Most of them were doing their jobs conscientiously and it seemed cruelly unfair of the employers to cut them off, making their lives so much harder. Yet in times of such high unemployment, it is not surprising that an employer would favour a bright, keen, clean, young thing over a tired, baggy-eyed, bad-tempered junkie. Two out of three of the women even felt that their employers' greatest fears were for the reputation of their businesses if the public were to discover the circumstances of their staff. They all gave flimsy excuses and one claimed concern for the woman's welfare, saying she would be better off if she had less money to spend on heroin. Some readers will, no doubt, agree with him, but junkies can become bitter when these things happen. Their confidence takes a terrible blow. They know that, overall, they are capable of carrying out their jobs and they resent the speed with which they are labelled as wholly irresponsible, worthless and undesirable. Employers resent the deceit and they are, understandably, nervous about allowing addicts to handle cash. Any junkie with a big habit who fails to pull out in time will find himself unemployed one day.

Sick and tired: carrying on against all odds

When a heroin habit is really well established and you have no job to go to, day-to-day life can be monotonous and fraught with fear. Pete explained it this way:

> Everything's in black and white and very simple. Life is just getting what you need and every time you come across getting what you want it's a big extra. I don't mean ordinary needs, just junk needs.

He talked about the difficulties of keeping up a supply:

> Regularly the guy doesn't turn up, or when he does, he's smashed and he's got nothing. It happens all the time. Nights are a lonely time. Days are just as bad. If you score you're not lonely. You don't even think about friends or somebody to talk to.

Junkies are regularly driven to put themselves through trials and inconvenience that most people would not contemplate. Pete described the frustration of waiting for a dealer to come home:

> Sleep. You can't go to sleep if you've got to wait for somebody to come home. Sometimes you really want to lie down but you know there won't be anything for the morning and there won't be anything for the afternoon either cause nobody gets up till 4 o'clock.

The cynical exaggeration in the last observation reveals the way unemployed junkies can live, awake all night and asleep until well beyond noon. Anyone who wants to score must do so after lunchtime. Before that there will be nothing down for them, unless they have come across one of the new breed of money hungry dealers who don't use themselves and switch on the vodaphone at 9 a.m. anxious for custom.

Scoring can be a miserable business and it often involves going to the worst areas of the city, like soulless housing estates or mouldering slums. You can find yourself hanging around on street corners just out of sight of a dealer's house waiting for him to open shop. This can lead to a degree of soul searching. You stand there watching the least privileged members of society pass you by. You have joined them, you are less well off than they are. You are not even bored. You expect no better, you are merely anxious, waiting patiently. My friend told me one day as we walked along these sad streets:

> Do you know, I'm even jealous of our dog. I look at him and I think, he's OK. He's got no problems. He's healthy and happy. He's fit and full of life, and most of all he doesn't need smack like me and I really feel jealous. Jealous of a dog.

If you can find a place to sit, you wait there being solicited by lonely middle-aged men, being dismissed by teenage girls as no competition. Young, married, Sunday-best-sporting black women saunter by, promenading with their kids who are well-groomed, sleek and healthy. Old black men chat in faraway tongues, looking pleasant, fatherly, not comprehending, perhaps not seeing you too well. Fat, destroyed, middle-aged white women marshal armies of noisy multi-coloured kids along the dry streets. And there you sit, watching the losers trail by, sharing a cigarette with your friend, ashamed of what you have made of your life that started out so much easier than theirs. That big fat woman is hard, abrasive, but she is coping. You are tearful, sweating, nervous, tired, waiting for your medicine – and you cannot afford enough to bring you up to scratch. You search the walls of tall, derelict, Victorian houses ripped wide open for you to scan their crumbling bowels, speculate on who lived there, see where students painted bright murals that spark a memory of your own happier history. You feel a momentary flash of insight into the lunacy of your position, then put your head back down to stare only at the feet that have carried you there to score. You watch for the police but you do not expect them to be interested in you. Users are ten a penny and the police are likely to consider that arresting you for a £20 bag is not worth the paperwork.

Once you have a well-established habit you get used to being ill, you learn to take a little turkey. There is nothing else you can do. If you fail to score, things will only get worse and so you disregard your aching body and you shuffle on in utter determination. In the end, you just about get what you need and you carry on listening to your body, waiting for it to call for more. When you are short of gear you wake early every day, sometimes at 5 or 6 a.m. Sleep is impossible. Your whole body feels stiff, aching and uncomfortable. The nerves at the back of your neck are jangling. Just getting out of bed is an exhausting and painful process. After you do get up you look around for what is left to sell. By now it will be things like books and clothes. You root through your belongings like a hungry cat at the bin, pack up the most likely items, wait for 9 o'clock and set out, sometimes on foot, to tout around the shops for cash. Some days yield plenty, but the minimum you need is £10. At least then you can hunt around for a friend who will team up with you to buy a quarter gramme. Many dealers keep locked doors and open letter boxes. It is pointless asking them for tick. The search goes on and on with good days and bad, and there is always the choice of turning to the clinics or pulling a big scam and setting up to deal yourself.

I have already made it clear that when heroin supplies run out the user becomes ill and unable to work or carry on his normal life. What I have not said is that this can go on for a period of anything up to two weeks or more, depending on the degree of his addiction. The first four days are the worst and during this time symptoms can be extreme, but even after that the user will not be back to normal health. He will also be unable to sleep. Genuine colds or flu often set in on the heels of early withdrawal, presumably because of the user's run-down condition and lowered resistance to infection. All this means that once a person with regular commitments, whether work, children or something else, has slipped into a heroin habit, it is very hard to find the free time to stop. That is partly why he carries on against all reason and common sense, to the shocked disbelief and disapproval of bemused or worried onlookers. This is why the struggle to get the money takes junkies so far from the pattern of behaviour they might otherwise expect from themselves. The loss of a degree of self-respect has its origin in the fact that junkies have put themselves in a position where they can no longer control their own lives but are being controlled by circumstances. As Brian remarked, 'My life's skidding away from me somehow and I don't really want it to ...' At the time of writing, his life is still skidding and he is still watching helplessly.

Sadly, a great deal of resourcefulness which might be better applied elsewhere goes into the hunt for drugs. Junkies sometimes comment wistfully on this fact: 'You can always get the money for drugs but never for anything else. You can't get enough to buy food or clothes, just drugs.' The hustle obviously means that pride is a luxury that junkies quickly learn to discard. All that matters is getting the money. Asking for loans can be humiliating yet one addict remarked, 'I have had moments when I would not have cared if someone had thrown a bucket of shit over me so long as they had given me the money to score. I would even have left having a wash until after I had got the gear.'

Funnily enough, despite these deprivations some people have told me that if unemployed, the search for smack is a way of filling their time. 'The hunt for smack gives me something to do. When I do come off I relapse because I've nothing to fill the empty days. It's like "do it yourself" Job Creation.' Now there is a thought for our worthy leaders.

Working drug users can hang on to a job no matter what the problems. Some even suggest that heroin has helped them to cope with the boredom and disappointment of routine. One ex-junkie explained, 'I used heroin as a palliative to make working life bearable in the way a frustrated housewife turns to valium.' For her, heroin had smoothed out the tensions of the working hours and provided a pleasurable retreat at home. Her life had been a balancing act between doping herself just enough to face the drudgery of the day and seeking escape to a private ecstasy at night. She told me, 'I drifted around the drug scene for years, sometimes missing police raids by hours. I was lucky. Through no skill on my part, I managed to avoid arrest and conviction, keeping my image sufficiently intact to stay employed.' She had survived, but she admitted to the loss of her car and her home. Drug users commonly have to make unpalatable compromises in order to carry on.

A heroin habit gobbles up a person's assets quickly, finishing off by consuming his or her body. Friends around me have faced the loss of whatever they had to begin with. One man lost a flourishing business. He is still taking heroin and has ended up in a bedsitter living on social security. Another local heroin user of many years' standing finally had to move in with his mother after losing his flat and sacrificing virtually everything of value that he owned. Some people, having eroded their health to the point of being self-made invalids, are virtually living on borrowed time. The struggle to stop offers little hope of an improved life for them. Others are dead.

The other drugs: what happens when the smack runs out

It is not, of course, only heroin that can ward off withdrawal. Other opiates, like opium, codeine or morphine will do the job just as well. Then there are prescribed drugs like DF118 (dihydro-codeine), pethidine and Diconal. If you know people who are registered, they may help you out with a swig of methadone, or sell you some so they can afford to buy heroin. You get to know the days when they pick up their script and look forward to buying whatever they can spare. Some people hang around outside chemists hoping to meet someone they know so that they can badger him for drugs. Once you get to that stage, there is not much lower to go. This is the time when those who are prepared to do it steal.

Some people hit doctors with bogus aches and pains. A feigned pulled muscle or a bad back can be worth twenty or thirty DF118 tablets which can be a help in desperate times. According to addicts I have spoken to, some doctors still sell prescriptions. Several years ago I knew of one who would prescribe Diconal, a synthetic opiate, in exchange for making an examination of a young person if he considered him or her attractive. If opiates cannot be acquired, tranquillisers, used sensibly and in moderation according to a doctor's instructions, can help enormously with the symptoms of withdrawal. If you can get some valium or Mogadon, indeed any downers, at least you can knock yourself out for a few hours. Some junkies drink in desperation although others claim drink makes them feel worse. Even patent medicines can be abused. Junkies might drink bottles of codeine linctus bought over the counter at chemists. It does little good unless your habit is very tiny. It also causes stomach troubles but some people will drink it when all else has failed. Occasionally, addicts cutting down on a habit will tail it off at the very end with Boots brand 'aspirin and codeine' tablets. This is just a desperate measure, although the aspirin probably helps to control the hot flushes that coming off seems to bring about.

Of the other opiates, opium is the least likely to be seen on the streets these days. Cleaning and preparing it for use is a lengthy and complicated process; it is much bulkier to smuggle and its effect is much less powerful than that of heroin. It is a dark, slightly sticky substance that is fairly malleable, a bit like black plasticine but harder. When it is available, it can be eaten but it has an extremely bitter and nasty taste, and can cause very severe constipation. It is not popular with English junkies, but I am told there are a few Chinese people who still use it, following certain traditional rituals and keeping their habit very private, even from the rest of their community who frown on their activities.

The liquid residue from boiling opium can be drunk or injected. This latter practice was not the subject of unreserved praise:

> It's nice as it gets you straight immediately but you get flushed, go red in the face and your fingers and toes feel as if they're going to explode. You ask if you look all right and everyone says, 'No, you look like a beetroot!' It relieves withdrawal for about an hour but you spend the whole time fighting all the other symptoms, like how not to blow up or be sick after a cup of tea.

Anyone who has not experienced the obsessive need to get heroin to keep the so-called monkey off her back will not be able to comprehend how someone could subject herself to this unpleasantness, yet my informant continued, 'Even so, if no smack turns up then you think, "Perhaps we'll get a bit more opium."' The ability to suffer all kinds of discomfort in the pursuit of 'normality' is the status quo among well-established junkies. Smoking or eating opium is, however, according to Ray a very pleasant experience. He reminisced about the 'warm cuddles' it had given him, adding ruefully, 'In the old days it was very available but you can't get it now. It's a pity because you can live a long time on it ... coming off is horrific though: you shake and twitch so badly that my mate pulled a muscle.' I was reminded of De Quincey's description of his days in a coffin fighting a crocodile. To understand the willingness of people to take these risks the outsider has to comprehend the relentless drive of the need for more junk. When the body cries out, the user will feed it. Remember, too, that most heroin abusers are already keen to achieve an altered state of consciousness. Ray once remarked, 'I realised I was a drug addict long before I took heroin.' When I asked him why, he replied, 'Because I just don't like being straight!' I have heard the exact same words, 'I just don't like being straight', from a number of very long-established 'incurable' heroin users. That is really the crux of the matter. In some users the potential for addiction is a fact of life.

Among the variety of opiates that can be exploited by junkies, methadone is the drug most commonly prescribed at clinics. It has for a long time been used to help wean addicts off smack or to maintain those users who are thought to be incurable. It may be given in amps which can be injected or as a liquid medicine.

The effects of methadone are not especially enjoyable but the drug stops withdrawal and when you are sick you are very glad of it. All it does in positive terms is produce a sense of garrulous well-being which allows you to continue with your normal life feeling comparatively good. Addicts receive a measured amount from their doctors which is usually a little less than they really need, as doctors tend to be cautious. This is referred to as their prescription (always shortened to script), and the allotted amount is picked up at a pre-arranged regular chemist on specified days once a week, or more often depending on how much the doctor trusts each patient to make the script last until the next one is collected. Most addicts take an extra large dose when they collect their script. On these picking up days the long-termers down their 'juice' as they call it and get down the pub for a drink with their mates. They may look a bit haggard but an outsider would have little inkling of the truth about them. Unless they have reason to suspect, most people would not be able to spot an addict if he was sitting next to them on the bus. Even addicts cannot tell when their friends are straight or stoned, unless they are really off their heads.

Methadone is not the drug of first choice for junkies and there is quite a bit of it available on the scene because addicts will sell it to get the money for heroin, swap it for other drugs, or even give it away to close friends who are sick. Any addict prefers smack to meth, but the meth keeps him straight longer and that is why most only sell a little to buy some smack for a treat. Despite rumours to the contrary, non-addicts would be unlikely to take methadone as the effects are not especially enjoyable. The sad reports of young children taking methadone may be the result of kids assuming that any controlled drug must be glamorous and exciting.

Having a script is one way to relieve the relentless money trials that beset junkies, and a few do stick to it. Others end up spending nearly as much on smack as they did before and taking the methadone as well. On the whole addicts would prefer a huge script for heroin but make do with a small one for methadone. Withdrawal from methadone is, in some ways, harder to cope with than withdrawal from scag because, although less intense, it lasts so much longer. The user can go for an almost unbearably long while before he can re-establish a normal sleep pattern and it could, in fact, be several weeks before sleep is restored. This problem intensifies the urge to relapse. Robbie, attacking the methadone programme, commented bitterly, 'You go there for heroin and you get something worse.' Nevertheless, there have been times when I have been very thankful to get hold of some meth. Well-established addicts with friends who are registered often have a symbiotic relationship with them. With a group of registered friends you can keep a steady flow of methadone for the bad days. It works out cheaper than smack because nobody buys it for pleasure and, as it lasts longer, it is better value for money, even though there is no strikingly good high to be had.

I remember one particular Friday night when I had run out of money, luck and ideas. I did not even have my bus fare, and it was too late to go looking on foot. I sat down feeling clammy, totally at a loss to know how I would manage in the morning, scared of facing withdrawal but not knowing what else I could do. Funnily enough, at these times it is rare that something does not turn up in the end. The next morning a friend telephoned offering to sell me methadone. I told him my situation and, reluctantly, he agreed that I could owe him the money until later. He called on his way to town to pick me up. By now I was in quite a state. He paid my bus fare and gave me money so that I could go into a cafe to wait while he picked up his script. I felt pretty pathetic as I sat there snivelling and penniless, spooning as much sugar as I could into my coffee. All junkies crave sugar when there is not enough junk in their system. When he arrived it felt like the relief of a siege. Without regard to observers, I took the bottle and swigged off the necessary amount. The neat, precocious, freckled little girl sitting with her mother opposite to us gazed at me with what looked like disapproval. Adults clearly did not swig from medicine bottles at table in her house. My companion advised me that a hot drink helped the drug to take effect more quickly. True or not, I drank my coffee obediently, hoping the drug would work soon. I chatted and smoked, ignoring the fact that I felt so wretched. It can take up to forty or fifty minutes for the effects of methadone to begin to relieve the symptoms of withdrawal. That can be a long wait. Once it does take over, all the pain and misery go. Your eyes are dry and you are ready for anything.

I have been describing what happens when meth is bought from genuine friends. I have known the person who features in the story above for fifteen years and I could be certain of the contents of the bottle he had handed me. Buying meth can be a real let-down, however, because, while some people are very genuine and remain that way, even though they have a drug problem, others are not. Methadone can easily be doctored or watered down. It is a bright green liquid that has a typical cough mixture taste, similar to Benylin but not as strongly flavoured. Night Nurse, a branded cold remedy, is a green liquid of an almost identical shade, although it is thick and syrupy. In any quantity it makes you fall asleep. Some addicts cut their methadone with this so they will have to sell less. So-called methadone might be 50 per cent Night Nurse. Locally, addicts joke about 'aquadone', a nickname for linctus that has been watered down.

These practices lead junkies to be very suspicious of buying linctus unless they have accompanied the seller into the chemist to see fair play. If another addict ends up with a bottle of methadone which has been cut she will be pretty cheesed off, especially when she is not only sick but falling asleep and she does not know why. Another reason she will be fed up, aside from the fact that she could have bought heroin with the money she has wasted, is because an addict often buys methadone at a time when she is trying to cut down or stop. If it is badly cut she will have to go out and buy heroin to get her through. If this happens, it can set her back and put her off stopping for another week, month or year.

The seamy side: groin shots, bad hits, overdose and death

In terms of everyday health and well-being junkies find that the symptoms of minor ailments are often masked. The discomfort of colds or even flu are effectively diminished, even completely cancelled out by a drug which is capable of assuaging the pain of the dying. On the other hand there are daily inconveniences like chronic constipation to be faced. It is an unglamorous fact that addicts frequently develop piles and, for some, going to the toilet is such an effort that it takes on ritual proportions. One drug dealer used to carefully line the whole of his toilet seat with cotton wool before settling in for what would necessarily be a very long and

uncomfortable attempt at an otherwise normal function. Even uri-
nating can be difficult. Heroin users frequently need to turn on the
tap so that the sound of running water will help persuade the body
to make the effort. The chosen method of taking the drug will also
have a bearing on a person's health. Junkies who snort gear regularly are prone to sinus infection and nose bleeds. Those who inject
themselves face all sorts of serious hazards, brought about by the
circumstances under which the drugs are taken.

Even when junkies fight against the odds to maintain a sem-
blance of dignity and a little self-respect, in times of real need most
will be willing to subject their bodies to an invasion of almost any
chemical sufficiently related to smack to keep them straight. They
quickly learn to recognise the names and shapes of tablets, like Palfium and Diconal, which occasionally used to be prescribed by
well-intentioned doctors, or which might appear as the result of a
raid on a chemist's shop or hospital drug store. It is often thought
that these robberies occur when addicts are high on heroin, and
decide to go on a wild spree. The opposite is more often true. An
addict who admitted to having carried out one such robbery told
me, 'I had tried all day and all night to get something. I was so sick I
didn't know what to do next. On the way home I passed a chemist
and I just started kicking at the door. It was insane but I kept on
kicking. At one point I was so fucking knackered I just leant in the
doorway and cried.' In the end, he got into the building and walked
around oblivious to the possibility of detection reading the names
on the supplies of drugs by the light of a blazing torch made from a
rolled up newspaper. He came away with an assortment of medicines, including Diconal tablets.

These are bright pink in colour and, like other tablets, are injected by addicts despite the fact that they are not fully soluble. An
addict will crush a number of tablets between two spoons and then
load the resulting powder into the barrel of a syringe. Shaken up in
water, Diconal form a vile pink silt that looks deadly even to the
untrained eye. Cranking up Diconal can be fatal. Everyday risks of
the practice can involve the blockage of veins which afterwards
shrink away and cease to be viable. People have lost fingers and
limbs when serious tissue damage has resulted in ulceration and
infection. Long-term addicts with a history of taking these risks
often end up in a position where all the surface veins into which
they can easily inject have become blocked or collapsed from

overuse. Undeterred, they graduate to injecting in the groin, seeking to hit the femoral vein. This runs fairly close to the accompanying artery and the knowledge that injection into an artery can be extremely dangerous has led junkies to coin the macabre two-line warning, 'If it's red, danger ahead. If it's black, whack it back ...'

Thus, junk folk law boldly advises on how to recognise from the colour of the blood sucked into the syringe whether the needle has penetrated an artery or a vein. As I have already pointed out, junkies are most concerned with getting the drugs into their bodies. Their comments show that they are quite prepared to face the consequences: 'Obviously, I've lopped off the end of my life, but what can I do about that now?' A possible threat to the intellect was dismissed with false bravado; 'Who cares about the brain cells? The more you've got, the worse you feel!' There is, in fact, a general feeling among junkies that life without drugs offers as many dangers and disappointments as their present way of life. Other fears took precedence: 'They're going to drop the bomb on us anyway so who's worried about taking a bit of smack.' Other drugs were indicted: 'I'm more worried about cigarettes. They're killing me and I can't give up. I can come off smack but I can't stop smoking.' Sadly, so long as junkies can acquire any form of opiate that will keep them stoned they will be willing to take the associated risks and bear the drawbacks.

I remember chatting with one addict as he probed around trying to find a vein in which he could still inject himself. As he slid the needle around beneath the skin, he muttered desperately, 'Oh please, God, stop coming out! I have to talk to them like they're plants at the moment,' he said, referring to his veins. It took him about twenty minutes before he finally managed to get the drugs into his system and then he held up the wounded wrist for me to see where the contents of the syringe had seeped out of his damaged vein to form lumps below the skin. 'Look at this,' he said. 'It's all fucking shapes and it's not muscle.' He cackled and added, 'I'll have to stop messing about with this fucking stuff.' He did not stop, however, until six months later when he telephoned me from a hospital bed. He had arrived there with a massive ulcer in his leg just in time to avoid hobbling out on crutches minus the leg. He spent a week in hospital while the ulcer was drained. After that nasty shock he stayed away from the needles for a month or so, sticking to prescribed linctus, but, like most people, he has drifted back to using a works wherever he can afford to buy smack. Beyond a certain point, there is no persuading junkies to consider possible damage to their bodies.

By this stage those junkies who have failed to give up heroin often become resigned to the belief that drugs will remain part of their lives until they die: 'I don't think I'll ever stop now. If I stay around that long, I'll still be doing it when I'm fifty.' Phil has now sought the help of a private doctor from whom he receives prescriptions for methadone. This arrangement spares him from dangers such as overdose, bad hits and infection from using a dirty works.

Hygiene is obviously of minimal importance to well-established junkies. It is commonplace for someone to fish out a needle from a dirty plughole, concerned only with being able to use it again, rather than with the germs it might carry. Couples nearly always share a works. If one gets hepatitis, the other probably will, too. Dirty equipment and dirty drugs can result in a bad hit. Most junkies who inject heroin will have experienced this unpleasant phenomenon. You take your injection, sit back to enjoy its effects and find yourself vomiting, sweating profusely and shaking uncontrollably for a period of several hours. Other junkies will cock an eyebrow, mumble about bad hits and offer you a blanket or an old sleeping bag to wrap yourself up until the malady passes. Junkies take these occurrences in their stride. They have to. While some doctors are sympathetic, others are antagonised by being asked to attend to self-inflicted wounds.

Last year, Bobby and I discovered an old friend slumped in his camper van only semi-conscious. It was very cold and we managed to dress him and carry him into the house. There we put him to bed, aware that he had taken an overdose of heroin. After twenty-four hours, however, he had a very bad fever, his temperature was up to 104° and he was completely delirious. He was clearly ill and we could not tell whether he needed more drugs or whether he was suffering from a serious illness. Further doses of drugs failed to relieve the symptoms and finally we called a doctor, who was, at first, very concerned by his condition. On questioning him, the doctor discovered the facts. The patient was a junkie. Without a word the doctor closed his bag, straightened up and said, 'Right, I can see that I'm wasting my time here,' and walked out of the house making no further attempt to offer advice or treatment. The man remained ill for several days, and, in due course, recovered without the ministration of medical practitioners. Whatever was wrong with him has now become a recurrent problem. He had been living abroad and may well have contracted a serious ailment.

Junkies are understandably nervous about contact with doctors, many of whom put them into a parallel category with the unfortunate menopausal female. When middle-aged women become ill, they are likely to be told that the menopause is the reason. Junkies are likely to be told that their drug abuse has caused their ills. They face another problem, too. They are nervous about the possibility of being admitted to hospital because they are rarely allowed to bring in their own drugs or given appropriate medication by doctors there.

When a junkie does find himself admitted to a hospital ward where he meets with an unsympathetic response, he will be likely to sign himself out as soon as he is able and shuffle off in search of heroin. Junkies who are not registered and who hope to avoid detection will telephone friends asking them to bring drugs in for them. Most other junkies would feel obliged to help. When Steve spent three weeks in hospital with a badly broken leg, Joey made regular visits carrying with him carefully prepared syringes full of smack for his friend to inject. Steve would slip off to the toilet in his wheelchair to do the dirty deed. In that way Joey helped him to keep his habit secret during his stay. As a professional person it would have been very hard for Steve to admit to his problem. As someone in severe pain already written up by his doctors for doses of morphine and pethidine intended for non-drug-addicted patients, Steve would have suffered terribly had he been made to go through withdrawal at that time.

Overdose is a lifelong threat for an addict who uses needles. When she does overdose, she knows little about it and that is one reason why she is likely to do it again. As far as she is concerned, she had a good hit and woke up in hospital because some fool panicked and took her there. Her first concern is usually whether there are still any drugs left for later. If you are present when someone else ODs it is, however, pretty unnerving. Most heroin users are reluctant to call an ambulance, bringing the authorities to the scene of the crime. People have been allowed to die because others, through fear of detection, have left it too late to get help. Fortunately, fatal overdose is comparatively rare. If, however, an addict repeatedly overdoses it probably does mean that she has really given up on herself. This kind of behaviour can be a plea for help. Some years ago one very sad local figure died cranking up in a telephone box while trying to call his girlfriend. Even other addicts tend to be a bit scornful of anyone who is completely out of control. People who squirt blood from a failed hit back into the spoon and start picking out the clots before trying to re-use it might raise a frown from some of the others.

One reason why junkies die is, of course, that, in the constant hunt for gear, they may come across something which is badly cut or not even smack at all. One local addict was crushing up brick dust and selling it to novices. In the light of tales like this a few junkies try to wait until someone else has had a hit before they risk it. Despite all this, when I asked one heroin user why he carries on taking smack even though it is bad for him he answered wearily, 'because so much else is bad for me. I don't stop to think about that. When I'm on it, I don't think about it being bad for me. That's why junkies don't smoke weed or trip. They don't want to think about themselves.'

Living inside damaged bodies as they do, junkies do not necessarily lose their streak of anarchic humour. Keith used to sit watching athletics on television, envying the huge rope-like veins and joking about hitting them up with a pointed straw and a bicycle pump. Addicts can even laugh about problems like getting rid of used syringes. Few junkies are irresponsible about this activity, many of the older ones being against spreading a needle habit among the young. They will try to flush syringes away down toilets, burn them on open fires or drop them down grids. Failing that, they bend the needles over and secrete them in rubbish where they feel they will not be discovered. Alan laughed about the time he tried to get rid of a carrier bag of used syringes by putting them in a bin at the back of a shop near his flat. The next morning he passed and noticed, to his horror, that the syringes were lying scattered all over the yard. A dog had unearthed the haul, and the old shopkeeper was standing aghast amid the debris scratching his head. The man scurried away and Alan rushed around scooping up the vital evidence of his folly and removing it back into his own flat. From there he heard the old man return and try to explain to his young assistant that the syringes had been there only a moment ago. The assistant replied scornfully, 'Yes dad. Never mind. They've taken themselves off now.' The young man thought he was drunk. Alan's secret remained intact.

One last self-inflicted torture that awaits junkies is the Marzine treatment. Diconal have been described as 'skull rattlers' because of the intense rush they produce. After they became scarce, addicts realised that the ingredient responsible for this sensation was contained in travel sickness pills called Marzine. Eagerly they took to crushing up these tablets, making them the basis of a horrible heroin cocktail. Junkies who cannot score smack have even been known to inject Marzine without heroin. Injecting crushed up tablets is, of course, extremely dangerous and involves some very serious health risks. For instance, tiny particles of the tablets may damage the lungs. When non-sterile material is injected, bacteria can lodge in the heart valves leading to the onset of a potentially fatal infection know as bacterial endocarditis. If Diconal or Marzine is accidentally injected into an artery in the arm or the leg, bits of the tablets can lodge in the fingers or toes causing ugly swelling, and setting up an infection so severe that amputation of the fingers, toes or even a whole limb might be necessary. Some drug users face these hazards without even being aware of the possible consequences of their actions. More foolhardy addicts always believe that someone else will be the unlucky one. Discerning junkies find these practices somewhat grim, but they are all part of the ongoing search for kicks.

CHAPTER 5

₡ Bearing the brunt of public contempt

The kangaroo court is in session

An addict is a victim; first of all, a victim of his or her own curiosity which leads to the addiction ... Secondly, an addict is a victim of the society which places him in a category of 'Unclean! Do not touch.'

An ex-user

Any addict is acutely aware that for 'straight' people he is *persona non grata*. At best he is pitied, at worst he is loathed. Heroin addicts are society's 'nouveau queers'. They have replaced homosexuals and conscientious objectors as the undesirable, antisocial figures who inspire public contempt. Like other minority groups they frequently become paranoid about their position and withdraw from social contact with non-users. Some feel shame or embarrassment but they still bitterly resent what they see as an unwarranted degree of aggressive public censure. They crack sour jokes making quips about 'new sports' such as 'junkie bashing', and some are becoming nervous about public reaction to them. One man who has used heroin for many years remarked, 'Taking heroin is the new political crime. It has become fashionable to hate junkies. I can see them stringing us up from lamp posts like defeatists in Berlin during the Second World War.' While he accepted that drug addiction has become a serious health problem he retaliated by drawing attention to the even more widespread social problem that attracts little emotional response saying, 'What about all the bloody alcoholics? You don't get thousands of people killed on the roads each year as the result of junkie drivers racing around off their heads. Most of us can't even afford a car.'

This resentment is shared by many addicts. Jimmy demonstrated very strong feelings on the matter. He jabbered on, heatedly giving vent to his frustration, saying, 'As far as they're concerned we're as bad as you get: worse than murderers, wife beaters, fucking child stealers, baby batterers, muggers, rapists, thieves, bigamists, cut-throats and satanists is a junkie.' To become a junkie is to abdicate claim to society's good graces. Society punishes those it rejects. Junkies are relentlessly punished – by doctors, by policemen, by judges and juries, by Joe Public and, of course, by themselves. In the end, they do far worse things to punish themselves than others could ever do to them, although there are plenty of others willing to try. Other addicts have complained that they are 'treated like nutters'. Many get steamed up about the dark picture painted of heroin users by the media and feel bitter because it is a widely accepted fact that junkies are the 'lowest of the low'. Those in authority tend to concur in the assumption. No one is above censure. Even an English aristo-crat convicted on a drugs charge was hailed as an example of the way that 'the highest in the land can fall to the lowest when drugs are taken'. If a junkie has a low sense of self-esteem to begin with, it will be even lower when society holds the mirror up to his face and starts to make pronouncements about his unpleasant reflection.

Junkies become weary of meeting with blanket condemnation from people willing to sit in judgment on them. They frequently find themselves being insulted but powerless to retaliate, while ignorance and smug self-congratulation often characterise the atti-tudes of those who bait them. Even doctors can resort to open antagonism. Is it fair for a psychiatrist to cast a glance towards a junkie coming for treatment and declare contemptuously, 'Not more dirty washing?' In the eyes of the world the junkie fails to strive, achieve anything, produce anything or consume anything except smack. He becomes a non-person with only minimal remaining rights. He is made painfully aware of this fact every day. It is not surprising that there is a general feeling among heroin users that seeking help from the authorities is a last resort to be avoided if possible.

It is certainly true that anyone with an iota of pride or initiative will not confess all readily. One woman declared vehemently,

> When I've been unable to get smack I've actually lain on the
> bed and sobbed. But I have never been able to swallow my

pride and go to the doctor. In the end I would suffer 'cold turkey' every time before I would go wingeing to them.

As the hue and cry gathers momentum, ordinary junkies are anxious to re-establish a sense of proportion. One man told me, 'It's becoming like the Wild West. We'll be getting tarred and feathered next.' Another announced angrily, 'They're putting dealers on a par with war criminals. It's over the top. Cigarettes kill more people in six months than junk does in years.' Jimmy made a plea for society to understand junkies a little more and criticise a little less when he said, 'Do not treat him as a leper and then punish him for his disease.'

Where heroin has become a problem for someone, those who are close to him tend to transfer blame for his condition onto his friends. Some junkies foster this situation in order to deflect criticism from themselves. It is quite typical for a man to encourage his wife to believe that he would stay away from drugs without pressure from friends. He may even believe it, but behind her back he will be pleading with the others to get him gear. Junkies find themselves made into scapegoats for the foibles of others. John described the attitude of his friend's wife like this:

She's dead straight and she doesn't understand. Mind you, it does turn people into monsters. That's what she sees when there's a load of us in her front room. All lizards crawling across her furniture, man. I bet she goes and gives everything a good wipe when we've gone.

Naturally, heroin users become sensitive about this sort of reaction. They feel vulnerable and defensive. They know that no one will take them seriously once they find out their situation. Addicts themselves usually assume that the others will be unreliable and likely to steal, but junkies understand one another better than their wives and families do. Anxious partners make fools of themselves by becoming rude and unpleasant when other junkies call. The visitors bear the brunt of the aggression and store up quiet grudges, strongly resenting the implication that they are not at all nice to know. Later, their friends will apologise and they will sneak off together to carry on taking their drugs, while the frustrated spouse or friend relaxes thinking he or she has routed the opposition.

What happens to women who take heroin

Drug addiction affects everyone in much the same way but women face a number of extra problems which do not affect men. Firstly, a woman's appearance suffers much more than a man's. Once the struggle to keep up a supply of drugs is under way users cannot afford to spend money on clothes and keeping up their appearance. Women soon lose interest in things that were so important before. By this, I do not mean the whole boring business of dressing up and looking pretty, I mean the very essential matter of caring about how you look, of minding whether you stand out in a crowd as grubby, dishevelled and spotty. A woman who embarks on long-term drug abuse soon looks drawn and haggard. We are all judged on our appearance, women more than men. A poor image will generate a negative response from others and that helps to undermine a person's confidence. In time, looking bad makes a person feel bad. That is the fate of the female drug abuser. Any insecure young woman who thinks that heroin will add glamour and mystery to her image should think thrice before acting on that misapprehension.

Many female addicts of my acquaintance are married women, most of whom came into contact with heroin because their husbands had developed a taste for it. I do not know any couples where the woman takes heroin and the man does not, although I do know of several where women who do not take drugs have to cope with a male partner who is dependent on heroin. In my experience the women who use heroin are often more intelligent than their husbands, but lack confidence and are unaware of what they could achieve. It seems to me that, for working-class women in their twenties and early thirties who have small children to look after and an irresponsible, somewhat inadequate male partner to contend with, heroin initially presents an antidote to stress and frustration. Such women find themselves in a position where they are unfulfilled and bored. Discouraged by the ineptitude of the male and conditioned to feel guilty about the prospect of outstripping him, these women are under enormous pressure. For a variety of reasons, both personal and practical, they are unable to improve their lot. Loyalty to the marriage and affection for their children bid them carry on but it is obvious that the only future is poverty, middle age and more of the same frustration and boredom which they are already experiencing. Many women find that as they lose their looks and pulling power, they fall into a noncategory of the old bag, the hag, the weird one, me mam. They cease to have independent value or status. In the mirror of life they have no reflection. Being a middle-aged woman can be a most debilitating social disease. Drugs provide short-term relief and many women settle for that.

In working-class households, women traditionally see to the chores and raise the kids. Unemployment and drug addiction do not necessarily alter this. I have seen female addicts scurry about the house struggling to keep going while their men sprawled about in peaceful drugged slumber like sated lions on a hot afternoon. Part of the woman's role is often the control of the purse strings. This means that she frequently takes on the burden of fretting about the money to buy smack. She has to balance the books, making sure that the children are fed and seeing that the supply of smack does not run out. There will usually be no money left over to pay the launderette. The kids run round in track suits that double as pyjamas, and a few urgent bits of washing hang dripping around the fire. A woman with a home to run can become very exhausted yet the man often sits by and lets her get on with it. He has his own problems and retreats behind drugs. The man often looks five years younger than he really is and the woman ten years older.

It is, of course, usually the man who goes out to buy the drugs but under some circumstances that burden can also fall to the woman. Frequently, the man is too stoned to bother or he may see scoring as another of the woman's jobs – like going to the supermarket. Another reason for the woman's involvement is that men often acquire a criminal record sooner than women. This can mean that a woman might elect to do the 'dirty work' herself rather than put her husband at risk of another conviction which could result in his going to jail. Women in this position are vulnerable to exploitation by anyone with drugs to sell. On a somewhat informal basis, they might be driven to exchange sex for drugs when they are short of cash.

A woman's health can suffer, too. Long-term use of heroin invariably results in the disruption of the menstrual cycle, and with heavy doses of heroin, amenorrhoea (cessation of the monthly period) is inevitable. Anyone who is frequently stoned can become careless about contraception. As the date when a period is due cannot be predicted with any certainty, a woman can become pregnant and fail to realise it. That can leave her facing an awkward dilemma, especially if she has let three months drift by and the question of termination has become more complicated.

A mother who is also a heroin addict is likely to be criticised for her failure to give up drugs. Some people tend to think that if she continues to take heroin she is demonstrating a self-centred lack of concern for the welfare of her children. That is not necessarily the case. Once she has become an addict it is usually very difficult for her to find the time to stop using drugs. Her children need her to be there every day cooking their meals, washing their clothes and comforting them when things go wrong. Thus, a desire to be a good, caring parent can stop a woman going into hospital for a cure. She may feel that no one else can look after her children quite as well as she can and, therefore, she is likely to make the choice to put their welfare before her own. She struggles on, determined to keep the family together. Without heroin she could not keep going and so she carries on using it, always worrying and wondering about what will happen if her luck or her supply of drugs runs out.

Women in this position usually shoulder a heavy burden of guilt, especially when heroin competes for money that could, in their eyes, be better spent on shoes, clothes or Christmas presents for the kids. The children can, of course, suffer too. Junkies are notoriously grumpy sometimes. Mothers are bound to get weary and may have less time to talk or to play than they otherwise would. This does not mean that their children are likely to be neglected but they might have a better time if their addicted mothers did manage to break the habit. Where junk rules, evening meals can appear rather later than expected and attendance at school can be erratic if it depends on mother accompanying her child to the door.

Despite these facts, many women believe that the right thing to do is to soldier on. It is possible that, without realising it, some use their children as an excuse not to come off. They convince themselves that they need drugs to cope with their role as a mother, so evading the unpleasant prospect of a cure. There is, however, no reason to assume that, overall, heroin addicts make inadequate parents. Many people without any of the problems that junkies have to face can give their children a less satisfactory upbringing. Indeed, a number of important issues surround the whole question of addicted mothers and I have discussed some of these in the final section of the book.

The deadly dealer

> I don't hate pushers. Why should I? I want to purchase a
> commodity and they supply it. They take the risks and I am
> grateful for their services.

Drug dealers figure in the public imagination as modern-day bogey-
men. Visions of slick, well-heeled villains who sip exotic cocktails
as they cruise about on gleaming yachts taunt the frustrated population. This description may fit the people who mastermind huge
import operations but these media-moulded 'Mr Bigs' are remote
from the scene. For the most part, they live safely, protected by status, power or wealth, and remain far beyond the reach of their pur-
suers. To explore the politics of their position is beyond the scope of
this book.

The middle men, via whose efforts the heroin empire dissemi-
nates its wares, are the people who come into the limelight. These
people do the 'dirty work' and bear the brunt of public contempt.
The man who passes for a 'Mr Big' in the average indignant newspaper report is, in fact, often no such thing. What misleads people
is the large number of noughts on the bottom line of the smack
dealer's sums. Thousands of pounds can pass through his hands in
just one week. It is, therefore, taken for granted that he must be an
up-and-coming young entrepreneur, salting away his ill-gotten
gains to purchase a mansion and a private plane when he retires. It
is not likely, however, that he will benefit from his labours on anything like the scale his critics imagine. Many dealers use heroin
themselves and this fact alone can strike out the majority of those
impressive noughts in the dealer's sums. Being a junkie tends to cancel out the profits.

The average dealer is quite likely to live in a high-rise block
where the lifts are awash with piss and shit, the walls are streaked
with human excrement, and things are smashed and damaged
everywhere. The picture of pushers leading lives of luxury is often
far from the truth, even for some of the dealers who move large
amounts of heroin. For these people their way of life frequently
ends up offering few rewards. It merely helps the dealer to block
out the harsh reality of his degenerating, slum environment. Taking
heroin means that he need not experience the land of the clockwork
orange with his full faculties zapping at him. Dealing in smack does

not even help him to get out, it just helps him put up with picking his way between the dog turds and the broken glass. Next time you read of an evil 'Mr Big' getting his just deserts, take note of where he lived. You may well discover his castle in the sky was at the top of an obsolete block that would have been blown up and replaced years ago if the council could have found the money to do it.

Dealers, of course, come from various backgrounds. Some may actually be well-established criminals looking for easy pickings. For a while, at least, dealing in drugs can present itself as a less risky, more lucrative line of business than robbing banks. Dealers need not, however, be seasoned villains. Some are law-abiding citizens fleeing from revolution at home. They are ordinary people who know that they have access to a commodity that is wanted here. They may arrive hoping to fuel a new life for their families with the proceeds from the sale of a suitcase full of heroin. Some dealers are riddled with greed and self-interest, others are idealists hoping to fund guerrilla warfare, finance terrorism or foster radical change. Whether funding revolution or supporting his own habit, every dealer convinces himself that the end justifies the means.

While established criminals run smack factories and employ 'mules' to carry in the drugs, many dealing rings are small organisations inspired, funded and run by little bands of vigorous, foolhardy individuals who see themselves as participants in a New Gold Rush. The whole business is another way to the top for the unskilled labourer. Young men set off in Range Rovers to risk their necks and make their fortunes in a Third World Klondyke called Pakistan. One cynic, weighing up their role, quipped, 'Really they're good capitalists. Half of them could qualify for a government enterprise grant.' Those who try Malaysia qualify for a noose.

For those in their twenties and thirties who feel that bricklaying or teaching will never provide them with the material comforts they would like, nor free them from the 9 to 5 grind, a one-off drug run can rank on a par with winning the pools. It figures in many a wild daydream and, for some, it becomes a desperate reality. Anyone who takes this sort of risk has usually sampled the drugs already, developed a taste for them and sees little real harm in sharing the craze with others. Such a person will set out on a so-called 'holiday' planning to return as a self-styled entrepreneur. His goals are usually fairly mundane and centre on intentions to buy a house or set up a small wine bar. As soon as the drugs are sold he plans to put the experience behind him and run a respectable business. Anyone trying this short cut to security needs to be both foolhardy and very lucky. If he succeeds once, however, he is sometimes tempted to try again using his ill-gotten gains to coax others into taking future risks on his behalf. The trade escalates as the heroin is carried in on the backs of those classic dreams of wealth, security and individual freedom. Working-class lads who have come up in the hard school can seize on this means of getting a speedy leg up to a position where they can enjoy the perks of the middle classes.

Although drug dealers come from an assortment of backgrounds and are motivated by a range of different attitudes, they all run their lives on a simple profit principle. Each man in the chain takes his own risk and adds his own percentage before passing on the goods. A pyramid structure springs up. The major importer sits at the apex of his own little chain of dealers. Each person in possession of kilos of smack seeks out people who will buy it from him and sell it in ounces to other dealers who will then sell it in grammes until we come down to street level where the pyramid rests uncomfortably on the thousands of hungry users who scurry back and forth in search of £10 or £20 packs.

Many of the people who would be regarded as big dealers by an onlooker are just users who have promoted themselves to dealing in order to support their own habit. Seizing the main chance, they have joined the ranks of our nation's small shopkeepers. They are not part of a huge and sinister network that has set out to corrupt the country's youth. Roger, a heroin user himself, summed up the role when he said, 'A dealer is just yourself in a different position.' Some dealers are even sincere in their desire to avoid starting others off on the same road as themselves, and refuse to sell their gear to very young people. Some are caring parents and disapprove of youngsters getting involved with heroin. They cannot, however, be sure where the gear will end up. What happens to it after it has left their possession is beyond their control. I am not suggesting that the average smack dealer is motivated primarily by altruism, but, like users, dealers are individuals with good qualities as well as bad. Dealers are people, too.

The 'teeny connection' is often used to discredit pushers as unscrupulous and wicked but young people who want to buy scag can be devious and ingenious in their methods and it must be remembered that peer pressure is what generally starts them off. It must also be acknowledged that many look and seem far older than their years. Smack dealers cannot ask their clients to show a birth certificate. There are also many instances of older users being stopped on their way to dealers' houses by young lads who beg them to buy drugs on their behalf because they have been refused by the discerning dealer. In these cases, the older users may be less responsible than the dealers. Laying scruples aside, most would be willing to help out. A teenage addict is no less desperate than any other. A weary veteran has neither the time nor the energy to give him a lecture on taking the cure. He looks into his face and sees himself; he gives up on the eager youth. If he does not score for him, someone else will. He takes the money and does the business. After all he cannot stop the inevitable spread of drug addiction single-handedly.

This sort of choice always faces anyone confronted by an addict. He can be cruel to be kind or he can simply be kind. Being cruel to a junkie achieves nothing except to punish him. Only an addict can choose when he will stop. Users and dealers often accept that taking heroin is wrong, admitting, 'You can't justify it. It's wanton hedonism and self-indulgence ...' Nevertheless, addicts tend to save their judgments for themselves. Once they have an understanding of the scene, they realise that even quite big dealers are often ordinary addicts struggling to get by.

Most small dealers are elevated to that role from amongst the ranks of the addicts. The process by which an ordinary user gets promoted to pusher status is simple. The rise and fall of the average dealer is often fairly rapid. His reign can span as much as two or three years if he is crafty and has luck on his side. Alternatively, he can set up and be closed down again in a matter of only a few weeks.

A user starts out buying scag from friends, moves on to scoring in 'safe' houses, graduates to the streets and ends up running the gauntlet of known hide-outs, freely allowing himself to be seen and hoping that the big hand will not fall on his shoulder. After a while, he is hard put to pay his way and begins to covet the ounces he sees on the tables of his suppliers. He may well become ambitious and decide to start dealing himself. By this point, he is used to living with the risks and the desire for a ready supply of heroin is greater than his fear of the law. At first, he is likely to buy comparatively small amounts of smack, perhaps as little as a gramme a day.

A gramme might cost between £60 and £80. It can be made into ten or even twelve small bags, each of which can be sold for £10. Other users will grumble about the size of the bags but if they cannot score elsewhere, they will carry on buying them.

Just by selling two or three grammes a day an addict can keep himself supplied. He will simply sell enough gear to pay for the next gramme and take whatever is left over himself. Selling three grammes a day can mean finding thirty separate individuals who are all ready to spend £10. Even so, it is usually possible to move that amount of gear to friends or personal associates avoiding the pitfalls of getting a name as a dealer. At this stage the person selling the gear might telephone other users or call round at their houses touting his wares. His friends may drop in for a coffee and buy a bag while they are there. Some will offer to sell the bags for him. Their reward is to take a little bit out of each one before passing it on.

Once someone starts dealing he can be carried along by the momentum and find that he needs to increase his turnover to keep up with demand. Those who know he is selling smack may bring friends and the word will spread. In response to pleas from the drug-hungry he may increase the scale of his activities and move on to begin buying quarter ounces or even larger amounts. In quite a short time, perhaps a matter of two or three weeks, the number of people calling at a dealer's house might have doubled or trebled. He may feel obliged to increase his turnover to meet demand: 'You might only start out to support your own habit but the whole thing escalates and gets out of hand. You start out telling six people you're going to do bags and within a week you've got twenty knocking at the door.'

The established clientele expect a service. His own habit will probably have increased and he will have become involved in a symbiotic relationship with his customers. Most small dealers quickly begin operating to regular hours. Users rapidly get to know the movements of their dealer. They will know what time he gets up and goes to bed, and which day he signs on. Some dealers are so efficient and well-organised that they rarely go out at all. If they do, they make sure that someone is there to man the door. Users soon tire of walking miles to a dealer's house and finding him out. If this happens, custom will drift away. Dealers, therefore, tend not only to keep long hours but regular hours too and, as much of their job is done at night, most do not rise or start business much before noon.

Making up bags is a repetitive, boring occupation that involves cutting paper into small squares and folding these so that they will hold the relevant quantity of heroin without springing open or letting it spill. It also means carefully chopping up the gear and separating it into deals. Small dealers usually have to score every day and so a typical day will require the dealer to get up and score at a regular hour, cut his paper, divide his gear, pack it into bags and be ready for his first customers by mid-afternoon. Some dealers buy in small amounts of gear and go backwards and forwards throughout the day to replenish the supplies, leaving the others to deal the bags and take the money.

Few make much out of their day's work beyond managing to support their own habit. Often a dealer will have not only himself to keep supplied but also his wife, his brother, and his best friend. Most dealers have a small entourage of 'helpers' who also require access to the stash. On reflection 'pusher' does, indeed seem a misnomer for the heroin seller as any dealer is constantly besieged by a steady stream of people looking for smack. If there is none for sale, the callers will be very disappointed.

Buying heroin is not the same as buying any other drug. If speed or cannabis are not available, the would-be buyer will be disappointed, but he will not be ill. If heroin is not available, the user can be devastated. He must hunt all over town until he finds an alternative supply. The wares can hardly be said to have been pushed on to him. He will be pleading with the so-called pusher to push his wares in his direction. Most addicts are puzzled by the media image of the pusher. They make sarcastic jests like, 'Let's get down the school gates and see if we can score!' Few have much to say about their dealers and often a really efficient operator is mourned by all when he is arrested or put out of business. Addicts will mutter darkly and with a wry grin remarks like, 'I wish they'd bring back Tony. He was great.' When I asked Paul his view of pushers he shrugged and said, 'Pushers! Well, they're necessary, aren't they! People want them. People are happy to have them. What more can I say?' Dealers themselves find it hard to come to terms with the commonly held view of them. One man confided, 'You see yourself described in the papers as "another man involved in the terrible conspiracy" and you think, "Do they mean me?" I mean I only think of myself as a boy.' Bobby highlighted the fact that dealers are just as trapped as their customers and just as ordinary: 'All dealers wear big thick coats with T-shirts underneath. Coats for when they have not had a hit and T-shirts for when they have!' They, too, are at the mercy of the drug.

People who deal smack in bags are often living on social security in grotty flats or run-down council accommodation. Some erroneously believe that dealing will make them rich. When they start taking heroin many are living aimless, directionless lives with no hope of finding work. Spurred on by visions of 'the big pound notes in the sky' they see dealing as an escape route from the social security snare. One dealer living in a high-rise block told me with chilling candour, 'I want to make so much money I never have to worry about money again. I just want to get up in the morning and not have to worry about money ...' His plan took him well out of his depth. He moved on to build a mini-empire that gained local notoriety, brought him to the attention of the drug squad and saw him behind prison bars within six months of the day when he sold his first bag. All he had gained was some new furniture, now confiscated by the police, a huge heroin habit and a heavy prison sentence. Referring to him one user remarked bitterly, 'I respected him and look where he is now. He's a loser. They're all losers. They're all divvies. Not one of them has made anything out of it.' Another explained, 'Money made out of smack is bad money. They all either end up nicked or on their arse.'

Dealers do command the respect of users for a time. The risks they run can add a glow of romance to their lives, just as rain adds a temporary shine to the grey streets. A dealer can figure as a Jesse James of the black alleys, but he is just as doomed and it is prison bars, not tombstones, that are in his eyes. As he crashes through the commonsense barrier of between twenty and fifty regular clients and starts selling indiscriminately to more people than he can be bothered to count, he becomes more and more vulnerable. To the police he is a sitting duck and it is only a matter of time before they pick him off. Somewhere deep down he must know this but, fascinated by the attention he gets and the power he has, drawn on by his temporary importance, and drugged beyond his wildest dreams, the dealer careers on in a collision course with authority. He needs a good flow of customers to take the gear from him and he ceases to care who sees them calling so long as they keep coming. He holds court, dispensing free drugs to those he has chosen to favour, withholding them from the others. Your best friend is the man with the gear. He is King. King for a day. Enter the busies. The King is nicked. The court moves on. Long live the King. The punters drift off to score another day. The King begins his bird. 'You see the dealer every day. He's your best mate. You know where he's going to be every hour and then, suddenly, you never see him again.'

I have never understood why dealers are so content to risk their liberty. They dream up all sorts of ruses and security measures to buy time but life is no more than an ongoing effort to outwit the opposition. Perhaps, like gamblers, they believe they will win. They back themselves against all odds and most are hopeless losers. For these people the fortunes that we read about in the papers are transient. The more smack they have, the more they take. The sums of money changing hands can be very large but one ounce of heroin can cost £1,400. Money ceases to have any meaning for a dealer who regularly moves ounces of smack. He may be using hundreds of pounds' worth of heroin every day. He can find himself sitting counting out dozens of £10 notes and asking someone to lend him a fiver to make up the money to score. Roger laughed as he reported one such occasion. 'I was down at Macker's and he said to me, "Lend us two quid for petrol. I've only got three grand and I need that to score."'

Once he has come to the notice of the police, a dealer becomes the human quarry in a kind of fox hunt. He is pursued and hunted wherever he goes. He is followed, invaded, arrested and busted until he is finally imprisoned. His life is diminished to the point where he does nothing but buy drugs, sell drugs and take drugs. He aims to be semi-conscious as much of the time as possible. His real friends shake their heads, try in vain to warn him to pull out, and wonder sadly how long it will be before the big top collapses and the circus is scattered.

In other respects dealers are often ordinary family men. Sometimes their wives are hoisted up on to the bandwagon and it rumbles on out of control with Mum and Dad both off their heads until it smashes into the big blue Black Maria and they tumble off into the outstretched arms of the police. Other women stand by neglected and confused watching their husbands destroying themselves. One woman told me, 'When I go out I have to get a babysitter to look after my husband, never mind the kids.' Her sister chipped in with, 'What can she do with a husband who gets up at 2 p.m. and smokes three grammes a day?' He had been popular and likeable but his passion for smack had changed him beyond recognition. David remarked wistfully, 'The Macker I've known hasn't even been there for the last six months.' Macker's dealing led him into jail. Prison seems to be the ultimate destination of most people who persistently try to get away with dealing in scag. Whatever the public are led to believe, even people moving as much as a kilo of heroin a week are not necessarily sitting back in luxurious surroundings to enjoy their ill-gotten gains. Some are living with threadbare carpets in dilapidated flats where the inside doors are hanging off and everyone is too stoned to mend them.

Furthermore, smack dealers do not have an easy time because they are surrounded by mistrust and dishonesty. There is no safety or security for anyone selling heroin and he does not know for certain who his friends are. The scruffiest, most convincing-looking junkies could be drug squad detectives working under cover. Dealers are at risk from all angles. The most obvious risk is from the police but, ironically, some dealers are more scared of threats from anti-smack campaigners within their own community than from the police. One dealer who was arrested on the street by plain clothes officers and later released related the incident saying, 'I was shit scared. I thought they were "Vigilantes". I thought they were going to kill me. I was dead relieved when I realised they were just the busies [police].' His fears were well-founded. Local vigilantes have been known to use considerable force in their efforts to evict dealers. These 'vigilantes', of course, are often desperate users who bounce in with baseball bats and relieve the dealer of his drugs – and anything else of value they fancy taking!

The police operate according to certain rules and dealers know this. It might be widely acknowledged that smack is on sale at a particular address, but the police need concrete evidence before they can prosecute. This means that they must break in and catch the dealer with the drugs. Some people brazenly fork out several hundred pounds having their homes reinforced with steel gates and putting metal grilles up at the windows. Locks, bolts and bars of every shape and size are the hallmarks of houses where smack is on sale. Dealers can carry on with their business for months by frustrating police efforts to gain access. While the police hammer in vain at the steel bars, the dealers calmly tuck into the remains of the evidence or flush it away before opening up to usher in the thwarted detectives.

In high-rise blocks where love for the law does not abound, several drug squad officers armed with sledgehammers tend to stand out even in a crowd. By the time they reach their target address the whole block is aware that the drug squad is on the way. Dealers even post look-outs to warn of uniformed strangers or other approaching trouble. Some get a couple of unruly Dobermans or German Shepherds to guard the premises and to wake them up if intruders should arrive under cover of darkness to carry out the notorious dawn raid beloved of drug squads throughout the land.

Scoring is one of the most hazardous activities for dealers who make their homes into fortresses. Inside they are comparatively safe but on the street they are not. Some go to considerable lengths and use all their inventive powers to dream up schemes and ploys to keep the police guessing and avoid being caught. Another danger lies in inadvertently supplying drugs to undercover policemen. This is less likely than it may seem as most dealers know the majority of their customers personally. New clients have to be introduced by existing ones. Even so, mistakes do occur and dealers have been trapped by this ruse. The whole business is like a savage boardgame riddled with setbacks and disasters that can be as random and unexpected as the toss of a dice.

Another problem is the likelihood of someone who has made a purchase being arrested and pressured into giving a statement naming the dealer. He may, for instance, be encouraged by promises of the vast benefits that await those who assist the police with their enquiries. An offer to retain his own liberty by turning in his dealer can be very tempting for a user who fears gaol and inevitable separation from the drugs he needs. Careful dealers, therefore, dream up all sorts of ways of selling their wares so as to minimise the risks to their customers as well as to themselves. The use of a public place to exchange money and drugs is a good ploy.

The seller will make it known that he can be found in a certain bar. His regulars will approach him there and a third party may be the one who scurries away to the stash to provide the relevant supplies. I remember one popular scene that centred on a betting shop. To cover their tracks all sorts of hitherto disinterested unlikely gamblers found themselves trying to place small bets while waiting for the man. Dealers will also drive around in cars, pulling up to do business if they see an acquaintance who is a user or responding to orders taken on their mobile phones.

When they first start selling gear and are operating from home, dealers begin by inviting their customers in. Everyone sits round chatting and taking drugs in a friendly relaxed atmosphere. In this sort of scene people often run up big debts which they will never pay. Some people will pursue the debtors with relentless and callous zeal, while others will write off hundreds of pounds, knowing that no money is available and being unwilling to harrass those who simply cannot pay. One big dealer could never bear to see anyone sick. Customers who turned up on his doorstep without money would be sure of a free turn-on however much they owed him. On one occasion he heard of someone mugging other users for their gear. Angrily, he sent the man a message, telling him that instead of attacking users he should come down and see him for a free hit when he was sick. This kind of generosity is perhaps not typical of dealers but the fact that it exists at all must come as a shock to anyone who has read the papers and been convinced that dealers are monsters whose closest relatives probably hailed from Transylvania. Indeed, some dealers find themselves accepting all sorts of unsolicited goods or services in exchange for drugs when junkies cannot find cash. I have known butchers swapping steaks and legs of lamb for gear, heard of joiners fitting shelves and cupboards and painters decorating dealers' homes. Bobby recalls people coming into Macker's house offering him all sorts of broken or half worn-out things. Often Macker would accept something and, when the owner had gone, he would give it away immediately to somebody else. Macker became a sort of junkie Robin Hood who was not too mean to forfeit some of his 'easy money' to help out the victims of his trade.

Macker himself was hopelessly addicted. Having come into dealing as a means of supporting his own habit, he would promise daily that tomorrow would be the day on which he would stop. He referred to heroin as 'this fucking shit', and when he heard that a teenage girl of his acquaintance had become involved with it, he invited her round and doled out methadone to her, putting her on a sort of reduction course until she was cured. This sort of concern helped to build the Robin Hood legend that surrounded him. After that, he refused to provide her with drugs, and banned her from the house. I am not suggesting that he was ready for canonisation, I am just pointing out that dealers are not necessarily all bad. Despite public outrage against them, they are by no means the worst members of our criminal classes.

In the end, cynicism overtakes most of them and they end up withdrawing behind their locked doors, resorting to techniques that keep the process impersonal and businesslike. A caller knocks, hears a mumbled enquiry as to what she wants coming from behind the closed door, puts her money through the letter box and receives the goods by return through the same letter box. The deal is done in seconds and the buyer may never see her dealer for weeks on end unless she catches sight of him in the street.

Dealers frequently find themselves at the receiving end of hopeless promises from sick junkies and dole out bags that are never paid for. For some, these losses are a disaster as they run on a very tight budget to begin with. Many of the debts are never collected. The dealer finds himself nicked and disgraced when half the time, he has been handing out free gear for verbal IOUs that are never filled.

Dealers are, of course, just as likely to be ripped off as their clients. They can be robbed like anyone else. When the pickings are rich those in the know can be tempted – and you can't run snivelling to the police when someone has just taken £2,000' worth of heroin from your back room. Smack dealers themselves tend to be fairly honest. In particular, they are usually fair about the quality of the gear they sell. They have been where the users are and they know the problems. Although they may make a little money and their hit out of the punters, they do not usually even consider giving out anything other than heroin. At the worst, the gear may sometimes be weak, heavily cut or of poor quality, the bag may be small, but it always works. If it did not, there would soon be dozens of hysterical, sick, angry users on the doorstep. Another reason why the smack salesman must deal straight is because, if he has a big habit, he will need to turn over the gear rapidly in order to score again and keep himself supplied. If the word gets out that he has bum gear no one will call. Although frowned upon as the baddies on the scene, smack dealers tend to be reasonably straightforward, comparatively honest and quite businesslike.

The lines of communication between drug users are excellent. If a dealer gets a bad reputation he will not survive on the scene. The junk grapevine is so good because those users who do not work spend a lot of time on the streets. Their mission in life is to move bits of smack of all shapes and sizes from one location to another. All day long they bob about from flat to flat to house to street to flat and back, buying, selling, consuming drugs and gossiping. Gossip serves an important function. If someone's flat is full of busies you do not want to call. You cannot score there and, if you do call, all that will happen is that you will be dragged in and have your name taken. Your time will be wasted, and your face will be noted, you may even be searched and charged with something, like the bit of dope in your back pocket.

You also need to talk to find out who has got what, who they are selling it to, and for how much. Like any businessman you may want to put in your bid, cut someone out, buy someone out, move up the ladder a rung, get yourself a better deal. News travels so fast that if two separate people, John and Phil, start dealing at mid-day, John selling strong gear in good-sized bags and Phil crappy stuff in small bags, by 2 o'clock all of Phil's customers will be queuing up at John's door. Phil will have difficulty moving his rubbishy gear. He may have to hang onto it until John runs out, increase the size of his bags, or sell it off cheaply in half or quarter grammes. At street level, junkies are acutely aware of matters concerning the quality and price of their drugs. They will go a long way to get the best and cheapest they can.

Each user visits a regular dealer but, when he runs out, it may be necessary to lay money on other people who know somewhere else to score. This can be a risky business. It is far more likely that a user at street level will he given a bad deal by other users than by a dealer. It is very common for users to pull petty tricks on one another in order to hustle a hit for themselves. For instance, buying a £10 or £20 bag is the most expensive way to acquire heroin. Technically, a bag is an eighth of a gramme, but most people make a gramme up into ten or twelve bags. If an inexperienced user sends someone else to buy scag for her, that someone else will be very likely to chip the bag, taking out a hit for himself. What the buyer ultimately receives is only worth about half of the money she laid out. A quarter gramme costs between £17 and £20. It is more likely to be a genuine deal and may contain the same amount of smack that would cost £30 if bought in bags. Users who cannot afford grammes aim to buy quarters rather than bags. A common ploy is for someone to take the money and return with two bags, saying that there were no quarters for sale and he thought the buyer would prefer two bags rather than nothing. What he has really done is separated the quarter into three bags and taken one for himself.

Some junkies sink to the point where they start stealing directly from others. They offer to score for someone, take his money and have no intention of returning with either the money or the scag. When the victim does catch up with them they invent stories about anything from getting arrested to being run over. There is no way the user will get his money back. Some pretend to buy the tales and shuffle off. Others put on a show of strength and wreak vengeance on the liar's nose. Either way they have lost out. It is quite typical that those who have blatantly ripped off their close associates will send their wives or girlfriends round with a fraction of the gear that should be delivered to make the peace. The unfortunate women have to grovel and apologise on the men's behalf, the logic being that the victim is unlikely to strike a woman.

The normal pitfalls involved in scoring can mean that the listener can never be sure that even the most preposterous tale is not the truth. One man told me a story about his own escapades and the lengths he had gone to in order to cover his deceit. He had been given a number of bags to sell by a small dealer but, being sick himself, had taken three and did not have the money to hand over to his supplier. He decided to tell him that he had been mugged and, in order to keep his male honour intact, he asked a friend to put a circle of 'love bites' around one of his eyes, so creating a convincing 'black eye' to back up the tale. He was believed and the dealer simply had to cover the loss. This is just one example of why the much talked-of profits from dealing are often not as great as people believe.

Enter the busies

It is almost inevitable that, at some stage, the police will enter a junkie's life. While no one is pleased when this happens, most drug users see it as an occupational hazard to be taken in their stride. Funnily enough, few users believe that possession of heroin should be legal. They merely hope to continue their own indulgence in secret, managing to evade the consequences of the law. Not one person to whom I spoke looked forward to a time when legalisation of heroin would occur. A few fantasised wistfully about the possible invention of a non-addictive narcotic but none suggested that free smack for all would be desirable. Most expressed the view that their lives would have been happier without it.

Obviously, drug users see the police as adversaries. Some fear them, others are resentful; most treat them with respect and aim to give them a wide berth. The police, too, have a difficult job with drug users, many of whom have committed no other crime and are, in other ways, model citizens. One addict actually found drug squad detectives who called on him virtually apologetic. One of their number told him that he was dissatisfied with his work on the grounds that drug users were not 'real criminals'. He complained that they showed too much camaraderie, tended not to inform on each other, and were basically 'normal citizens' who took drugs instead of a few pints.

On the whole, however, the police do not demonstrate a great deal of amiable bonhomie towards drug users and when an addict is arrested his biggest fear is that the drugs he needs will be confiscated and he will be left to face the rigours of 'cold turkey' in a bare, comfortless cell. A registered addict described being locked up, denied access to his prescription and repeatedly questioned by detectives. In due course, he had had a fit. Only after that were the drugs returned to him and a speedy discharge organised. That is typical of the lack of sympathy addicts can expect. Those who are registered have some chance of receiving medication. For the rest there is little likelihood of their being given more than tea without sympathy.

While the police ostensibly concentrate their efforts against dealers, if a junkie crosses their path he will not be ignored. He might be picked up on the street as he goes about his business or visited at home if he has a record of previous offences. Once he falls into their hands he will almost certainly be subjected to a strip search. This can include an examination of every orifice in the body. I cannot imagine that the police find this part of their duties very pleasant but an addict feels vulnerable and self-conscious in the extreme when told to 'Bend down and spread 'em.' The forfeit of the right to keep the body covered in front of strangers cannot be taken lightly. One veteran of numerous searches said savagely, 'The police must be bloody perverts. They spend half their time peering up your arse.' The minimum indignity to expect is a rather sordid investigation of socks and undergarments. A mother of two in her thirties described a search. 'It's so bloody embarrassing standing there with some snotty, juvenile WPC telling you to drop your drawers.' It seems so degrading for a middle-aged woman to be asked by a fresh-faced girl to remove her knickers. Flagging self-respect can droop even lower under circumstances like these.

Women can be asked to undergo a vaginal examination by a police doctor. I need not describe their views about this. Most women do not enjoy facing these examinations even under normal circumstances. Considering the fact that most of the searches are fruitless, it is not surprising that addicts resent them. Drugs are rarely found because the knowledge that searches can form part of standard procedure has meant that most users do not hide their drugs. Only novices traipse around with the gear firmly wedged into inaccessible pockets or down socks: in an emergency, there is no hope of retrieving it in time to ditch it before a search takes place. They often carry small amounts in their mouths, wrapped in cling film ready to slip easily down the throat if they are approached, or in their hands ready to throw away. Swallowing gear is not, however, completely without risk. Packs that are too large to swallow readily have been known to cause damage to the throat or intestines, particularly when foil, rather than cling film, has been used as a wrapper. Overdose also becomes a potential hazard for anyone swallowing more than their usual daily supply of drugs.

Those who live safely on the right side of the law do not realise the sort of humiliation to which drug users can be subjected. Television glamorises the roles of police and law breakers alike, but the reality is often tawdry, depressing and vulgar. The public tends not to consider the fact that policemen are often recruited from deprived inner city areas. Their roots are quite likely to be the same as those of many of their clients. They can be hard, loud, brutal and downright offensive. Occasionally they are sympathetic. Sometimes they are bullies. There is not much room for sentiment in their job. In some respects, it is true that 'the police and the crooks are two ends of the same stick'.

Even if they are not regular dealers, most junkies sell a few bags now and again in order to survive. On the heels of the buyers come the drug squad and when they arrive they are likely to be toting sledgehammers and, occasionally, guns. It is common for them to begin their visit by obliterating the front door before the occupants have had time to decide whether or not they will open it. Any hesitation on the part of residents will be construed as time in which evidence is being destroyed. That could well be the case, although it is equally likely that the victims are asleep, in the bath or on the loo. If they are, it is hard luck on the front door. Once inside, the police restrain residents and systematically search both their bodies and belongings. After a bust, the only questions ever asked by other users are, 'Did they find anything?' and 'How much?' People do sometimes complain privately that the destruction of their property goes beyond reasonable limits and amounts to harassment. Expensive furniture can be slashed in the hunt for drugs, wallpaper peeled off or floorboards ripped up. The contents of plant pots and drawers can be strewn around the floor. Whether intentional or not, the drug squad often leave a very nasty mess in their wake.

As the swinging sixties gave way to the seventies the dreaded police drug bust became the scourge of student lives. In those days, the object of their attention was usually cannabis. Large numbers of young people forfeited jobs or promising careers, to say nothing of their liberty, because of a liking for that drug. Nowadays, possession of small amounts of cannabis has, in practice, been demoted to the status of a misdemeanour. The drug squad have been known to take the decision not to prosecute offenders. Heroin is the current bogey drug and the anti-smack cavalcade rumbles on crushing anyone in its path. Youngsters in possession of scag can find themselves in youth custody, exposed to contamination by the full range of young offenders and facing an uncertain future. Young lives are sacrificed to the greater good as the desperate battle to stamp out opiate abuse rages on. Few take the time to question the nature of the crime or the appropriateness of the punishment. A short examination of the facts shows that prison does not cure drug abusers. It merely takes them out of circulation for a while. Most relapse when they are released. A more humane and worthwhile alterative to imprisonment needs to be found if drug users are to be rehabilitated. If society cares about drug abuse, it must care for drug abusers. Force must be tempered by imagination. Money, ideas and greater understanding are badly needed.

Violent vigilantes

Fear of arrest by the police has been superseded by a comparatively new threat: the formation of vigilante groups. Some of these groups may be parents or relatives of drug users. Such people feel genuine concern and anger. They give information to the police and form useful self-help and support groups. Others are no more than greedy thugs who have caught on to an excuse for robbery with violence. In an area like Liverpool 8, they gleefully home in on the houses of anyone rumoured to be dealing in heroin in the expectation of seizing drugs, money or both. They are a cowardly shower of back-street buccaneers who arrive in force, armed with knives, sticks and other weapons. Some are masked with balaclavas to conceal their identities. They put out a smokescreen of self-righteous lies, billing themselves as frustrated citizens driven to taking the law into their own hands. They use the money they confiscate for their own ends and much of the heroin they take ends up back on the streets. It is more likely to be sold for profit than taken out of circulation and destroyed. The press thunders support for the motives, if not the methods, of the vigilantes. Meanwhile the thieves sit back rocking with laughter.

If a group of unscrupulous young thugs knows the address of a smack dealer they might be tempted to call without hiding their real intentions under the banner of righteous indignation. They burst into the unlucky drug user's house wielding knives, threatening his wife or girlfriend, and carrying off anything they fancy. On these occasions, women have been raped. One gang actually attempted to carry off a screaming woman. She was only saved by the fact that she hung on to a lamp post outside the house until the noise she made roused the neighbours. Dealers have been badly beaten and slashed with knives as they tried to defend their homes and families. Unless compelled by their own needs such people would never continue. Yet the determination not to give up heroin can overcome all opposition. I recall seeing one man struggle with firemen and run back into a blazing house to retrieve his smack. He was actually ready to risk his life to save it.

Occasionally, as residents of an underworld that makes its own rules, dealers can find themselves attacked from all sides. The police form the smallest threat. One man was robbed of several hundred pounds by so-called vigilantes and related the incident saying, 'When I saw them, I threw my wife in the back room and locked the door. One of them shouted, "cut the bastard" and the other one went for me with a knife. He only missed my balls because I was wearing a loose track suit. These people are lunatics.' Later that week when the original suppliers called he was dangled from a top floor window by his feet. They wanted their money and did not care how he had lost it. Under pressure like this some people crack up. Others arm themselves with anything from meat cleavers to guns and the whole mess escalates.

The unlikely survival of humour

Junkies do not look amusing to outsiders. It is not surprising that junkie humour is only likely to be funny to junkies. Healthy people find it hard to share a joke with a dying man, especially when he is laughing at himself. They are, naturally, too embarrassed by his predicament. The same applies to junkies. Most people disapprove of their lifestyle or pity them. Few see the funny side of what looks like lingering death. Nevertheless, on the junk scene there is laughter and there can be fun. Many junkies laugh in the face of the sad or unpleasant aspects of their world. Junk humour can be dark, powerful, self-mocking and, at times, self-denigrating.

Dougie, reading an article on experiments into the effects of opiates on the nervous system of the rat, burst out, 'The government are giving rats drugs to see what they do. Fucking hell, man, why use rats when they can use us?' To another junkie this would represent an entertaining fantasy scenario to get free drugs. To anyone else it might be a depressing confirmation of the depths to which a junkie can fall.

This sort of black humour is common among junkies. Like nurses of the dying, junkies have to stay cheerful. Bravado reigns. They laugh about the worst things they have done, gleefully exchanging horror stories like fighters returning from the front. They delight in shocking. Recognition of their own bizarre behaviour lessens the tension and diminishes the fear of the consequences. Any subculture needs to establish its own norms. Humour assists this process.

Addicts laugh about their own inadequacies and inability to function as they feel they should. I remember a group of young men making enthusiastic plans for a climbing expedition. Gradually, they began to realise that the need for junk and their own lack of fitness would impede their progress. One of them suggested that a raid on an emergency outpost for injured mountaineers might furnish them with some morphine to help them carry on. They all fell about laughing at the absurd contradiction in their position. The trip was never made.

As life takes on the proportions of a 'Tom and Jerry' cartoon, the real people seek relief in laughter. Destructive humour appeals to the self-destructive. Drug-culture jibes help to release tension, and explode the myths generated by a savage and private underworld. Humour negates the old romantic hero image of the drug addict and heals the real wounds inflicted daily by an abrasive scene.

CHAPTER 6

ℭ *Heroin: the other cost*

The enemy within: the Trojan Horse effect

Heroin is purchased with three separate kinds of currency: physical, financial and personal. I have already examined the price of drug addiction in physical and financial terms and tried to explain some aspects of the effects on an addict's inner life. To an observer, however, the drug user who has anything more than a passing acquaintance with heroin will begin to manifest gradual personality changes. The stress of secrecy and inevitable debt may, in part, explain some of these, but the effects of the drug itself account for others.

It is true that junkies can and do lead quite normal lives, but heroin will take its toll on the user. She will find herself more irritable and less forbearing in stressful situations. This is not a permanent condition, but when in the grip of a bout of drug-induced ill-humour an addict can be unreasonably snappy and bad-tempered. Those in the know will recognise the symptoms, acknowledge that the user has the 'morph-grumps' and humour her until the malady has passed. Any confrontation could result in tantrums and tears. Addicts can become extremely distressed if something upsets them when they are in this hypersensitive state. A tiff between lovers could degenerate into a vicious battle terminating only when the dinner plates start to rattle the walls.

Regular use of heroin can sometimes result in uncontrollable swings of mood. Excitable and enthusiastic at the start of the day, an addict can become depressive, irrational and aggressive later on, her moods dictated by the level of the drug in her body. The same junkie who seemed expansive and generous can quickly become argumentative, unco-operative and disruptive. One day an addict will flee from confrontation, the next she will appear to seek it out. Little things start to matter terribly. An otherwise good-natured and easy-going individual can develop a pedantic obsession with detail, becoming tearful if thwarted. Her view of the world changes and she becomes defensive and suspicious. This stance can lead to misunderstandings and violent rows which are usually followed rapidly by guilt, recriminations, apologies and tears. In general, an addict becomes over-emotional and, sometimes, excessively senti-mental. Bewildered friends do not know whether to expect an effu-sive, lively companion or someone who is sullen and withdrawn. The instability of an addict's inner life can mean that even she becomes confused by her own responses. Jimmy explained, 'Your emotions change a lot. Emotions swing violently from one to another. One minute you're quite all right, the next you're crying over nothing. Even a silly film. You just start crying for nothing.' Another addict described similar feelings when she said,

> I can't stand this life. I dream only to wake up screaming. I get over-emotional and cry at anything. I become sentimen-tal and very vulnerable to changes of mood. A dog story, a baby story, a death story, a tale of triumph or success. Absolutely anything can reduce me to tears.

Junkies can become very tired owing to the disturbance of their sleep pattern, and this can result in a general inability to cope with pressure. In time, junkies withdraw as much as possible into them-selves, aware that their altered emotional responses can give them away. Susie commented, 'You become self-centred, irritable and potentially hysterical. Everything seems too much trouble and you worry all the time about forgetting something or not doing some-thing right.' On the one hand junkies just want to curl up and doze, on the other they have a million pressing tasks to perform (usually only one or two) and it's 3 o'clock already and they have only just got up. They must go. It is all too much. Things are terrible. They are late 'but don't tell anyone'. Secrecy and paranoia become facts of life for junkies. On a bad day, almost every statement can have an admonition not to tell tagged onto the end.

While aware of the changes taking place in themselves, junkies cannot control their emotions as successfully as they would wish. This leads to a loss of confidence. Kate reached a point where she described herself as having 'lost all confidence, both in myself and with men'.

Self-respect dwindles under these conditions, and others find it hard to relate to their junkie daughters or workmates. David reflected on what he had lost through drugs. His tone was wistful as he told me, 'I lost my self-respect; probably the respect of my family ... three years of my life, from 22 to 25. The chance to make something of myself.' He added calmly, 'I'm a lot more cynical than I would have been. It's destroyed my trust in people.' Paul felt even more strongly about the changes in himself and his position. He confided angrily, 'It just made me become a bum. There isn't any lower you can really go! You haven't any social standing when you're standing in the sewer with the rats.'

Circumstances can make a junkie selfish and unreliable. Smack has to come first and that means that someone gets let down sooner or later. Junkies tend to lose their judgement as they become unable to stand back and look dispassionately at a situation. Rows develop and friendships founder. Trust evaporates after a while. Petty spite and bitchiness creep in. When they feel wronged, junkies tittle-tattle and tell tales on one another. Addicts come to feel wrecked intellectually, emotionally, physically and spiritually. A heroin habit opens up an abyss of mental and spiritual death. Junkies forget so many other things they can even forget the way out.

Life shrinks in on the user until she has lost sight of the life she once expected to have. David expressed it rather well when he said,

> One's social life dwindles to the point where it's you and smack and nothing else matters. It's a speedy decline. A flimsy bridge across quicksand. You feel it going and suddenly you're in there. Burroughs summed it up when he talked about 'smack time'. Everything runs to your next hit. To me it just means a diminishing life, a dwindling life, until it's just you and smack.

Exit family and friends

As heroin takes precedence over all else, you start to become uncomfortable in the presence of old friends who will make demands on you and confront you with your old self. You, therefore, cut them out. And they tire of you. The process may be set in motion from two sides. It may even be more on theirs. They simply start being bored by you without knowing why. They will seek you out less and less. Gradually, the relationship will end quite naturally. You do not seek out your former friends as you can never afford to make arrangements in advance, knowing you may need to score. To them you become distant, cagey, stand-offish, erratic and downright unreliable. Junkies seek only the company of other drug users because they expect nothing and make few demands. Any unusual behaviour is accepted as normal by other junkies. Everyone shares the same understanding that gear comes first. Scoring is the most important event for all. People unite in the cause. They speak in code, learn not to talk on the telephone or what to say if they have to. Junkies never interfere with each other's outrageous behaviour. In glass houses themselves, they do not criticise or judge. They are used to crazy changes of mood, tears and hysterical outbursts in themselves and in others. Whatever you do they will not be shocked. Sometimes they may be angry but never shocked. Among them you are at ease and free. With others you have a dark, difficult secret to conceal. The gap between you and the rest of the world widens, a chasm finally opens up and you are on the other side.

Users all spoke about their recognition of losing credibility and the respect of others. Paul explained the way that friends drift out of your life:

> You lose credibility because you become unreliable in other people's eyes. They might even think you're odd. People who called round regularly to see you suddenly visit more infrequently till you don't see them at all. They stay away for one of two reasons. Sometimes they know you're a user and they stop coming because they know you're not communicating with them. Straight friends instinctively know something is wrong. They are often gone forever. They will always look at you with a weird look.

He confirmed the fact that users spend all their time with dealers and other junkies and he felt that these relationships were disappointing and inferior to former friendships: 'Your whole social life changes. You don't go out. You don't have meals with them or go to the pub. To call these people friends is a joke. You only see them when you're scoring.' He concluded by saying, 'When you're taking it you're actually having a relationship with the drug. Heroin

always comes first.' Tony also acknowledged that he had abandoned the struggle to keep up normal relationships, commenting
wearily, 'You soon give up the fight of trying to keep normal people
around you. It's too much like hard bloody work!' Later he
revealed that he had been hurt by the rejection that telling his
friends had brought. He confided sadly,

> One of the bummers is if you tell a friend and decide to reveal
> your life-line secret you usually find if they're close – or you
> thought they were – they just agree with everything you say.
> Then they go away and weeks or months after you've
> revealed your little secret you find they didn't understand
> anything. They just think you're a self-indulgent creep.

He carried on to expound his theories on why non-users find
junkies so hard to cope with. He told me,

> You break certain social conventions and so people think
> you're dotty. It would be all right if you could just be yourself
> and go out of the room for five minutes when you wanted to.
> That's where all the myths come from about drug addicts
> being more weird or aggressive than everyone else. Ordinary
> people think that if you leave the room you've got to say
> where you're going. You might just be doing something. You
> might be getting carried away – having a wash and deciding
> to wash the sink for instance.

He chattered on, desperately trying to justify the stoned junkie's
obsession with irrelevant detail as 'normal' behaviour. Somehow
his attempt to make his actions seem sensible foundered, and it was
not hard to see the situation from the point of view of the bemused
onlooker as he continued,

> When you're with people that are straight they get pissed off.
> You can't tell them 'cause they think you're fucking insane.
> You think, 'I can't tell them I've been washing the sink at
> half-past ten at night when I've got company,' 'cause they
> can't fucking handle it. By the time you've thought that,
> someone says, 'Where've you been?' Then you're in a right
> pickle 'cause you've got to think of a good lie. Immediately.

You know you shouldn't have cleaned the fucking sink. The lie is worse than the truth. You say something like, 'I had something to do outside.' Nobody believes you. They all imagine you've been taking more drugs or doing something weird and you feel even worse.

Carol went into less detail than Tony but felt the censure of others just as keenly. She stated bluntly, 'They see me as an idiot. My mother, brother, my husband's family. I'm even losing the respect of my kids.' Most junkies feel extremely self-conscious about their position. They expect others to be contemptuous of them and sometimes avoid even those who might be sympathetic rather than risk further humiliation. Paul showed typical junkie resentment about finding himself vulnerable to criticism, aggressively rejecting sympathy as a kind of insult. He told me, 'My parents have been sympathetic. My wife's don't know. Mind you what does sympathy count for? It comes somewhere between shit and syphilis in the dictionary.' He complained about the way in which people he considered to be his friends had reacted on finding out that he was using heroin. He declared bitterly,

I lost my friends mainly through their narrow-mindedness, or because of their idea of what a drug addict was. A few people actually didn't want to know me and a few actually mixed it for me [made trouble]. The slightest thing I'd do or not do would be attributed to drugs and one person broadcast it all over in public; almost rubbed their hands over it. It's made me really bitter. They won't trust you any more. You lose people's trust. They think that if you're using or strung out you can't be trusted to do anything. In a way it's true but they could have a bit of tact. They don't have to be so fucking blunt and just interpret the failings you have as being down to under the influence of heroin. There's no need to just call you a junkie and all that means – don't lend him any money, don't trust him behind your back, don't leave him alone in your house.

Like all junkies, Paul found that his social life suffered in every area. He told me, 'My social life took a dive. It just became non-existent. There was no social life ... unless you call sitting in a room with twenty other people waiting for the man a social life.'

He reiterated Tony's message that junkies soon find themselves mixing only with other junkies, explaining, 'The only people you see are people connected with smack.'

Chris described a visit to the home of a junkie suffering from hepatitis. 'A night at Bic's ... Don't drink out of the cups, don't touch anything, drink straight out of the tap ...' He went on to relate the story of an evening he and his wife had spent with another couple, both of whom were heavy heroin users.

> Junkies trying to socialise ... God! We went over to that fucking pit where they lived. Anne had made this meal and she was too stoned to cook the fucking meal and when she did turn it out, I was sick all over the plate. I don't know what Pauline [his wife, a non-user] thought! Joey was mortified, bless him. He'd actually got the hoover out and dusted. He made an effort, but the three of us were all out of it. I was sick on the floor at the dinner table. We'd all fallen asleep in the chairs. We trudged home early. I can see it now. Anne's long red hair hanging in the curry and the plates getting smashed ...

Everyone I spoke to, men and women, spoke of a decline in their sex lives after taking drugs for a period of time. Mick confided, 'It destroyed my libido for months. That was another thing I really hated. I couldn't get it up for months.' Phil made similar comments. He added, 'I've always come across with sex for Debbie but I've been less interested lately. When you're turkeying, sex is only ten seconds. Smack is like a mistress you must have.' One woman joked, 'If I was locked in a room with Daly Thompson for a month I think I'd ask him what it was like being in Borstal but I wouldn't want to make love to him.' Joey lost his girlfriend altogether. Their lives had degenerated into drug-induced chaos and their relationship did not survive the strain of police raids, hospitalisation and court appearances. He told me, 'The worst thing was losing Anne, losing someone I loved. I turned nasty and was always arguing. After we came off she went weird. She wouldn't have me back. It was my own fault.' He accepts that he is to blame and grieves openly for his loss. Like most addicts, he does not expect others to put up with him. He accepts that he has become unlovable and unloved.

Normal life becomes a thing of the past for junkies. The losing of friends and acquaintances is an everyday reality. Hobbies and

sport are abandoned, and outside interests go by the board as energy and time are poured into the hunt for drugs. Talents and abilities
waste away. The drug user finds that she cannot make arrangements to stray far from home and her suppliers. Those who do
attempt to carry on as normal and try taking holidays wish they
had not bothered. They find that suffering cold turkey on a hot
beach is considerably worse than staying at home. Junkies learn
that lesson fast. They free themselves from all interference and
make sure that new acquaintances find room in their lives only if
they know a new place to score. Once life declines to this stage,
drug users are usually seeking a way out and quite a number are
lucky enough to find one.

When a heroin user has discovered a way to cure herself she can
reflect on her worst moments and evaluate the experience. Few
junkies in this position see themselves as permanently off drugs.
Most feel they are preparing for another bout of indulgence.
Nonetheless, the knowledge that they have been able to stop at all
gives a degree of confidence and hope.

The 'good' side: are there any gains?

Surprisingly, most people could find something positive in their
experiences. Paul felt he had gained a degree of wisdom. He
described his new outlook like this:

> Any experience so profound must have some value. There are
> things I see more clearly now. But it's not something I would
> have gone and looked for. I'm not necessarily a better person
> – a bit wiser, that's all. I felt like I'd aged ten years in two
> years. I felt a lot older and wiser. You feel as if you've
> matured. I feel like I grew up awfully quickly. Your needs,
> your real needs are in sharper focus. People say I'm a differ-
> ent person. They tell me I'm not the hell-raising person I was.
> I want deeper conversations now, not just about booze or
> women, which some of my friends still talk about ...

Jimmy, despite everything, also felt that heroin had changed him for
the better, and strengthened him. He commented, 'It's changed me
for the better because of coming through so much.' Mick felt that

taking heroin could lead to a clearer understanding of oneself. He remarked, 'The last person you can fool is yourself. You find out there is no point in being anything but honest, not in the long run.' In general, addicts I spoke to seemed to share a certain ability to come to terms with their experiences and a lack of regret for what they had suffered. They shared a willingness to build on what had happened to them rather than any desire to reject the bad times. Viv articulated this view when she said,

> Being a junkie can have a good side. You get so low that it's humbling. That need not be destructive or negative. It can make you appreciate ordinary things much more. Life becomes simple again. Walking in the country or sitting in the sun ... Ordinary things take on a new importance.

Bobby summed up his views on a cautionary note. He seemed to have failed to resolve some of the conflicts in his own attitude. He complained,

> Life seems to be a permanent battle not to get strung out. You cannot go back and be the person you were. Nothing you do can be the same. It strips you of your innocence permanently. That's something you cannot get back.

I disagree. Once a user gets free from a heroin habit she can experience new joy in simple things. Just being alive and well can be a satisfying novelty. Winning the fight against heroin can give an ex-user more confidence, hope and determination to succeed than she ever had before.

How family and friends can help

For a drug addict the knowledge that someone else believes in her can be very important. It is unlikely, however, that a junkie will manage to come off drugs simply because someone else asks her to. The process is a little more subtle than that but the confidence and concern of those who are close can help the addict to regain a degree of self-esteem and that can be the first step to a drug-free life. If someone else can see her as worthwhile, valuable and important, a junkie is more likely to value herself. The support and love of others can, therefore, be of crucial significance in giving the impetus to quit drugs. If you believe in someone and they believe in you, your chance of success is increased.

Helping an addict is not easy. The strain can be enormous and anyone who sets out to do it needs to be strong but tolerant, loving but firm, supportive but determined. The role is a hard one to fill and will take a great deal out of the helper. The rewards, however, can be just as great. There are addicts who owe their lives to the fact that somebody stayed with them and carried on believing in them even through relapse and the bad times. Only the helper can decide whether the person he knew is someone for whom he is prepared to fight. If you are prepared to go through with it, it might be far easier than you imagined. Once you have faced up to the shock that someone is an addict, you may even find that your lifestyle and theirs are little altered by that fact.

The friends and family of an addict face an assortment of difficulties. They have to contend with both practical and personal problems and some complain that addicts have become strangers who are unreliable, who lie, cheat and steal. I would certainly refute any suggestion that this is true in every case. Many heroin users, as I have already pointed out in earlier chapters, never behave like that. Those who do, however, can make alarming companions and their selfishness can shock. When someone has given all that he can to help finance an addict that person may still turn and bite the hand that feeds her by stealing money or goods. Users who get to this stage will even be talked about, frowned upon and shunned by other junkies, but their relatives and friends will be most at risk from their actions.

If you do find that someone is stealing from you, the first thing you must do is take evasive action to protect your own position. Make sure that you do not leave cheque books, building society books, money or valuables in easy reach and try not to leave the house unattended for long periods of time. The second thing you must do is to work out whether theft is likely to become a regular threat or whether you have been the victim of a random, one-off, desperate act. That will help you decide how to proceed. Involving the police is rarely helpful. Punishment and revenge are not constructive. If you do inform the police that a crime has taken place they are likely to prosecute the offender even if you change your mind and decide to forgive and forget. Once they are involved, the matter is usually out of your hands.

The best course of action is probably to try and talk to the person who is causing you all this pain and distress. You will need to find out the extent of their drug problem and consider solutions together. Remember that he or she will be in a very vulnerable position; the need for drugs and the addict's conscience may be at war. An aggressive approach from the wronged party could lead to alienation through guilt, a consolidation of the addict's fear that 'nobody really cares' and the complete loss of the opportunity to help at all. Addicts need to know that someone is there to offer help if it is needed. It is of vital importance for them to maintain their relationships with those they care for. That is one way for them to hold onto an identity and the concept of life in a drug-free world. It is also worth bearing in mind that theft might be occurring because the addict has not tried to get help of any kind. Shocked and scared, she reaches out to take what she needs. Doctors will, however, provide fairly lengthy reduction courses of appropriate drugs that help to alleviate the craving for heroin while allowing the addict to stabilise her lifestyle.

There are now a number of agencies and organisations willing to offer help and support of every kind both to addicts and to their families and friends. It is therefore worth seeking out help and advice yourself and trying to persuade the addict to do the same. It can even be a good idea to go along to a clinic or centre with her to offer much needed moral support and encouragement. Remember, however, that the decision to seek help must, in the end, come from the drug user. You can show her what she is doing to you and how she is damaging herself. You can try to persuade her to change her ways, but unless she chooses to go along wholeheartedly with any suggestions you make, your efforts will fail. That is why support, rather than aggressive determination to stamp out the addiction at all costs, is what is needed.

Anyone who discovers that someone close to him is an addict should examine his own attitude and try to rid himself of certain prejudices straightaway. He should disregard hearsay, ignore dramatic newspaper reports and believe only in the messages from his own eyes and ears. Parents probably find it hardest to cope with addiction in their children, especially when those children are teenagers or in their early twenties. Just when the job of bringing them up seemed to be over, just when the worry and the struggle seemed likely to end, the situation becomes worse than it ever was. Parents must get ready to cope with conflict, aggression, instability, upheaval, disappoint- ment and real fears for the safety and welfare of their son or daugh- ter. What they should try to avoid, however, is panic. There is no need to assume the worst. The case need not be hopeless. Heroin is only a chemical like tea and coffee, and, like them, it can be refused. It has no mind of its own; it can be controlled.

The hardest thing for parents to do is to accept their addicted children as they are. The most obvious urge for a mother or father is to separate a son or daughter from the drug immediately, whatever the difficulties. Some parents claim to have tied up their children, even put chains on their legs to stop them going out to buy heroin. Others have resorted to physical violence. They claim that they have been successful in keeping their children off drugs. Perhaps, if they have succeeded, it was the intensity of the love and concern they showed that impressed their children the most. Perhaps it was a reci- procal affection that made them conform to their parents' wishes. Perhaps it was simply fear. Certainly, wielding a length of chain is, in the long run, no way to win a debate. The most important thing for helpers to do is to accept the truth, avoid the urge to moralise or condemn and to get on with trying to cope with the situation in a humane way. Learning to live with the knowledge that someone is an addict and that she wishes to stay that way, for the time being at least, can be an important step towards helping her.

This can be very difficult for some parents. Many feel acutely embarrassed by the discovery that heroin has invaded the family home. Shame, humiliation and guilt can be very real stumbling blocks for parents to overcome. Some, understandably, feel angry and betrayed. They feel like throwing out the ungrateful child, leav- ing her to fend for herself. Some might be tempted to believe that drastic action of this kind would produce favourable results. The likelihood of this cruel rejection succeeding in achieving a positive goal is, however, very small. Under such circumstances the addict would be left with even less reason to stop taking drugs. Faced with total rejection, addicts can become self-destructive. They may feel bitter and turn to crime in an effort to finance their habit. That could land them in even more serious trouble and, ultimately, bring worse shame to the family's door.

The way in which parents discover the truth can, of course, be very painful, especially when they are told by a third party or find out by accident, and the hurt can lead to hasty actions which might be regretted later. The best thing is to stop and think carefully before making any decision. Parents should remind themselves that this is still the child they loved. They should remember that they are not alone, that thousands of families all over this country, throughout Europe and in America, have faced or are currently facing similar problems. With sympathy, common sense and support from others a family can work together to overcome addiction. It need be no more than a temporary setback in the family's comfortable existence.

Problems for couples

Couples sometimes face addiction together, but when one is addicted and the other is not it is very hard for them to maintain their relationship. Resentment builds up in the injured party. He or she can feel hopeless, helpless and betrayed. The addict's behaviour can seem irrational, unreasonable and utterly selfish. Promises frequently come to nought; debts accumulate; trust can be destroyed. There are often problems paying bills and frustration increases as heroin competes for any available funds. Disgust and anger can beset the non-addicted party. In this situation there can be relief in sharing your troubles with others. When a husband or wife can let off steam by talking to friends or finds a support group where he or she can freely discuss problems, this safety valve can make it possible to carry on.

There is, of course, always the option of offering an ultimatum along the lines of 'me or the drugs'. This is a dangerous course. Such a choice can be too hard for an addict to face. If the situation seems out of control it is better to offer support and encouragement while persuading the addict to seek medical help which can relieve the strain; despite the drawbacks, the provision of legally obtained drugs on prescription can help to minimise the addict's personal problems and avoid a financial crisis. This can be the best option for many addicts as it reduces the strain for them and for everyone around them.

Couples must keep talking. It is essential that they do not retreat into separate worlds. The partner who does not take drugs must try to realise that the addict may be stressed, embarrassed and uncomfortable under certain circumstances, such as a party at the home of an old friend who knows nothing about the addict's drug problem. Naturally, the addict may feel ashamed, fear detection, or find it harder to relate to people because of the 'guilty secret'.

It is, therefore, unfair to punish the addict by sulking or by criticising if he or she refuses to attend parties, weddings or other gatherings. You may feel 'let down' by having to go alone, but it is unhelpful to come home and inform your partner that you felt utterly humiliated explaining about his or her 'headache' once again. You must learn not to blame your partner for the situation. If he or she is to blame in your eyes, that negative approach will result in resentment on your part – building to a point where hatred will take over and the relationship will be beyond repair.

The addict is, at all times, in grave danger of losing his or her partner's respect. He or she should therefore work at retaining an active and useful role within the relationship. An addicted mate who is unemployed might, for instance, do some decorating or keep up with the housework. Both partners must realise that addiction does not mean that an addict cannot achieve anything. It is probably a good idea to plan things together, things that you both feel comfortable doing. The addict will have to be willing to keep the habit under control. Both partners should sit down together and work out a plan to tackle the addiction. The partner who does not use drugs should not expect overnight success, but should look for overall commitment to getting the problem under control. Binges are almost bound to occur. A lapse does not mean failure. There is always another day. People learn by their mistakes. There is always time to try again. Couples can move closer to each other as they work together to build a new life without drugs. They will have to begin by finding a way of living with them.

Health problems for helpers to bear in mind

Medical problems for an addict can include malnutrition and complications caused by using dirty syringes. Those who want to help might, therefore, be well-advised to take an interest in the addict's diet and general circumstances. Sometimes, when money is available, stocking up the larder can be a more useful form of help than giving money directly. If they keep a watchful eye on her physical condition family or friends can alert an addict to a health problem before it gets too serious to treat. For instance, an addict whose leg had become badly ulcerated attended hospital just in time to save the leg only after 'nagging' from friends who had noticed swelling in his thigh and become concerned about the fact that he was limping.

Addicts who inject themselves can, occasionally, overdose. When you share accommodation with an addict it is, therefore, a good idea to be aware of her activities. Keeping a watchful eye out if you know someone is taking a hit can mean getting to her in time in the unlikely event that she overdoses. If this should happen, you will find her slumped in a chair or collapsed on the floor, apparently unconscious with the syringe still in a vein or lying near by. If attempts to rouse her fail, check to see that she is breathing. If in doubt, you can do this by holding a mirror close to her face to see if it mists over. When breathing has stopped, immediate action is necessary. An ambulance should be called straight away but there is no time to wait for it to arrive. Basic mouth-to-mouth resuscitation techniques are easy to learn and have saved the lives of at least two of my friends. Resuscitation should be started at once if the person is not breathing and continued until she begins to breathe for herself again or medical help arrives, depending on which happens first.

If no-one present is capable of rendering this sort of assistance, the individual might be dead or brain damaged by the time professional help is available. Anyone close to a heroin user, therefore, would be well advised to make it their business to acquire basic first aid skills. Once it is clear that she is breathing, make sure that the mouth is clear and turn her on to her side into what is called 'the recovery position'. It is probably a good idea to keep the patient warm by covering her with a blanket. While you are waiting for the ambulance to arrive you can look around for evidence of what she has taken.

You are once again faced with an awkward choice. Telling the hospital the full facts could result in prosecution for your friend or child if the police happen to be around. It is, in fact, unlikely that such a case would reach their notice and, even if it did, the addict's life must come before fears of legal action. Addicts have been known to leave other users lying on the nod, and sit about chatting, quite unaware that the patient was silently dying. It is, therefore, always safer to get help if you are in any doubt about an addict's condition. For most addicts, however, overdose is not a frequent event and so there is no need for friends and relations to live in constant fear.

PART THREE

The Cure

CHAPTER 7

ℭ *Making a choice*

A lot of assumptions are commonly made about heroin users. Among them is the notion that addicts want to be cured. They do not. They want to take drugs but when the going gets rough they will accept a cure as a last resort. Some are, of course, sincere when they say they want to stop but they are in the minority. It is usually circumstances that generate a choice. Arrest, overdose, illness or another crisis can precipitate the decision to give up drugs. Once discovered, addicts are expected to seek a cure. In this way they can atone for their sins against public morality. Society expects them to repent, and since the path to public exposure is usually through the courts, addicts often comply.

Hard-working legal representatives frequently treat the world to a thorough account of the addict's shame and remorse. He has always seen the error of his ways. He is always eager to make amends. The judge is grave, the court hushed, the addict hangs his head. He must be punished but he will be re-admitted to the bosom of society now that he has eschewed allegiance to the deadly drug. Cleansed by penance, he will be ready to go forward. His critics drink a toast to his reform.

When he leaves gaol he cannot wait to be reinstated as a normal, healthy, happy young chap ready to fight the noble fight against degradation and unemployment. Sometimes he believes in his own reform but he may be equipped with no more than a cheery smile and a wholesome determination to stay straight. He sets out clutching a crisp, new UB40 to his temporarily drug-free heart.

Privately, he wages an ongoing war against the urge to relapse. The longing for heroin grows like an unseen virus until it bursts out and common sense is totally laid waste. In truth, he cannot wait to be a junkie again.

Taking smack is like driving a car towards a wall at a hundred miles an hour. It does not matter if the wall is one minute off or a decade away, in the end you will hit it and the result will be the same. You will end up surrounded by the wreckage of your once-promising life; feeling fed up and defeated. Until that happens, junkies rarely face up to the fact that the only way to improve matters is to learn to live without drugs. At that point life becomes a major salvage operation which involves healing the physical body and rebuilding both your personality and lifestyle. 'Until you admit you're lost you can't hope to find yourself' is a cliche often bandied about by old campaigners in the junk war. It is certainly true that no junkie can free himself from addiction unless he reaches a point of crisis where he feels he must choose between drugs and something else which he feels is crucial to his happiness and which he cannot, willingly, relinquish.

For a long time, junkies compromise and try to fit life in around heroin but there is always an inescapable moment when there will be a need to choose between heroin and a partner who has issued a final ultimatum. Financial ruin or another crisis might be looming. Whatever the choice, the apparent gains from stopping must be great enough to precipitate a positive decision.

Addicts will muster all their mental energy to justify their need for drugs. New excuses and reasons why a cure would be desirable but cannot be faced are always found. Times may have changed but the psychology of the opiate user remains the same. In the nineteenth century De Quincey wrote, 'I hanker too much after a state of happiness', explaining that he was 'little capable of encountering present pain' in order to attain future satisfaction. He never broke the habit of consuming opium and most addicts share in his refusal to face the short-term discomfort in the hope of achieving long-term goals. Addicts are caught in the paradox of their own feelings for smack. They do not want to be junkies and suffer all that the term implies but because they love taking heroin, they repeatedly fail to find the resolve to leave it alone.

If non-users want to comprehend the situation they must forget the notion of viewing heroin abuse like a hobby or indulgence that people should learn to control. Refusing heroin is not like turning down a free ticket for the opera. It is not a simple matter of having more willpower and doing the honourable thing. A heroin habit pervades the user's being until it has become a part of him or her, as natural and essential as eating. Hence the comment, 'Stopping taking heroin is like giving up sex, like somebody suddenly telling you sex is a bad thing.' Junkies are not noted for their controlled, ascetic approach to life. It is, of course, the very lack of a firm belief or philosophy that leaves room for smack to enter. The lack of a solid internal framework means there is no reason to reject it. The problem is worsened as the drug acts on the user.

The effects of its presence make the possibility of finding something to believe in less likely. That knowledge leads to this remark:

> From the start you're robbed of any incentive *not* to do it. You have to have something to replace it and when you're into it it's so much harder to find anything ... Perhaps I've got to stop wanting smack before I can want something else. I cannot imagine a time when I won't want it but one has to hope for a state like that or life would be unbearable.

To say that life would be 'unbearable' may be a little strong, but users do realise the risks and common sense informs them of the way they should respond.

What junkies hope for, in particular, is that they will really want to stop. Anyone who genuinely wants to come off has a good chance of succeeding. The rest have an excellent chance of relapsing before they are even fully cured. Most junkies come off many times, by which I mean that they manage to overcome the physical symptoms of withdrawal from the drug. That is comparatively easy, but conquering the temptation to relapse is an almost impossible task that leaves many people feeling embarrassed and ashamed as they find themselves drifting back into old habits that not only die hard but seem not to die at all. Some people try to salvage something from this dispiriting pattern of cure and relapse that becomes the 'norm' for addicts. They blunder in and out of states of addiction failing to find the conviction to remain drug-free and casting around hopefully for proof that the failed attempts count for something:

> I've taken heroin almost continually for the last two years. In that time, the longest period without daily use has been six weeks. I've managed to stop twice. For me, these periods of stopping were very important. They proved I could actually do it. That's important because I have many moments when I

believe I can neither stop, nor stay stopped. Sometimes the case seems hopeless now and I think, 'Why don't I just admit heroin permanently into my life?' Then I remember that heroin not only gives, it also takes! I never indulge in sport, jogging, swimming, parties, pubbing, clubbing, socialising or spending time with friends. I don't go out in case I'm sussed out. At work I have to keep a low profile, and I work extra hard to make sure I am pulling my weight. When I am stoned, I wonder whether everyone can tell. I know they can't but some of my relationships are suffering because I am irritable and sometimes aggressive or difficult. Others seem irrational but there's always that moment during a confrontation when you realise someone is humouring you and you are in the wrong. All this convinces me I have to stop. I just don't know when ...

Hunting for a reason to stop that outweighs the drive to stay hooked is the major problem. During one soul-searching session I neatly listed advantages and disadvantages of taking smack. Potential consequences of using heroin included being charged with an offence, starring in a scandal, losing home, job, health, wealth, friends and credibility of every kind. Advantages were impossible to find. The following statements appeared on the list of reasons not to stop: 'It makes life easy'; 'I'm scared to stop'; and 'I don't feel like it.' A moment's thought contradicted the first two and left me confronted by the third. I did not 'feel like it'. I did not stop, but logic had not assisted the choice.

I examined the list of things I would do without heroin and found them attractive. They included trips to the ballet and the theatre, holidays abroad, buying new clothes and getting a new hairstyle. At the bottom of the list, as if it did not matter as much as the rest, came the simple statement, 'Change life.' It stuck out like a sore thumb. It was the crux of the matter. A new hair-do could not outweigh the hunger for smack. The command to change seemed ludicrously grave and quite impossible to carry out. Nevertheless, I got on with the cure, motivated, like many others, primarily by impecunity. I waited impatiently for the moment when I could relapse. Perhaps, as Dougie said, 'The only reason anybody stops is lack of money!' True or false, the people who stay stopped are those who find a more genuine and valid motivation. For years, the addict behaves like a stupid animal, putting his nose on an electrified fence and failing to recognise the origin of the electric shock. Junkies are doomed to repeat the pattern over and over again until something jolts them out of the cycle.

Many addicts either stated or implied that the offer of a job would be the answer to their problems. Some felt that without a job to go to the effort of stopping would be wasted as they would only drift back to drugs. One commented, 'I don't know why they bother to make out they want us to be cured. They might as well just give us a gallon of methadone each and a straw.'

Few addicts recognised the need for inner change. Most cited concrete goals like jobs or large sums of money as the things that would make them stop. An addict on the dole told me, 'If you said to me, "I'll give you a grand," then I'd stop.' A few did, however, look inwards for answers. One remarked, 'Is it possible that you've been a cheat all your life and all it boils down to is you just haven't got enough balls to cut the cake?' Another asked, perplexed, 'What am I hiding from? Why do I need this? Why aren't I normal?' It certainly does seem true that without a degree of soul searching, the discovery of new insights and motivation for change is impossible. Without it, addicts are unlikely to stop. Most do not have much self-love. Perhaps the answer lies in finding out that you are ordinary and learning to forgive yourself for not being special or unusual. Most addicts are just ordinary people whose interests direct them towards experimenting with drugs rather than playing cricket.

Addicts sometimes need to be reminded of this. Before they can succeed in a cure, they have to believe in themselves. They have to learn to disregard the destructive and unhelpful aspects of the picture that the media and public paint of them and, perhaps most importantly, they need to have a vision of some sort of desirable future life to aim for and work towards. Without that, any cure is very unlikely to succeed.

Once the addict faces up to her predicament and makes the choice to stop, the first hurdle is always going through the rigours of physical withdrawal. Cold turkey has traditionally been the major stumbling block to cure. Films still show people shuddering and twitching. Bodies drenched in sweat, faces contorted in agony, they writhe and kick. Legs flying out involuntarily, they cry and roar, beat the pillow, scream and beg for help. This stark vision of private hell fascinates and haunts the public imagination. The truth, for most addicts, is much less dramatic. They will freely admit that, while the symptoms can be pretty unpleasant, the physical side of coming off smack is not the hardest part.

It is still true, however, that it can take weeks of breaking your own resolve and shelving repeated promises to yourself and others, before the day comes when you wake up feeling ready to set off on the gruelling road to 'kicking the habit'. You have to steel yourself to make a start and sometimes you simply cannot face it. There are days when you would go to any lengths just to carry on for one more day: tomorrow can fend for itself. You will feel stronger then and be more able to cope. Each day slips by without a decision being upheld until, perhaps, after several half-hearted attempts, you are ready to throw off the warm pink blanket of addiction and reveal the naked, shivering, goose-pimpled thing beneath.

Cold turkey: what is it really like?

The severity of withdrawal depends largely on the amount of drugs you have been taking in the months preceding the attempt and on the overall length of time you have been an addict. Each withdrawal may be slightly different. Some are quite intense while others are relatively mild. One of the problems is that, if withdrawal has been faced before, the addict knows, more or less, what to expect. Waiting for withdrawal to begin is a bit like sitting in the dentist's chair expecting the drill to start.

The addict will experience a series of symptoms which usually succeed one another in a particular order. When the smack first wears off, the user will become exhausted. A long, peaceful sleep will follow and she will awake as withdrawal sets in. After that, peaceful sleep will be a thing of the past for up to a fortnight.

Throughout withdrawal, the user finds herself in the grip of an ongoing craving for heroin. As her pupils begin to dilate her eyes will water and her nose will start to run. The throat and nose begin to tickle and bouts of violent sneezing begin. By now the user will be half-way through the first of the four days during which the worst of the symptoms usually burn themselves out. She will be wondering whether to leave coming off until tomorrow. If she has made her plans well, if she is fully motivated, she will keep up the resolve to soldier on into full cold turkey, all the time trying not to think about the fact that the worst is yet to come.

The pendulum of opinion regarding withdrawal has recently swung towards the point where the process is dismissed as no more than a bad dose of flu. Up to a point, the comparison is a useful one as the external symptoms are similar in both conditions. One thing that is very hard to describe, however, is the overall feeling of discomfort that accompanies the obvious symptoms. Everyone has their own way of explaining this aspect of coming off. I have always been aware of an acutely irritating sensation at the back of the neck. I imagine all the nerves of the body meeting at the base of the skull. I see them as the strings of a puppet or a set of electric wires. In my mind's eye, at that point, they converge like roads at a junction. A big fist seems to seize them pulling them together tightly and, tugging them backwards and forwards, creating havoc throughout my whole body. My teeth are on edge. The aggravating ache has the same quality as the fear when a tooth is being drilled; only occasionally does the drill actually catch a nerve and the sensation is not acutely painful, just extremely irritating. It is difficult to sit still. That mounting tension is the hardest thing to bear. Pain would be preferable.

Along with that distressing feeling goes a terrible restlessness of mind and body. The user fidgets and twitches and is quite unable to concentrate. Reading is almost impossible. The sensation grows throughout the first two days and rises to an unbearable crescendo on the second night as the addict boogies around a sweat-drenched bed, thrashing, tossing and turning; weak, listless and uncomfortable. No position gives relief, nothing can induce sleep; emotions run out of control; depression pushes tears out past bulging eyeballs; silent sobs shake the desperate body. Joints in arms and legs ache and creak like unoiled hinges. Every nerve jangles. The skin seems to sting when touched. Contact, even with the bedding, is unpleasant. Panic comes in waves. Panic about yesterday, about tomorrow, about last year, next year. All the cells below the skin seem to develop an ability to move about on their own. They feel as if they are jiggling about independently. You find that you are shaking all over, sometimes quite violently. The sensation is quite disconcerting, although not of itself unpleasant. This is accompanied by rashes of visible goose pimples that raise themselves up all over the body and disappear as quickly as they came. The skin feels cold and wet to the touch, dripping like warm ice melting. These are the uniquely unbearable aspects of withdrawal. The bad dose of flu means nothing to all this.

On day one, if the habit is bad, nausea follows the early bouts of sneezing. As all the body's juices start to flow again the tickle in the throat sets up a dry cough. The user hacks away uncontrollably until she vomits. When your habit is getting serious and you have had to wait to score it is quite possible to be sick in the street on the way back before you can get home to take something which will reverse your symptoms. For addicts who are short of cash, life does tend to be geared towards reversing the symptoms of withdrawal rather than getting high. When the nausea passes, the addict will suffer hot and cold flushes, sweat profusely so that her hair and clothes stick to her and, in general, she will start to feel as if she really does have flu.

Regular doses of heroin minimise bowel activity leading to constipation. Withdrawal means that the bowel will start to return to normal functioning. This entails a degree of discomfort which ranges from unpleasant tummy ache through to severe stomach cramps that double you up and make you groan. Diarrhoea follows the discomfort and, during those initial few days of withdrawal, time spent on the toilet can add up to a number of hours. It is quite handy if the bath is close to the loo as there is no need to leave in order to be sick. This arrangement of bathroom furniture has proved convenient to several people with whom I have discussed withdrawal. As far as I know, flu is not normally associated with these particular symptoms.

Withdrawal begins slowly; the first night is very unpleasant, and the second day and night are usually acknowledged as the time when the nastiness peaks. Gradually, the symptoms start to ebb away and by the end of the fourth day, they will have almost completely abated. During the whole four days they tend to come and go in a cyclical pattern with some symptoms disappearing and then returning in full force, building to a point of almost unbearable unpleasantness and then retreating gradually. When withdrawal is particularly severe it is hard to keep up the resolve not to go out and get heroin. Knowing that you could be feeling 'on top of the world' in minutes presents a temptation which is difficult to resist. Once the first day is over, you are, however, usually far too ill to make the effort to score. There comes a point of no return after which all you can do is lie down and take it. You feel far too weak and exhausted to do anything else.

Once in full swing, withdrawal proceeds on its predictable course. The discomfort and depression seem unbearable and, every so often, there comes a little respite when the light at the end of the tunnel is visible. Throughout the four days you wish your life away. As soon as you wake, you start to count the hours until you can return to bed and, if you are lucky enough to have some, knock yourself out with sleeping pills. The day progresses slowly. Every ten minutes you look at your watch again. The inevitability with which each new symptom joins the rest tantalises. Frustration is the overriding emotion. The harrowing ordeal unfolds in its own good time and will not be hurried. There are moments of sheer anguish and sometimes you rock backwards and forwards as your body shakes with sobs, and tears mingle with the sweat on your face. Self-pity rises to an excruciating crescendo as the minutes tick by. Music bellows and jars, conversation dwindles to monosyllables. Every ounce of concentration is used up fighting the symptoms and keeping the teeth gritted against reaching out to relapse.

In time with its own slow rhythm, dusk creeps in and night throws its heavy curtains across the sky. You feel worse but you take more downers and crawl into bed. This must be the worst night. With the strains of Dylan's 'I Shall Be Released' ringing out hope inside your aching body you seek a fretful, febrile sleep.

When dawn coolly prises you from your bed you comfort yourself with the knowledge that the pain must soon pass away. Clinging to all the promises of a fine and better future you have made to yourself, you survive to reach a calm plateau where you realise that pain is gone and you are not a junkie today.

Obviously, it is difficult to do very much during withdrawal and so most people who actually plan to withdraw, rather than have withdrawal forced upon them, try to anticipate their needs and prepare as well as possible to cater for them. They will, for instance, try to organise congenial company, although it is hardly much fun spending a wet weekend withdrawing and anyone who shares the experience with you has to be either very close or very patient. Couples sometimes withdraw together although they run the risk of encouraging each other to give in and score. They also run the risk of splitting up following the violent rows that can ensue as they both become bad-tempered and sick. One thing anyone who is trying to come off must do is make sure that there will be no one around who has gear. It is almost impossible to come through withdrawal successfully if there is gear within easy reach.

Food is another problem to be considered. During withdrawal an addict has little appetite and would probably prefer not to eat at all. If she does get hungry, she will not have much energy to cook or prepare food and this means that an experienced user will anticipate her needs and buy in a selection of appropriate convenience foods in advance. Cereal, bread and cheese, spreads and pâté, biscuits and fruit are ideal. Even so, during severe withdrawal the user will eat very little and will confine herself largely to a series of snacks. Sweets, biscuits and chocolate satisfy the craving for sugar that besets junkies.

Although cold turkey is not an 'illness' as such, the symptoms described by addicts are pretty similar. Each person has a particular symptom that she hates the most. Paul gave a thorough account of his experience of 'turkey' which came pretty close to my own:

> You get a hot and cold feeling which gets worse till it turns into real hot and cold flushes. You're sweating profusely yet shivering with cold. You're all goose pimply when you're boiling hot. All the nerves in your skin and body seem opened up and exposed. You sit there shivering, dithering, feeling trembly with butterflies in your stomach. You get insomnia for three days. You're actually fatigued but you still can't sleep. The bowels are the next thing to go. Churning over and invariably you have diarrhoea and stomach cramps like gripe. And, of course, you've got the cold symptoms. Constantly pouring nose and the yawns. Enormous long, gaping, jaw-dislocating yawns. My eyes stream like I've got hayfever and my hair's all stuck to me. I look a right picture ...

Another addict who had been using vast amounts of gear went through a very bad patch after the police raided his flat. He described the symptoms of withdrawal and the emotional problems which followed:

> I was laid out on my back unable to walk. I had terrible pains in my back and my legs and terrible headaches. I was unable to sleep. My legs were kicking violently hence the expression 'kicking the habit'. You start sweating and the cold gets to

you. You go all goose pimples, all your hairs stand up on end but the worst thing about coming off are the feelings in the head. Manic depression. Suicidal tendencies. I was going to cut my wrists. I had social problems that compounded my troubles. My woman leaving, the police, getting thrown out of my flat. I had to come off 'cause I had no gear, I just couldn't support my habit.

The emotional problems mentioned here are very real. They are, in a sense, another 'symptom' of withdrawal, but they are a symptom that others cannot see or sympathise with.

From the outside, someone undergoing cold turkey would spend most of the time sitting or lying about looking pale and listless. There would be few noticeable external symptoms; the observer might be aware of a little shaking or might notice rashes of goose pimples scattered across visible bits of the user's body like wrists or legs. The running eyes and nose are hardly likely to impress. For the observer, therefore, cold turkey seems something of an anti-climax. It is certainly not usually anything like we have been led to believe by over-the-top TV programmes. Even so, the user feels so miserable, depressed and uncomfortable that, for her, a bout of uncomplicated, simple flu would be preferred to cold turkey every time. There is no comparison; it is so hard to bear.

I have already explained that heroin insulates the user from pain and shifts her focus on life. When the drug is withdrawn, therefore, new sensations and emotions rush in as the process of running away from pain is reversed. She finds herself in a cul-de-sac and has to turn and confront her problems and fears. It is this which can be most traumatic. Emotions are raw and vulnerable at this stage. Responses are exaggerated, even distorted. The user will sob or laugh aloud, prompted by the vaguest of stimuli. It takes time to re-adjust. She has to work very hard at suppressing panic, sitting it out and easing herself back into a society from which she long ago abdicated.

According to some people, cold turkey gets more unpleasant and severe each time the addict has to go through it: 'I've stopped on a dozen occasions but it has seemed to get progressively worse. Each turkey seems to get progressively worse.' The mournful repetition underlines the addict's fear of facing 'turkey' again. That is one thing that keeps really long-term abusers shelving plans to quit. They do actually come to fear the physical symptoms they will have to face. Indeed, after long-term use, symptoms of the first four days of turkey, when the discomfort is usually most unpleasant, can last up to a week and general debility can continue for six weeks or more.

Strategies for getting through withdrawal

Most addicts prepare for battle with themselves by trying to antici-pate both their physical and emotional needs. Addicts go about doing this in various ways, some of which are more likely to suc-ceed than others. One man describing his attempts to stop said, 'I've tried everything: straight cold turkey, clonidine and valium, DF118s [an opiate called dihydrocodeine given in tablet form] opium, amphetamine and cocaine. I've used all of them in an effort to cut it down. But that isn't the problem. That's the first week. It's staying off that's so hard.' The use of other drugs to help withdraw can, at least, minimise the unpleasantness. Some addicts believe that cocaine or speed can help to distract them from their misery but the combination of withdrawal and the cocaine come-down is such that it is better to avoid them: 'Using coke to come off, and weed, just to get over the worst, can be OK. Hospitals should use these things to get people over the worst. Mind you, you have to come down to feeling ill, twenty years older than usual, dead and empty.' Downers, on the other hand, are very useful. One of the main difficulties of withdrawal is surviving the long, anguished nights. Some addicts combine small, decreasing doses of heroin with the use of sleeping pills or tranquillisers:

> The worst night started. It was a Saturday evening, feeling impossibly horrible, I took to my bed. Dave gave me a tiny, tiny line and, where everything else had failed, that worked. I slept like a baby for two or three hours. I awoke dripping with sweat and dropped two blues and a yellow. I slept for two hours. I took another two blues, then another two. Then at 6 a.m. I gave up.

It must, of course, be remembered that many sleeping pills and tranquillisers are, in themselves, dangerous drugs and addicts should realise this and use them responsibly. Addiction to one drug does not necessarily imply tolerance to another. You should use unfamiliar 'downers' with great caution. With some brands of sleepers overdose can result from taking a very small number of tablets. Mixing sleeping tablets and alcohol can also have very serious consequences, even when a seemingly low dose of both substances is taken. When it comes to any drug, it is always sensible to take only one tablet and wait for an hour or two to gauge the effect before taking another. Addicts who were able to tolerate very high doses of opiates have been known to die from the effects of taking sleeping tablets, which were presumably only intended to ensure a comfortable night's rest. In such cases inhalation of vomit has been known to kill because the person has failed to wake up in time. When you are trying to quit drugs, all you want is a quiet night and a little relief from the nastiness of withdrawal during the first painful week. Used wisely, 'downers' are a great help; misused, they can end your heroin problem permanently.

Days are not so unbearable, but often you are too weak and ill to get dressed at all. Strategies for survival include watching films if you are lucky enough to have a video, and listening to music. Some people like to smoke dope as they believe it reverses the psychological effects of heroin, opening up 'the doors of the mind' and renewing an interest in life. Music can prove a panacea:

> I sat about feeling pretty poor, listening to enormously loud, almost deafening music: The Tubes, Dylan, Grateful Dead, and watching the racing on TV with the sound turned down. I kept changing from my nightie to my clothes and back, lying under the duvet on the settee. One minute hot, the next cold. I was sweating, shivering, coughing and sneezing. Billy called but I was too ill to talk so he went away.

Coming off is easier when you have a partner in crime. Couples can join forces against the world to help each other through. Provided they are both resolved and if there is true affection between them, they can each hold out for the sake of their partner. Neither wants to be the one to abandon the attempt first, or take the blame when the recriminations start.

What can the doctor do?

Many addicts stoically set about curing themselves and get on with it. Those who feel that they have gone beyond the stage of finding the resolve to take that step alone seek help from doctors, clinics or other organisations. The doctor's surgery may be the first call. When approaching the GP, however, addicts have, for a long time, been likely to meet with a negative, unhelpful response. If a doctor does show sympathy, junkies tell their friends, and the unwitting GP will find that she has a list clogged up with addicts keen to hit on her for free drugs of any description. The doctor then has the awkward job of weeding out the genuine cases who need help to stop from the others who are after cheap drugs. If she prescribes too often and too much, there could be trouble with the powers that be. The Home Office might call the doctor to account and ask her to justify her policy on prescribing. Such a rap on the knuckles can be acutely embarrassing. The doctor's role is a difficult one as, on one hand, the government calls for strict and careful controls to be observed, and on the other, panicky patients clamour for prescriptions. If you do hope to get a prescription from your doctor it is as well to understand the situation clearly.

The doctor's legal position regarding the prescribing of controlled drugs in the United Kingdom is based on the 1971 Misuse of Drugs Act by which production and distribution of all scheduled drugs is controlled. Any doctor who is 'fully registered' with the General Medical Council is permitted to prescribe or supply any controlled drug (other than LSD or cannabis). Thus any doctor can prescribe heroin to a patient. Addicts, however, will find that, in practice, their GP will not usually even consider doing this when treating a drug addict. That is because there are special regulations set out in a Home Office leaflet entitled *The Medical Use of Opiates in the UK* which state that a doctor may prescribe controlled drugs for 'any condition other than addiction'. This effectively means that anyone except a patient who is addicted to opiates might receive a prescription for heroin if the doctor considers it appropriate, for example for the treatment of severe pain. To the average addict, the situation seems ludicrous but government reasoning hinges on the desire to keep track of all people who are habitually abusing opiates and to limit the quantity of prescribed drugs reaching the black market. It is for these reasons that there are special controls.

When a doctor is confronted by a heroin user who requests a prescription for opiates she is still allowed to prescribe a number of alternative drugs. The Home Office guidelines state that, 'A doctor who considers that his treatment of an addict calls for the prescribing of a controlled drug may prescribe any drug, other than heroin, cocaine or dipipanone.' The doctor can, for example, offer the addict a prescription for methadone, or for DF118 tablets. In practice, few GPs are keen to treat addicts for their addiction, considering them nuisance patients, and that is one reason why doctors frequently refer patients to a special clinic where they can be treated by doctors who have considerable experience of the problems of drug users. Thus, prescribing drugs to addicts tends to be largely the responsibility of special clinics. Besides the clinics there are, of course, a number of private doctors who work with addicts. Their views and the treatment they offer vary so that an addict might, if prepared to shop around, be lucky enough to find the treatment to suit her in the private sector.

Nationwide, whether private or NHS, there are only about 120 doctors licensed to prescribe heroin for the treatment of addiction and that figure rarely rises beyond 200. Current trends in treatment strategies do not, in fact, seem to favour the view that prescribing heroin to addicts is an effective treatment in more than a very few cases. Whether an addict attends a clinic, visits a private doctor or goes to a GP, if a prescription is given it is, therefore, most likely to be for a drug such as methadone rather than for heroin. This is the case even though few doctors can produce really conclusive evidence for the widespread preference for the use of methadone. Home Office guidelines clearly state: 'the substitute drug of choice for opioid misuse is oral methadone mixture'. The excessive prescribing of heroin in the early 1960s by a small number of doctors has resulted in the controls we see today. It has also left most of those doctors who are licensed to prescribe heroin to addicts rather wary of doing so. Even the Home Office regulations point out that 'very few doctors now exercise that prerogative'.

Despite the complexities of the situation, some family doctors are, of course, still prepared to help addicts by, for example, offering a reduction course of appropriate drugs and, sometimes, giving out tranquillisers or sleeping pills. Even if your GP does not wish to treat you, you will usually need a referral letter from the doctor in order to attend a drug dependency clinic. It is, therefore, always worth visiting your GP if you are desperate for help and not sure which way to turn.

Most addicts do not like presenting themselves at the surgery, however, and admitting that they are beyond their own control. Paul explained, 'I was mortified sitting in front of someone and saying I used heroin. It wasn't a good thing. It prolonged it. You mustn't be fooled into thinking you can substitute smack with another drug.'

How do the patients feel?

One heroin user I spoke to attempted a cure using a drug called clonidine. His doctor was keen to help and also arranged sessions of group therapy for some of the people on his list. Paul admits that his attitude to the whole business was wrong as he was still refusing to face up to the fact that there are no easy ways out of a heroin habit. Nevertheless, clonidine has been found to have some rather nasty side effects. Paul explained,

Clonidine and valium was the treatment. Clonidine! Yeuch! They make you so depressed and disorientated and like a drunk. You lurch around bumping into things. I was crying for days on end. We were sitting there wrapped up in blankets and seeing double through those clonidine and feeling as if our feet were trapped in lead boots. I couldn't even get to the chemist's for the prescription. Jimmy had to help me back.

The physical symptoms of withdrawal abate after four days but a serious habit leaves an inheritance of depression and disorientation that is difficult to handle. There may be accompanying physical problems such as colitis or other stomach troubles. The urge to relapse is powerful, and Paul continued, 'I can remember sitting there one night. We'd had nothing for two weeks and I said. "We've cracked it. Let's go out and get a bag." For the next three weeks the pair of us were just fucking rampant, off our heads.' Clearly, attempts to deal with the psychological aspects of withdrawal had failed. The comments on group therapy showed this:

There were three of us in the room. The doc turned on the tape and it said, 'You are feeling heavy. You are all relaxed.' He drew the curtains: 'You are feeling warm all over ...' I just roared laughing and said, 'I can't handle this'. He put the light on and everyone had a big grin on their face.

It seems that until addicts are prepared to try and resolve the conflicts that foster their drug use, attempts to help them come unstuck. If you do succeed in breaking free from addiction, trying to pretend it never happened is no good. Only facing up to the truth and learning to understand yourself a bit better can help:

> You get sick of hearing about it. Yet I'd like to think that I can talk about it and not rush out and buy some. I'd like to think the drug hadn't beaten me. I am just having the odd bag now, and hope that maybe a big drought'll come up and I can just phase it out of my life altogether.

Phasing heroin out of your life altogether is the hard part. The worst of the physical symptoms are completely over in a maximum of two weeks. After that the addict faces a long hard climb back to normality. Many fail.

> It's staying off that is the hard part. It takes a lot of willpower. But seeing smack eats away at your willpower it makes it very hard. When I stop I just feel vacant with no direction or energy and that lasts for months.

After withdrawal is over, addicts are often left weak and sometimes poorly:

> Last time I came off I was ill for weeks. The whole summer I suffered bouts of stomach cramps and couldn't eat without pain. I was frequently doubled up and unable to continue with whatever I was doing.

The months following physical withdrawal are a crucial time. During that period, addicts need considerable support to reorientate their lives if they are not to simply slip back into their old ways. Having a job to go to or some useful way of occupying your time is crucial to psychological welfare and, ultimately, to survival in a drug-free world. Addicts often say this, although in reality they know it is unlikely that they will be offered a job. For this reason, such remarks are often tinged with bitterness:

> Having a job is fundamental, especially at the end of a cure. People should be guaranteed a job. If they gave junkies jobs when they'd cured them they'd have a chance. It's a simplification, but it's so important. Just kicking them back into the environment they came from is a complete waste of time.'

Remarks made by some drug users showed that they had lost all hope of getting a job. They had given up on themselves, and merely expressed anger that society wanted to remove the drugs that were making life bearable. One wonders whether the addict is to blame or whether the society that makes him feel this way is perpetrating the greater evil. Something must be wrong when ordinary people draw conclusions like this:

> Why stop people taking drugs? You've got a large number of unemployed people who are never going to suddenly achieve something or become brain surgeons. Why not let them take smack if that's what they want? Let them just get on with it. Why harass them? It's their only source of pleasure ...

The speaker quoted here is an addict himself. Political animals will be provoked by his cynical and defeated stance. The fact remains that nobody is going to rush out next week and offer jobs to the thousands of unemployed junkies. In the meantime they will be taking smack.

Why do cures fail?

Most long-standing addicts will talk freely about the numbers and types of cures they have attempted. Most have tried everything from cold turkey to reduction cures. Although there is a time for all addicts when they are enjoying drugs and do not want to stop, in due course almost every one of them comes to believe that life would probably be preferable if drugs were not dictating the terms:

'All users really do is use drugs. There is no time for anything else.' That realisation can be the root cause of disillusionment and increase the desire to stop.

After the physical problems are over, the battle to re-adjust begins: 'Coming off smack's like coming out of the nick. You think it's all going to be different but nothing has changed.' That is the crux of the matter. Unless something has changed the addict is unlikely to make it. Each time he comes out from under the blanket of smack he carries so much more pain with him. He finds it hard to face the thought of going forward into the danger of potentially negative experience that may be even worse than before. The past makes him afraid, the fear that his position is now worse than when he failed previously makes him terrified. The pain of past losses relived afresh with full senses is too much. The result is to relapse.

He dislikes himself for failing, for taking smack and for believing he will fail again. He suspects that failure is tattooed across his soul. Despite the importance of having a job to go to, no temporary solutions such as bright new opportunities can permanently cover that scar. If he is to succeed, the addict must learn to change from within. He must alter his attitudes to life and to himself. He will feel vulnerable and hypersensitive. He must learn to control his emotions. Junk imparts an identity of sorts. Without smack it is suddenly gone and the former addict has to work out a new persona through which to relate to the world. His inner life is in turmoil and, under pressure, he will fall apart and reach out for a bag of smack.

Rehabilitation back into the real world is slow. Being in public places is, for the new ex-addict, an oddly exposed, over-bright, 'naked' experience. After two or three weeks when you really feel you are off heroin and the anxiety starts to fade you feel an odd combination of pleasure and fear in these new, more intense experiences, recognising your old self in them. When you are a junkie you see everything through a cosy, protective film of mist. A dome of perspex over your mind insulates you and keeps the world at a safe distance. You float around in a bubble of smack into which nothing and no one can intrude. Smug in your high, falsely euphoric at times, you relate to people differently. But you also relate differently to your environment. You notice less, you are less attracted by, or interested in, the things around you. This is how a junkie can decline badly in appearance and not seem to notice. When you are strung out you do change and your priorities become fewer. A clean pair of socks may no longer seem essential, only desirable, then, finally, irrelevant.

Objects take on a different perspective. Without heroin even the pictures on the wall have a different significance. They might seem more or less appealing, or more emotive. They speak quite differently. Something that seemed reassuring may become trite or crude. Something that did not interest may become alive, vital, almost three-dimensional. The world seems bigger and more spectacular. People and things are shiny and in full technicolour. A scene in a pub might resemble a hologram, the walls painted with glycerine, the characters like cardboard cut-outs. Mouths are large and menacing, laughter brash, brittle and over-loud. Clear-headed now, you are confronted by an amazing world full of new and striking stimuli. You become aware of all sorts of little details about the people around you. You notice holes in people's clothes, become shocked by the dust on bits of uncleaned furniture. You feel part of everything again, bright-eyed and sharp.

Coming off is always a new adventure. You are excited and optimistic. You look back on smack with scorn and aggressively reject it. That attitude is a necessary part of the process of cutting it out of your life. When you are really resolved, you believe that you will stay off forever. You tell yourself what a fool you have been, congratulate yourself on your success and inwardly patronise your addicted friends. You are inspired by thoughts of all the exciting and satisfying activities you will undertake. Who wants to be rocked in a comforting embrace that becomes a restraining clasp and, finally, a life-threatening, crushing bear hug? You become convinced that you never want to be drugged again. You want no more diabolical, anti-life potions near you. You are utterly happy to be normal, lively and energetic. You feel ten years younger and ordinary, everyday things give so much pleasure. Just walking about, going shopping, taking a bath are so enjoyable. Every morning you wake up thinking about getting a hit and then remember that you do not need one. That miraculous freedom alone gives so much satisfaction.

Spring is the best time to come off. In the winter it may not seem worth the effort but in the spring the flowers are bursting and glowing. Rebirth is possible. Nevertheless contradictions abound. The heat from the sun warms, then burns uncomfortably. The breeze cools and turns cold. The rain moistens but stings. Like a puppy toying with a wasp, insecure and shaky, you reach out. Unlike the puppy you have been stung before, unlike him you know fear but you are no baby and there is nobody mothering you. You are struggling through your hardest lesson on your own.

The euphoria following a successful cure is punctuated by waves of depression. The urge to relapse seems to strike without warning and with inexplicable ferocity. Familiar objects trigger an irrational longing. Wrapping the meat in tin foil brings on the urge for a smoke. An innocent glass of water waits for a syringe. Every situation prompts the urge to relapse.

A friend once told me that he found giving up smoking particularly hard because every situation prompted him to smoke. If he felt like celebrating he wanted to smoke. Concentration, study or relaxation heralded the need for a cigarette. If he was stressed or contented, hungry or full, in company or alone, he wanted to smoke. Every minor shift of emotion initiated the urge to light up. The ex-junkie finds himself in a similar situation. He can last for a while without junk. It may be weeks, months, even years, but he is always under threat of relapse. Any day, a combination of circumstances could conspire to place him and junk together. If the moment is right, if he is especially happy or especially bored, particularly crisis-ridden or on an even keel, however he feels he will feel like a hit. He will believe he is in control but once he falls, it may be weeks, months or years before he is ready to stop again. One man's reason is another man's excuse. Today you are happy: you will want to celebrate with a hit. Tomorrow you are down: you need a lift. You have worked really hard: you deserve a treat. A hit is always what you need. A hit is always what you think you want.

Junk and Jesus: the search for inner strength

Addicts can find the inner strength they need to come off drugs in religious faith. Others can take a cynical view of this discovery of God, feeling that peddlars of dogma have moved in to exchange one state of dependence for another. Whether or not the cynics are right those few junkies who find faith believe in their form of salvation. The pursuit of altered states of consciousness in itself shows a desire to exploit those aspects of the human mind that reach beyond the mundane and everyday realities. Faith can fulfil that need.

When the light at the end of the junk tunnel fades, desperation sets in. Everything is fear, lies and hassle. Sometimes even despair deserts the desperate. After all, without hope, how can there be despair? This is a time when junkies start to die. They might take to injecting crushed up tablets indiscriminately. They might succumb to a terminal binge. If they wake up or are pulled out of it in time, they will be so hollow and empty, so lacking in confidence, so utterly abject that, in private, they may gingerly and secretly reach out for God. In their own terms, they have tried everything else.

Leonard Cohen, referring to Jesus sang,

And when he knew for certain
Only drowning men could see him
He said all men shall be sailors then
Until the sea shall free them

Junkies can sail on until it seems that only death can free them. It is no wonder that, broken and forsaken, utterly human, they sometimes reach out to God.

Junk has been compared to white light or white heat. My school motto, translated from the Latin, read 'To the light through the cross.'

In his poem 'Prayer Before Birth', Louis Macneice spoke of his need for 'a white light at the back of my mind to guide me'. With heroin the light blinds; it fails to illuminate. Lost in the dark, blinded by too much light and totally at sea, drifting and cursed like the Ancient Mariner, when junkies first sight land it can be the Hill of Calvary that they see.

Bob Dylan, who has reflected the consciousness of his generation through his music, appears to have made that transition from hedonist to Christian. Over the years, his lyrics move along the path from desolation, fear and despair, to a recognition that, 'You have to serve somebody.' He states his case like this: 'You either got faith or you got unbelief. There ain't no neutral ground.' Junkies have 'unbelief'. For a junkie to have meaning in his life after so long is a minor miracle. Who can be surprised that some find what they need on the road to Damascus? Like Bob Dylan they may call out,

...Shine your light on me,
You know I just can't make it by myself,
I'm a little too blind to see.

In the early years of drug experience you are unlikely to compromise your ego by something so unfashionable and apparently unexciting as religion but after you have repeatedly failed yourself it does finally dawn that there may be another path. You may start to look outwards for signposts erected by others. You will recognise that all you have done is to follow your nose into a cul-de-sac. However painful, there is nothing to do but turn round and attempt to go back. At this stage, help from outside is not enough. You require something to give you inner strength. You need Faith. You need to believe that, even broken and disgusting, you are worth more in essence than the mess you have made of yourself. If you cannot believe in yourself there is no cure for you. Ever. At a time when your mind and body are too feeble to make plans, when you are sick, aching and scared, you pray. Like someone confronted by death you beg for help, even from a God in whom you claim you do not believe. I have spoken to several people who have admitted to doing this. They believe that they have received help.

It is not only Christianity that can provide this sort of direction and meaning. Yoga, meditation, Zen Buddhism, some kind of a cause, even curing other junkies, are all examples of the sort of thing that can become the rope with which to haul yourself out of the pit.

CHAPTER 8

ℭ *Treatments*

A double dilemma: 'Help me quit drugs – but not yet!'

Many addicts, although highly motivated to give up drugs, persistently shelve plans to begin the process. There are a number of reasons for this, including fear of the physical symptoms and an even stronger fear of failure. They know from experience that their greatest battle is not coming off but staying off. Many see no reason to go through cold turkey again unless they are sure of success. They usually start seeking help from doctors or clinics during times of crisis when the struggle to keep themselves supplied with drugs is proving too hard. This means that their first priority is often getting a prescription for drugs rather than coming off. To anyone without experience of addicts and addiction the fact that the addict purports to want help to stop yet frequently hopes to acquire a prescription for more drugs might present an almost incomprehensible contradiction. That, however, is often the case. Many addicts do want help to come off but just as many want help to stay on. Part of the doctor's role is, therefore, to prepare the addict to face life without drugs. In practice, doctors tackle the problem from two sides. They prescribe drugs to ward off withdrawal symptoms and depend on counselling or some form of therapy to effect changes in the addict's attitude and build up her confidence in preparation for coping with the break from drugs. Addicts are often not fully aware of the doctor's aims and, sometimes, when they are not happy with the treatment offered, they become resentful.

Once an addict does decide it is time to seek help, what is on offer will depend very much on where she lives. She will be likely to start off with some preconceived ideas about what she wants. What she wants and what she can get are almost certain to differ. If a prescription or a hospital bed figure in her hopes she will probably have to wait quite a while before getting any help at all.

In theory, getting help for a drug problem is fairly straight forward. Addicts simply turn for help to one of the well-publicised treatment centres. There are even hotline numbers for users to call. But on closer examination, getting help is not as simple as it may seem. The official version of the situation is somewhat at odds with experiences reported by addicts. I will, therefore, briefly outline the position as it appears from the outside and then look at the sort of treatment that is available from the point of view of the drug users themselves.

Where to get help: what's on offer

The first place an addict might go for help is to a local advice or information centre. These usually operate on a drop-in basis. Some of them are government-sponsored, others funded by various means. They are usually staffed by fairly pleasant, helpful folk who churn out endless leaflets to justify their existence and do their best to be sympathetic. Sometimes they are ex-addicts themselves and, at least, they understand the problems. They can be helpful in explaining clearly what treatment options are available and they also advise social workers, relatives and friends of drug users, teachers and even doctors. At one centre, they told me that harassed GPs have been known to call them asking what type of drugs they should prescribe to an addict!

The trouble with these organisations is that they cannot provide the one thing that is frequently uppermost in the addict's mind, a prescription. As one woman said of her local centre, 'They're really nice down there. They do their best but the trouble is, all they can do is sympathise.' Many centres can and do provide counselling, help with personal and social problems, indeed all sorts of help other than the provision of emergency drug supplies. They are by no means superfluous to NHS provision or other facilities but if medical treatment is what you are after, you will have to move on.

Where you try next will depend on your circumstances. If you have cash there are, in the private sector, a number of doctors who treat addicts. If you can find out who they are, and the advice centre may help you there, you could make an appointment to see one of them. At least that way you will get individual treatment. You may even get what you want. Private doctors, however, are still accountable for policy and prescribing to the Home Office. There are no open doors to endless supplies of free drugs anywhere.

If you do not want to or cannot afford to see a private doctor, you are left with the task of beating a path to your local drug dependency clinic. The system can be irksome and confusing. If you go straight to the clinic they are unlikely to see you. They will generally send you back to your GP for a referral letter. It is, therefore, better to start off by making an appointment to see your own doctor. If you convince him that you genuinely want treatment and that you are not casting him in the role of a supplementary drug dealer to be visited during the bad times, the doctor may prescribe something for you. If this happens you are likely to be asked to attend for therapy or counselling as well. Alternatively, the doctor will refer you to the clinic. Hopefully, you will not have to wait too long before you can see a doctor there.

Such clinics are funded and controlled by the National Health Service in Britain and may be attached to a hospital out-patient department or housed in a separate building altogether. Either way, you will usually be asked to see the doctor on a regular basis and he (most of these clinics are controlled by men) will almost certainly prescribe drugs to help alleviate the symptoms of withdrawal. Obviously, there is a range of drugs that could be offered. The type of drug, the dosage, and the method of administration are all matters to be worked out between the doctor and the patient. Treatment varies with the views of each doctor and his assessment of each patient. It is, however, a disappointing truth that while each individual doctor is officially free to prescribe according to his or her own conscience, purchasers and others who have influence over the way in which funds are spent are using their power to manipulate prescribing policies. For example, in the Mersey region, the cost of funding heroin prescriptions, which is considerably higher than the cost of methadone – but still a tiny fraction of the cost of drug related crime – has been used as an excuse to force addicts receiving heroin to accept methadone instead. Two clinics which made heroin available to addicts have been forced to close with disastrous consequences for some of their former clients. Fashions tend to emanate from London via its 'coterie' of senior psychologists and pressure to fall in with policies approved by them is felt by most doctors in clinics throughout the UK. Indeed, other consultants defy them at their peril and in doing so are likely to bring the weight of an inflexible establishment down upon their heads. You may hope to get a long-term prescription for injectable dry amps of heroin and come away with a short-term script for reducing amounts of methadone linctus. Most clinics prescribe on a 'take it or leave it' basis. Regimes tend to be strict. Urine analysis tests are often given. When they reveal traces of drugs other than those being prescribed scripts are likely to be stopped. Attendance at group counselling sessions is often compulsory, although at some clinics people with full-time jobs are exempt from this.

Most clinics aim to reduce the client's intake to a point where she can be finally withdrawn from drugs. For many people, especially long-term abusers, withdrawing in this way is difficult, if not impossible, and a residential place in a hospital or special clinic has to be found. The role of the out-patient clinic is often to help drug users to stabilise their lives. The constant need to hunt for drugs and the exhausting struggle to find the money will be over. That in itself allows addicts more time to think about themselves, to take more care over their personal appearance and to plan for the future.

Getting registered

When addicts attend a clinic for treatment their details will, of course, be passed to the Home Office. The fact that this will happen has led them to refer to themselves as being 'registered'. 'Getting registered' used to mean that an addict would be ensured of a regular 'maintenance' dose of drugs, usually methadone, over an indefinite period of time. There are addicts who have been maintained like this over a number of years and, because of their long history of maintenance, some of them are still receiving regular prescriptions. More recently, however, many of the doctors who treat addicts have come to believe that maintaining them in this way is not really a useful form of treatment. Many doctors now subscribe to the theory that addicts should only be offered a short, reducing course of drugs intended to wean them away from their dependence as quickly as possible. Regular maintenance is, therefore, no longer available in some parts of the country. Reduction courses ranging from between three to eight weeks are more commonly offered.

Thus, for addicts who do not wish to stop taking drugs, attendance at a clinic often fails to provide them with the sort of help they hope to receive. When they are in crisis, quite a number of them will accept a reduction course geared towards 'curing' them. Many have no intention of giving up drugs permanently but use their script as a stopgap to provide a little respite from their harrowing lifestyle.

Knowing that their details will be passed on to the Home Office makes some heroin users nervous about 'getting registered'. Seeking help from a doctor can give rise to concern about the future. Junkies worry about the possibility that information, once filed away, might fall into other hands and jeopardise their opportunities in one way or another. It is, therefore, a good idea to understand the situation fully.

The Home Office sets down official guidelines for doctors which require any doctor who is treating an addict for drug addiction to notify the Home Office of that fact. He is 'required to notify details of the case to the Chief Medical Officer at the Home Office', and this applies 'irrespective of whether the doctor intends to prescribe a controlled drug to his patient'. The Home Office publication explains, 'The purpose of notification is partly epidemiological and partly to provide a central point from which doctors can obtain in confidence information about an addict previously unknown to them.' In other words, they just want to know what is going on! Many addicts are not reassured by this or by the following statement: 'Notification, which is often wrongly interpreted as "registration", does not confer any official or special status upon an addict.' The information is said to be available only to a doctor who can prove an interest in a particular case. The police, reputedly, no longer have access to the lists of notified addicts. When notification first began, the police used to be informed of an addict's situation. It may be this fact that has left a residue of anxiety in its wake. It is certainly hard to believe that the information is so closely guarded that it would not be available to the police or other interested parties under special circumstances. Furthermore, the law can change. What is private today can be public tomorrow.

Some addicts, therefore, still prefer to avoid what they see as the perils of becoming a notified addict. Many prefer to make plans to wean themselves off drugs without medical help at some indeterminate future date. It is estimated that for every notified addict there

are as many as four or five other addicts who are officially unknown to the Home Office. It does, therefore, seem likely that a
good number of addicts do succeed in stopping on their own.

Some people actually believe that 'getting registered' prolongs
the process, making addicts feel that they are now less in charge of
their own destinies and reducing the pressure that makes them stop.
Once 'registered' they are no longer so vulnerable to the legal
penalties and the financial struggle is less of a problem. There may
well, therefore, be advantages to addicts if they choose not to 'get
registered'. If they do 'come out', and their details are notified to
the Home Office, these facts may be on record indefinitely. Every
addict has to make the choice about which path he or she prefers.

Hospitals and residential communities

Hospital detoxification on the NHS may be the next step for an
addict who really wants to stop but cannot come off as an out-
patient. Hospital beds are limited, however, there are long waiting
lists for them, and treatment varies from place to place. Patients may
be offered a two- or three-week stay, after which they are pushed
back into society wide-eyed and nervous, often to relapse within
weeks. Alternatively, a lengthy stay in hospital which includes considerable efforts to restructure the addict's personality and lifestyle
may be available. There is no guarantee that either tactic will work.
Many addicts simply cannot cope when their world is drug-free.

That is why some doctors are very keen to promote participation
in ongoing self-help groups like Narcotics Anonymous. At least,
then, addicts are involved in a network of caring relationships with
people who are still living with the aftermath of problems like their
own. One doctor told me intently, 'You walk into an NA meeting
and straight away there are fifty people who all love you and care
about you.' That seemed a bit far-fetched to a cynic like myself but
NA does claim a good success rate. Participants probably need a
high degree of motivation, but, given that fact, the kind of support
provided by regular attendance at NA meetings can be essential to
the continued progress of some ex-addicts.

When someone is using drugs they gradually lose touch with
their contacts in the 'straight' world. This means that anyone who
does manage to become drug-free is left with the option of spending

time with old friends who are probably still using drugs or trying to find a new set of associates. That is where the residential community can be of valuable assistance. It can provide the bridge across which an addict can travel back into the 'straight' world.

There are a number of organisations that provide long-stay residential places for newly detoxified addicts. They all have their own specifications about how long an addict should be drug-free before entering the community. Some require the addict to be fully 'cured' before arrival. Others will help addicts through the first days of withdrawal, provided they have been drug-free for at least twenty-four hours (in some cases forty-eight hours) before entry. Some houses are run by Christian staff with all that implies. Others rely heavily on discipline and expect residents to earn privileges and respect, requiring them to work their way up through a hierarchical structure. Some try to promote love and sharing; others mount an abrasive regime using encounter group techniques where addicts insult and yell at one another. Many therapy sessions, whether gentle or intense, end in tears. Growth can be painful. Weeping is usually taken as a sign of progress. Much supportive hugging often takes place but in some houses sexual contact between residents is banned.

The range of tactics and techniques is sufficient for most addicts to find a place that will suit them. Getting help really depends on doing your homework and working out which system is most likely to be the right one for you. Quite a number of people enter one of these communities only to panic and flee within the first few days. Such a setback must be both painful and soul-destroying. As far as possible, you should try to make sure that you are committed before you join a community. Otherwise it will be disappointing both for them and for you.

I have tried to give a brief outline of the sort of help that is at hand. Getting any real assistance requires an honest, realistic approach and plenty of effort on the part of the addict. When it comes down to it you are on your own. You get yourself into it. People can help you, but in the end, only you can get yourself out.

The system in action: watch out for the red tape!

Obviously, the treatment an addict receives varies according to the views of the staff at each particular place. In London alone, there are, at the time of writing, 14 different clinics dealing with addicts, each of which demonstrates its own preferences regarding treatment strategies. Overall, methadone is still the drug of choice among doctors in London, although there are increasing numbers of community based drug projects that are pressing for change, such as greater variety and flexibility of treatment strategies. Thus addicts should, ideally, try to check out their options before approaching a doctor. The treatment they finally receive will depend on where they go for help.

In theory, once a choice has been made an addict pops cheerily into his GP for a speedy referral to a drug dependency clinic. In practice, even the time lapse between visiting your GP and getting an appointment at a clinic can be over 12 months. The addict's immediate need for drugs is rarely seen as very important. Sometimes addicts find themselves passed around from one place to another always being politely told that this is not the place where they can receive the help they need. Often nobody knows who has the scissors needed to hack through the red tape with which the addict is tightly bound.

One friend of mine recently decided that, after thirteen years on the street scene, he had to get help. Bravely, he handed in his notice at work and approached his family doctor. The stunned GP, somewhat junior in years to the addict himself, explained kindly that he was 'a little out of his depth here' and would seek advice before prescribing any drugs or taking other action. He calmly sent the patient home to wait two days for his next appointment. In the absence of a prescription for 'safe' drugs, the patient purchased palfium tablets on the black market and spent the next two days crushing them up to inject at further considerable risk to his already flagging body. Two days later he telephoned the doctor's surgery, hoping that emergency aid in the form of a short-term prescription would be at hand. The doctor was not due back for a further two days. The addict visited his local drug dependency clinic in another attempt to get help. They could not see him because a letter written by his doctor was still in the post. It had been sent second class and did not finally arrive for another three days. Without that letter the clinic could not even pencil in his name on the appointment schedule. They told him that he would have to wait about four weeks and that, once in receipt of the letter, they would give him a date for his meeting with the doctor. He moved on wearily to the Advice and Information Centre next door. They were sympathetic. They made fruitless calls to a couple of doctors. They wrote a letter urging his GP to help by issuing a prescription. The GP was not, of course, at the surgery that day. The addict shuffled off to crush up some more palfium tablets, and wonder whether anyone wanted to help at all. Nearly a week had passed. He was still scoring drugs on the black market, waiting for someone to find those scissors to cut him out from under those yards of red tape.

Such an experience is quite typical. Another friend waited 11 months before his local clinic would even give him an appointment. Addicts usually approach the doctor when they are at their wits' end to know where the next hit is coming from. Clearly the NHS does not exist to issue free drugs to be abused by anyone who fancies them. Junkies, however, are in a difficult position. Without drugs they will suffer varying degrees of physical and emotional trauma. In panic they may risk their health, their liberty, their all. In the most extreme instance, an emergency prescription could save someone else from being mugged. Purely on humanitarian grounds a prescription could be issued to spare an addict days of extreme discomfort, despair and distress. Leaving addicts to face cold turkey when they need not do so has been described by one caring medic as 'an inexcusable piece of barbarism'. There is quite a lot of 'inexcusable barbarism' on the scene today.

Thus, all those good citizens who assume that helpers with open arms await the addict at every doctor's door are as off beam in their thinking as the people who see 'moustachioed pushers' at every school gate. Do not believe all those glib statements about all that is being done to save the undeserving junkie by a caring system. Getting help can be a lengthy and difficult process requiring patience, tenacity and dogged determination.

I have already discussed the role of the GP in an earlier chapter. He can prescribe some drugs to addicts, provided he operates within certain guidelines and follows the correct procedures. Most addicts who visit a GP these days will, however, find themselves referred on to a drug dependency clinic. Above all, addicts require flexibility of approach by doctors. Each one needs individual treatment. While treatments differ slightly, most clinics seem to pursue a policy line and the patients there will find that only certain types of treatment are on offer. Elsewhere, they could be treated quite differently. From the addict's point of view, the trick is to present herself at the right door for the treatment she hopes to receive.

This is not, of course, to suggest that addicts always know better than their doctors what is the best treatment for them. It is, however, true that unless their wishes are carefully considered and taken into account, what little point of contact there is between them and the doctor is likely to dwindle until a complete breakdown in goals and co-operation occurs. When this happens the addict will either disappear voluntarily or the doctor will kick him off whatever programme he is on as a failure who should be cut off before he wastes more of the doctor's time.

Doctor–patient relationships: a conflict of interests?

Many doctors believe that, when one drug is prescribed, 'cheating' by consuming another is a serious breach of the doctor–patient trust. Even though treatment is usually given on a 'take it or leave it' basis where a desperate patient will agree to try anything rather than receive no help at all, the doctor usually wields his metaphorical axe and chops off the patient's drug supply cleanly and decisively when a breach occurs. From the doctor's point of view, the patient must meet him halfway. When she fails to do so, the doctor must take action or be seen as a 'soft touch'. Addicts, however, see it differently. The naughty, self-deceiving junkie has bitten the hand that writes her prescription. The doctor, in a fit of professional pique, tears it up.

On the whole, from the addict's point of view, scripts are used to blackmail junkies into attending for therapy. To addicts, this usually means mismanaged public humiliation sessions geared towards helping them to face up to how awful they are. Addicts have not conformed to society's idea of model citizenship. By one means or another they must be cajoled, persuaded, bullied or threatened into reform. They shall give up their drugs. They shall go to the ball and the glass slipper will fit if they have to lose every toe right up to the ankle. As addicts see it, most drug clinics exist to arrange for this sort of surgery.

Thus, addicts can demonstrate a considerable degree of 'paranoia' about what they believe are the patronising or antagonistic attitudes taken by their doctors. They often assume that doctors dislike them, look down on them and even want to punish them. Occasionally such fears are well-founded, but often they are quite groundless. Addicts sometimes confuse the doctor's professional stance with his private opinion. While doctors get on with carrying out their policies addicts can take their actions personally and assume that they alone form a persecuted minority of one bearing the brunt of the doctor's unwarranted malice. Their own guilt, embarrassment and lack of self-esteem may well contribute to their suspicions. A perfectly valid frustration with the treatment meted out can also foster the resentment felt by some addicts. They can become bitter and feel that they are being manipulated and humiliated in exchange for a prescription. To a certain extent, they are. Doctors may well believe that they are acting in their patients' best interests but no one enjoys being 'held to ransom' by someone else, especially when that person has the power to make them feel well or leave them feeling ill and wretched. The whole doctor–patient relationship is, therefore, fraught with tension; accusations, conflict and recriminations are regular features of it.

Many doctors feel threatened by addicts. They do not want to be reduced to the level where their only strength lies in the fact that they know how to spell dihydrocodeine or methadone. Most want to be more than the body on the end of the arm that guides the hand that fills out the prescription. Some care passionately about the addicts they treat. They believe that being drug-free is their only hope and want to achieve that end as quickly as they can. Sometimes they are over-zealous and hard on their patients. They must be cruel to be kind. Patients have lost sight of a drug-free life. Doctors must be their eyes. Spare the pain and spoil the programme. Commitment, discipline and success are required. There is no place for failure, backsliding or weakness on the ladder to health.

Addicts are liars. Every doctor knows that. Large pinches of salt scatter the doctor's desk. Under pressure addicts shrivel like snails on spring cabbage. Sometimes they lie because the truth is so preposterous that the doctor would think they were lying. He does anyway. They tell the truth. He gives up. They must think him really 'green'. More salt on the cabbage; more shrivelled snails. The addict must invent a truer lie next time. Before the doctor's desk addicts wheedle, plead, beg, complain, insist, demand, sulk and rage. They can be aggressive and downright insulting. Outside they boast. They were brave, assertive; they sorted him out. They told him he could not treat them like that. The doctor grits his teeth. Perhaps he will have better luck with the next patient.

Sadly, doctors and heroin users often fail to see eye to eye and are frequently disappointed by each other. Despite this, some of the doctors to whom I spoke defend their patients staunchly, saying that their personalities drove them to be addicts and that too many people failed to recognise drug addiction as an illness rather than a symptom of selfishness and self-indulgence. They put forward idealistic theories for the reform of their patients. One told me enthusiastically, 'First we get them off drugs, then we deal with their personality problems, rebuild their lifestyles and return them to society so that they can take jobs and lead a normal life.' He gave sound reasons for his suspicion of maintenance programmes, saying, 'It wasn't stabilising people or keeping them at work. Their lives were still chaotic and it was just contributing to the black market.' He explained that his policy was to advise total abstinence from opiates. He stated idealistically, 'Life for drug users is not fulfilling or productive. Our programme is all about encouraging people to be well and to take responsibility for their own wellness.' He admitted, however, that he stopped prescriptions for anyone supplementing their legally obtained methadone intake with heroin, and he further agreed that 'the clinics are a shambles', adding, 'There is no decent research and there are always valid disagreements to all policies.'

Most doctors are bound by the policy of the clinic at which they work and one told me that he felt powerless to help some patients as he was unable to prescribe the quantities of drugs needed to assist them to come off. Doctors do sometimes feel, however, that complaints from addicts about the treatment they receive are the result of the addicts' own aggressive behaviour. One told me that 'the attitudes of doctors are caused by the addicts themselves being very greedy about prescriptions'.

Addicts can certainly be fairly scathing in their condemnation of their treatment. They complain, for instance, that doctors always assume that they are not telling the truth. Chris explained, 'I told him I'd cut down my intake of drugs voluntarily and the doctor replied, "That doesn't make you genuine. I think you're taking something else!" Your experience is irrelevant. They are inflexible. Their minds are closed. They decided years ago what junkies are about.' One woman told me, 'You get to feeling all right then you go to the clinic and they convince you that you're one of those weak, dirty, degenerate people who's got problems.' Her husband chimed in angrily with, 'It's about time these people were found out. You think they're motivated by compassion but it's power that turns them on.'

Junkies, on the whole, show themselves to be highly suspicious of anyone trying to help. They tend to believe that doctors look on them with contempt and, indeed, some doctors do. Jenny told me, 'You have to sell yourself to them as their idea of a junkie – a snivelling, lying, thieving junkie. Otherwise they won't give you a script.' In some parts of the country, addicts who were formerly maintained on methadone have been forced off. Some show considerable resentment about this. Chris complained, 'So many people come down to London who have been maintained, usually in the north, and are forced off. They end up losing their jobs and scoring in the streets.' That had also been his experience. He is now unemployed and using heroin again. While maintained on methadone he had held down a full-time job for over three years.

Many addicts, while generally critical of their doctors, become even more vociferous in their condemnation of therapy. I have not spoken to one who does not resent it bitterly. When it comes to therapy, addicts are like injured dogs. They would rather bite you than let you tend their wounds. If they do have personality problems, getting them to look at them proves too painful for many to bear and vicious resentment sets in. Jenny confided, 'They really blackmail you. They work on the inadequate personality theory. They do a profile of you and make you feel that you are inadequate. They really make you feel bad. I was upset for ages.'

It is true, however, that addicts have little say in the treatment they receive. Chris was not far wrong when he said, 'It's all down to fashion. We're all the victims of fashion.' Indeed, some long-term methadone users feel that the state has got them addicted to a drug which is even harder to give up than heroin. In their terms, they too could be called 'victims of fashion'.

Whatever complaints addicts level at those who treat them, the doctors have, after all, made the choice to work with addicts. If no one wanted to treat them, addicts would have no doctors to complain about. Some doctors were very much on the addicts' side. One fairly liberal doctor told me, sincerely, 'We tell people they are not weak-willed. They have an illness called "chemical dependence". Anybody can get addicted to heroin if they take enough of it. They need to recover by being abstinent from all chemicals.' So far so good, but the problem lies in convincing addicts of that fact. Some doctors seem too eager to force addicts to run towards a drug-free life when they are not yet even ready to walk in that direction. That is the root of the conflict between them.

On the surface, doctors and patients can seem to have different objectives and there is often little satisfaction in the situation for either party. Few doctors are sympathetic to the addicts' sense of urgency about acquiring a script. Some feel that, whatever happens, addicts should get on with it. When I asked how he felt about women turning to prostitution to finance a habit one told me irritably, 'If a woman wakes up in the morning with a man whose name she doesn't even know it might help her to realise that she really will have to change her lifestyle.' I wondered whether he would add venereal disease, unwanted pregnancy and cervical cancer to the list of things that would merely help her to 'change her lifestyle'. The comment reinforced my general feeling that, when it comes to treatment, addicts really are victims of the whims of those in charge. One thing is certain: whatever theory is applied, not even the most widely practised theories have been proved to be a conclusive success. Some doctors may be sincere, well-meaning and committed but they are not always right.

Methadone: friend or foe? Reasons for the doctor's choice

Heroin produces a noticeable 'high' which wears off in a relatively short time, as little as four hours in habitual users. This is followed by depression and the need for another dose of the drug. Thus, the addict's day is a series of highs and lows; she is rarely 'normal' and, as doctors see it, she would have more chance of considering a drugless existence if these swings were eradicated and her emotions were on an even keel. This is one reason why methadone is preferred by most psychiatrists dealing with addicts. Methadone is a synthetic opiate, first produced during the Second World War, and, while it stops withdrawal symptoms, it does not produce a high in the way that heroin does. A large dose will merely send a person to sleep. It is also a long-acting drug, working in the system to ward off withdrawal symptoms for up to twenty-four hours. In practical terms, a daily dose of methadone can enable a regular heroin user to lead a normal, comfortable life. In terms of daily swings of mood, she will be more emotionally stable and, in particular, she will learn to live without experiencing the heroin high. This, in the view of many psychiatrists, gives the addict a chance to come to terms with herself and start to understand the reasons for her addiction while allowing her to avoid, for a while at least, the pain and distress of withdrawal. Methadone also allows the addict's physical functions to return to something like normal. The severe constipation associated with heroin use does not occur in methadone users. Sleep, too, follows a more normal pattern when an addict uses methadone rather than heroin. One patient discussed these matters saying, 'When you're using heroin, these things don't mean a jot, but when you change to methadone you realise how much smack was cocking you up.'

Methadone itself has come in for a degree of criticism. Addicts have complained that withdrawal from methadone is more difficult than from heroin. Onlookers have criticised the administration of the programme, suggesting that methadone is being overprescribed, sold on the black market in large quantities, and that it is being obtained under false pretences by people acquiring urine contaminated with traces of heroin in order to 'con' doctors about the extent of their own drug use. Most of this criticism is exaggerated, unfounded or unfair. Methadone is sometimes sold on the streets but usually to other drug users who need it. Addicts who sell part of their prescription usually do it to help a friend in a crisis or to get money to buy heroin to replace it. Recently, however, friends in London have observed an increase in the likelihood of people seeking a prescription for methadone with the primary intention of selling it to make money. In these times of high unemployment such abuses seem inevitable no matter what kind of drugs are prescribed. (Sleeping tablets and steroids also filter through to the black market as those keen to 'make a fast buck' show willingness to cater for the demand for whatever drug is required.) In general, prescriptions tend to err on the low side. Scandals in the 1960s usually involved doctors who knowingly chose to overprescribe. I have not heard of people buying contaminated urine. Only some of the newspapers seem to tell that story. Addicts who have cheated and taken heroin while on a urine analysis scheme might try to get hold of 'clean' urine to avoid being put off the programme, but most would find that hard to come by. Their friends all take drugs and anyone else would be amazed if someone asked them to hand over a carton of piss.

One consultant psychiatrist with whom I spoke pointed out that, particularly in the present climate of panic and concern about drug abuse, there is always someone ready to criticise any attempt to tackle addiction. He commented wearily, 'In this field whatever you do is wrong.' He appeared to be both sincere and dedicated. I felt that he was pained by the destructive, often ill-founded criticisms bandied about by those with no experience of drug users and little knowledge of treatment policies or the thinking behind them. Another area of controversy in drug treatment policies is that of maintenance. Maintenance in relation to heroin users is the name given to the policy of supplying addicts with regular quantities of heroin or methadone in order to maintain their habit without pressuring them to stop using drugs or to reduce their intake. This is a policy which is not, on the whole, advocated now. The goal of most 'helpers', whether doctors, social workers or relatives, tends to be the complete separation of the addict from the drugs. This makes maintenance an unpopular idea. There are, however, a few advocates of the policy who believe that when people are determined to continue taking drugs it is better to accept the fact and make clean, safe drugs available rather than drive them back to the black market where they must continue to buy impure drugs at savagely inflated prices. Some doctors will, in effect, cater for those patients who require what is virtually a maintenance programme. For their patients that seems to be the most appropriate course of treatment.

This brings me to another point put forward by critics of methadone. It is the suggestion that what amounts to spiteful calvinism on the part of those in charge (i.e. the government) informs the choice to give methadone rather than heroin. By this, critics mean to imply that the authorities both show their disapproval of the hedonist and also punish him by prescribing a drug which stops withdrawal but is not exciting or enjoyable. It is, of course, quite possible that the state would be uncomfortable about the prospect of peddling untaxed ecstasy, but caring doctors have given sound practical reasons for their choice of methadone and that seems to refute this argument. I have known addicts who pressed for a change of prescription from methadone to heroin and then actually changed it back to methadone once their wish was granted. They did so on the grounds that they preferred the long-acting drug that allowed them to get on with their lives uninterrupted. Other addicts, however, still complain that they would prefer heroin to methadone. Their main objection, a view which is widely held among users, hinges on the fact that it is harder to stop taking methadone owing to the long-term sleeplessness and depression which seem to follow withdrawal. They cannot all be wrong and their views should be investigated more thoroughly.

I raised this point with one of the doctors to whom I spoke and he countered with yet another practical point: the problem of how to administer heroin. Methadone can be taken by mouth and, in most cases it is, therefore, prescribed in liquid form helping to rid some addicts of dependence on the ritual of injecting themselves. Heroin, on the other hand, is not very effective when taken orally. Snorting, smoking or injecting are the methods which 'work' the best. All carry a degree of risk to health. Doctors would naturally be very nervous about handing out large quantities of heroin which would almost certainly end up being injected. The danger of encouraging new addicts to use a hypodermic syringe would be immense. This fear should be taken seriously by everyone. As things stand, some young addicts never do graduate to the needle. It has, in fact, been shown that with the co-operation of pharmacists such as Mr Clitherow in Liverpool, heroin cigarettes known as 'reefers' can be produced. A number of addicts have been successfully treated over a period of time with these 'reefers' and some prefer them to injectable heroin or methadone. More widespread availability of 'reefers' may well help to steer people away from injecting. From the point of view of those treating addicts, heroin 'reefers' must, therefore, seem to be a preferable form of treatment to injectable ampoules of either heroin or methadone.

In the 1960s methadone was hailed in the United States as a way of controlling crime. It had been suggested that addicts were largely criminal (i.e. that a direct cause and effect relationship between heroin and crime inevitably existed). The link between crime and heroin was a fact, but it was a matter of circumstance rather than of cause and effect. Because of the illegal status of the drug members of the 'criminal classes' were more easily exposed to it. It seems most likely, therefore, that in some cases at least, crime or prostitution came first and heroin after. Nonetheless, workers in the field were concentrating keenly on attempting to eradicate drug-linked crime. Drs Dole and Nyswander were acclaimed as successes in this battle against crime.

More recently, however, Edward Jay Epstein, in his paper entitled 'Methadone: the forlorn hope' which appeared in *Public Interest* magazine, disputes the results of research carried out by these doctors in the 1960s. Dole and Nyswander ran a methadone clinic in New York City in the mid-1960s and had made grand claims for their success in reducing crime in their patients. A parallel investigation by the Addiction Research and Treatment Corporation suggested alternative conclusions. Epstein's paper seriously queries Dole and Nyswander's report, arguing that evidence for the success of methadone was unconvincing. An account of his argument is given in O'Donohue and Richardson (1984), pp. 88–92).

The crux of the matter seems to have been the suggestion that methadone reduced crime among addicts, which Epstein shows could not be proved from the figures. Mind you, in the under-31 age group drug offences, forgery and prostitution were reduced. What this does show is that prescribed drugs reduce the pressure on the individual and I would consider sparing young women from prostitution a very worthwhile achievement. Even so Epstein has brought into disrepute one of the arguments used to justify the methadone programme. He attacked the policy as a form of 'chemical parole'. It must not, however, be overlooked that in this country addicts themselves choose to go onto the programme. On the other hand it is, in most cases, methadone or nothing, which leaves addicts the option of struggling alone or accepting methadone. Quite where that leaves us I am not sure. Methadone is far from a perfect answer to the problem. Prescribing heroin would also have its problems.

If, on the other hand, we choose not to help addicts by prescribing any drugs for fear that our motives may be seen as sinister, that leaves the addicts in a desperate state. Coercion to join a closed residential centre would hardly be a satisfactory alternative. Furthermore, it is a matter for concern among some doctors that while methadone remains the established 'drug of choice' for treating addicts, some alarming facts are beginning to emerge regarding its usefulness and its safety. Police surgeons in London have found that prescribing methadone is 'ineffective in stopping illicit drug use'. They have evidence that methadone is sometimes 'sold on'. Methadone has been found to be 19 times more toxic than heroin; it produces disturbances in weight and is responsible for greater numbers of fatalities than heroin.

A paper produced by Dr Russell Newcombe in 1995 summarises the main proposed short-term and long-term health problems associated with methadone use as follows:

Probable effects: constipation, dysphoria, tooth decay,
                addiction, nausea, dizziness
Possible effects: insomnia, depression, sedation, low libido,
                sweating, brain damage

He comments, 'in short, the literature on deaths among opiate users lends reasonable support to the hypothesis that there is an increased risk of death among opiate users who take methadone compared with those who take heroin'. He points out that such findings must be 'treated with caution' but recognises a possible 'urgent need to reduce the level of methadone prescribing' may arise if research (continues) to confirm the 'greater mortality risk' from methadone.

Another danger lies ahead. If methadone is discredited as a maintenance drug it does not follow – as its detractors often hope – that heroin will be accepted as its replacement. It is more likely that maintenance itself will be thrown out, rather like the baby accompanying the bath water down the drain, and instead of improved treatment for heroin users in line with their hopes and expectations, we could end up with fewer options and little treatment (in terms of prescribed drugs) available at all. Addicts could be faced with the choice between a brief 2–6 week detoxification, a straight 'cold turkey', or a one-way ticket back to the black market.

Where does that leave us? It leaves addicts confronted by an establishment policy that may put their health at risk; it leaves doctors without the freedom to prescribe a drug (heroin) that may cause less risk to their addicted patients than methadone. Indeed, research into prescribing heroin along the lines of Dr Marks' experiments in Warrington and Widnes on Merseyside is currently under way in Switzerland. If results there are successful, we may see changes in policy here and in other European countries – although, in the words of one disillusioned addict, 'I wouldn't hold your breath.'

One or two other factors must be mentioned before I leave the subject of prescribing to addicts. Methadone costs Health Authorities far less than heroin because a single company holds the licence to produce diamorphine legally, which keeps the price artificially high. One 100mg ampoule was listed as costing around £19 when I checked the catalogue last year. A single individual might receive between one and eight of these daily at a weekly cost that far exceeds that of methadone syrup. It is not difficult to see that, when pressed to make savings, doctors and Health Trusts might look more favourably on methadone as a treatment for addicts.

Will money talk to the policy makers?

Finally, I must mention two major American studies which set out to investigate the relative costs of drug treatment when compared to those of law enforcement. Both found that treatment was a highly cost effective and desirable option with the potential to save the tax payer vast sums of money. The RAND Institute (1994) studied cocaine users but felt that their results would be just as valid for other drugs. Their study showed that each dollar spent treating heavy cocaine users saved society $7½, 'over 15 times the saving from enforcement against drug dealers'. In the States, 73 per cent of the anti-cocaine budget is directed towards enforcement and only seven per cent is spent on treatment. 'The benefits of treatment have been underestimated', says the report, 'because previous studies have focused on how many users emerge drug free, failing to appreciate the benefits of keeping people off [street] drugs while in treatment.' It suggested that, 'diverting a ¼ of the enforcement budget to treatment could save the USA over ten billion dollars a year in the combined costs of cocaine use and anti-cocaine programmes'. If proportionately huge savings could be made here, much more attention should be given to treatment.

We have seen, however, that methadone is by no means the perfect treatment and it has become clear that some addicts reject it altogether while others supplement their legal supplies of methadone with street heroin whenever they can – as many as 95 per cent of clients at some clinics are believed to do this. It follows that if a wider variety of treatments were offered, more addicts would present themselves at clinics. If prescribing heroin encourages users to seek help, the government should reconsider its position and those doctors who are not in favour of prescribing heroin or other drugs to addicts should review their policies.

In the State of California, 'the most rigorous, retrospective out-come study ever' of drug abuse treatment was released in August 1995. Its methods differed radically from those of the RAND study but major findings were remarkably similar. Incredibly, the same cost/benefit ratio was observed; each dollar spent on treatment saved the tax payer $7. Neither report attempted to evaluate the relative merits of different types of treatment, but if all forms of treatment have been found to result in such vast savings, then sure-ly the primary objective should be to attract addicts into a treat-ment programme in the first place? It follows that making a wider range of treatments available will attract more addicts away from the black market and into treatment, with the result that our sav-ings will be great. Restricting our choices to a 'methadone or noth-ing' regime seems very short-sighted in the light of these facts.

How to stop on your own: the DIY cure

If you think you want to stop, the first thing you must do is to tack-le your attitude. If you are to make it through withdrawal without backsliding you need to be ready to combat any excuses for chang-ing your mind. If you are not fully prepared, you will only give up the attempt as soon as you start to feel ill. I suggest the following strategies might be employed with a view to ensuring a strong resolve. Take a pen and paper, sit down quietly somewhere, off your head if you like, and make a list. You need not, of course, actually write it down, running over the points in your mind will do, but some of these considerations may have a sobering effect:

List the drawbacks of using heroin.
List the gains of stopping.
List all the things you will be able to do when you stop.
List the disadvantages to your health/appearance if you carry on.
List all the unpleasant things that have happened to you because you use heroin.
List all the people who look down on you.
List all the people who shit on you and belittle you for using drugs
List what will happen if you go on. Draw your lifestyle to its logical conclusion!

List all the people you know who have died, suffered losses or
gone to prison because of heroin.

List any advantages of taking heroin. If you think hard enough
you will not find any.

List all the people you admire. Ask yourself whether they take
heroin. If so, has it done them any good? Would they have
been better off without it? (You will find they would.)

Think about the things you do not enjoy any more like music and
dancing.

You may want to face turkey without medication although most
people prefer to get something to help if they can. If you are prepared to 'come clean' but do not want to go to a clinic, your own
GP may help you by prescribing DF118s which contain dihydrocodeine, a poor relation to heroin, weaker in real terms, but useful to ease you out of a habit. If your habit is small a few of these
can help to ease the symptoms of withdrawal. You will not get a hit
unless you take a lot, and even then the feeling is unpleasant. You
get breathless and feel weird. It is not a recommended indulgence. If
your doctor gives you sleepers or valium you will, at least, be likely
to get a few hours sleep. Sometimes people try to get through withdrawal by using alcohol. As with cannabis, other people find that
alcohol makes them feel worse. It is, on the whole, a bad idea to use
drink because its ready availability and social acceptability mean
that an addict can start to lean on alcohol following withdrawal. If
this happens, the addict will be changing one habit for another and
drinking will turn into the same sort of problem that heroin was.
Once you have tackled your attitude and are convinced that you are
ready to make the effort to stop you need to consider where you
will stay and whether you will seek company or spend the time
alone.

You will need to find somewhere where you will not be dis-
turbed. It is bad enough having to cope with withdrawal without
trying to deal with a string of visitors at the door or put on a brave
face when your auntie happens to drop by. What you need is complete privacy, somewhere warm and comfortable where you will be
completely undisturbed for at least four days. You need to stock up
with anything and everything you are likely to require during that
time. As you will not feel able to go out and do any shopping you
must buy in stocks, but all you will probably need are convenience

foods like cereal, biscuits, and tinned or frozen goods. You will not feel at all like cooking big meals of any description. A bar of chocolate is probably preferable to a steak for most junkies coming off. Plenty of toilet roll and tissues are a must. If you use toilet roll for your running nose you will end up with a sore face.

You will also need something to do to take your mind off the way you feel. As you will have little energy and will find it hard to concentrate, music can help. TV is excellent. You can stare blankly and let the sweaty hours roll by. A stock of video films you always wanted to see can be a great help. If you have decided to turkey with a friend, cards or scrabble can be useful. At least then you will not need to talk. Try to have spare bedding handy if you can. You may need to take off the soaking wet sheets in the middle of the night. If you are short of bedding, a few large towels placed on top of the sheet can be useful as they can be changed more easily. If you have chosen to turkey with a friend, make sure it is someone who knows what to expect and will not expect anything of you. There is nothing worse than a well-meaning, hearty acquaintance admonishing you to 'get up and look lively' or wrinkling their nose as you decline the plate of steaming roast they have thrust at you. Whoever you choose to be with, they must know the score or you will end up hating them forever.

If you fail to get any legal medication it can be helpful, if you are really strong and determined, to buy a small quantity of heroin for the worst moments. You will be surprised at how small an amount will actually work when you feel really wretched. A tiny (no cheating) line at bedtime can save you from an agonised night without impeding your overall progress. One thing to avoid at all costs is telling yourself that you will have a really good binge the night before you stop. A lot of people make the mistake of deciding to get really wasted the day before coming off. After all, they want the last hit to be a good one. That, however, is a mistake. The result of a final binge is usually to wake up late the next day feeling so awful that you change your mind and decide to abandon the idea of stopping until next week. These so-called final binges can be repeated once a week for months until you decide to stop kidding yourself and shelve the whole idea of stopping until next year.

The last thing to do is take the phone off the hook. Tell everyone you will be away for the weekend and refuse to answer the door. Once turkey is under way, there is nothing to do but get on with it.

When you are flagging remember that four days is a small price to pay to redeem the rest of your life.

Things to do
Write a diary.
Play games.
Pamper yourself.
Bath, shower, hair wash.
Read.
Look forward to your new future – count the money you will have and plan the things you will do.

If you are a non-addict helping someone through, follow these rules:

1 Do not expect them to behave as normal. They will be ill. Treat them as such, even if they look OK to you.
2 They have decided to stop. They know better than anyone all the reasons why it is necessary. Do not nag them. They are doing their best, even if in your eyes it is not good enough.
3 Do not expect them to get up at a particular time, eat any meals, wash up after themselves if they do, take a bath, indeed do anything at all.
4 Do not be offended if your attempts at conversation fall on deaf ears. They will need all their concentration to cope with the symptoms.
5 Do not complain about the heat – or the cold. They will probably spend the time turning the heating on and off. You will have to put up with that if you want to help.
6 Do not watch them all the time expecting them to relapse. If they want to relapse, they will anyway.
7 Be patient. They will be bad-tempered, fretful and probably drive you up the wall. If they do need to talk, the kindest thing you can do is listen. Do not expect to tell them all your troubles in exchange. They will not be listening.
8 Try not to share a bed with them. They will probably be awake all night and if you sleep in the same bed so will you.
9 Never wake them up. If they are lucky enough to get some sleep, do not go bounding in with a nice, hot cup of tea just

because you have decided it's time for the day to begin. The happiest time for junkies who are sick is when they are asleep.

10 Do not insist that they will feel better if they wash their hair, smarten themselves up or go for a walk, etc., etc. This will only add to their distress. They know what will make them feel better and it is none of those things.

11 Do not be drawn into an argument or succumb to the temptation to give them a good talking to. If they are well enough, playing games like cards or scrabble is, on the whole, less dangerous than heavy bouts of boring soul searching that are likely to end in tears.

12 Do not let their tears and depression get you down. They will probably succumb to bouts of anguished sobbing. If withdrawal is new to them, they will not realise that this depression, although very real, is just another symptom that will come and go like the rest. If you get upset as well it will only make them feel worse. Try not to let them depress you. Stay buoyant and strong.

13 Do not just sit there watching them or trying to make conversation. Have something to do yourself such as reading or any quiet indoor pursuit. That way they will not feel pressurised. Your presence alone can provide the moral support they need.

14 Unless they want to talk, ignore them. The kindest thing you can do is to leave them to get on with it in their own way. They will tell you when it's time to celebrate.

15 After the first few days have passed they will feel a lot better, but they will still not be very fit or strong. If you are that way inclined, that is the time to start pampering them, feeding them up and making your plans for a better future. That is the danger period when you will want to keep their mind off drugs.

PART FOUR

Addiction in Context: Do We Really Know the Enemy?

CHAPTER 9

ℭ *The nature of addiction:*
'will the real villain please stand up?'

Heroin breeds contradictions: pleasure and pain; optimism and despair. Those who begin by running towards it often turn and flee for their lives. Tolerant liberals who have never taken it have been known to suggest that heroin should be legalised. Inveterate junkies are likely to assert that, while they want it themselves, it must remain a controlled drug. In part two, where I explored the junkie's eye view of smack, I acknowledged the paradoxical nature of the heroin experience and suggested that complete outsiders might find it hard to come to terms with contradictory reports on the subject. These apparent contradictions are inherent in the situation and I recognise that they exist alongside one another in the text. I have tried to embrace the truth by representing different aspects of it. I trust that the reader will accept any seemingly unresolved conflict as part of a complex message.

When it comes to matters like social policy, treatment, drug laws and penalties for possession of illegal drugs the conflicts and tensions are even greater. There is a very wide range of opinion and what the observer sees depends very much on where he or she is standing. In this final section of the book I delve into the hornet's nest of public opinion in an attempt to explore some of the issues surrounding drug addiction.

In the text so far I have discussed the use of 'street' drugs as things stand in the UK at the time of writing. In the concluding section I consider the possibility that circumstances could be different. I cannot stress too much the fact that the greatest dangers faced by addicts at the present time often stem from the lifestyle they are forced to adopt. The quality of the drugs available to them, the high cost of those drugs and the methods of their administration have a direct bearing on the addicts' health and well being. The burden of secrecy is enormous and can have a detrimental effect on the lives and personalities of drug users. On the bottom line, society makes the choice about the way addicts must live. In my conclusions I will try to show that alternative choices do exist.

Heroin, the great seducer: irresistible or not?

Throughout the book I have talked of the seductive power of heroin and traced the route by which people travel from simple curiosity into serious addiction. Of course, no one book can embrace every motive for using drugs or present a profile of every type of addict but I hope I have, at least, revealed some of the truth of the experience of drug addiction as it exists in Britain today. What I hope I have not done is made heroin appear to be an even more formidable foe than it really is, because heroin alone does not make people into 'drug addicts'. Some people have no desire to try it while others sample it but quickly reject it. A few people manage to use it in the same way as the average person uses alcohol. For them it represents an occasional treat for weekends or special occasions but never takes a grip on their lives. Others remain blissfully unaware that they have even come into contact with members of the opiate family. The elderly rheumatic or the man with a badly broken bone pop their pain-killing DF118s into their mouths quite ignorant of the fact that they are using a drug often prescribed to heroin users to ease them away from their addiction. Patients who have had surgery might leave hospital without knowing that morphine was the drug that eased their post-operative pangs. Through no fault of their own, the terminally ill can become opiate addicts. Regular doses of these useful pain-relieving drugs will lead anyone into a state of physical dependence.

But the drugs themselves do not do the greatest damage. If heroin poses a problem, the origin of that problem almost certainly lies with the attitude of the user. Those who gravitate towards mind-altering chemicals will be likely to welcome heroin into their lives. Once they discover that it dulls not only physical but also emotional pain, would-be junkies see heroin as a comforting helpmate whose assistance they readily accept. They can gradually build up a relationship with the drug that would be unattractive to others. It must, therefore, be apparent that even when people are exposed to heroin, there remains an element of choice. There are those who elect to plod on into addiction as it is popularly understood, while others walk away, seemingly unscathed. Thus addiction is, in essence, a double-edged phenomenon comprising elements of both physical and psychological dependence. Those who do not seek out a drug to partner them through life's merry dance can bop happily alone. Only junkies become convinced that it takes two to tango!

I do not mean to suggest that the needs or attitudes of drug users are, necessarily, inferior to those of people without a penchant for drug abuse. It is, in fact, quite typical for junkies to suggest that, at a former stage in their lives, heroin held no appeal for them. It may well be that the same person might at one time reject heroin but at a later date choose to seek it out. Our views develop and change: even junkies can lose interest in drugs and, after years of trials and tribulations, many do. There is actually a popular term for this process. Doctors refer to it as 'ageing out'.

I have already tried, in earlier chapters, to explore some of the reasons why people find heroin attractive and it is clear that fashion and peer pressure play quite an important part in fostering drug abuse in young people. Once they realise their mistake and find out that addiction is not much fun some youngsters can recover quite rapidly. Feeling that they have been rather silly, they put the experience behind them and start looking forward to getting on with their lives. Sadly, many do not get out so easily, and addicts can reach middle age without finding a cure. In countries where opiates have traditionally been more readily available, it is still not uncommon to find elderly addicts who have used drugs for most of their lives. Thus, heroin addiction can burn itself out as no more than a juvenile fling or dog a person to the end of her days. It is hardly surprising that there is so much public resentment against it.

Addiction: the obvious pitfalls

Yet few members of the public seem to be aware that both history and medical research have shown that it is possible for addicts who have ready supplies of opiates to lead stable, comfortable and even useful lives. During the last century there were actually many well-known and widely respected long-term opium addicts in Britain. If people can and do continue leading bearable lives while using opiates regularly it is not too unreasonable to query the thinking behind society's determination to come between them and their drugs. Addiction is a complex and diverse issue and far too many people cling to rigid and over-simplified notions of what it actually involves. If we can bring ourselves to suspend our instinctive judgments for a while it is, therefore, worth stopping to consider what it is about the state of drug addiction that alienates and worries the bulk of society so much.

The question might seem superfluous, especially since there are a string of obvious and simple answers to it. Everyone is aware that, when misused, heroin can kill and the diseased, unhealthy casualties of the scene are no advertisement for their drug. Furthermore, addiction is, quite simply, undesirable. The lifestyle that addicts must adopt limits their options and many drug users become bitterly depressed and disappointed about their situation. There are also very real fears that heroin abuse might become a major epidemic, creating problems on a much greater scale than anything we have recently witnessed. If that were to be the case, no doubt, petty crime geared towards financing the habit would also escalate. Of course, no wholly accurate estimate of the number of people already using heroin can be made but it is thought that as many as 150,000 British people may already be involved in heroin abuse. (Indeed, a quarter of a million may well be closer to the real figure.) Nobody can gauge how far the craze might spread and there is no doubt that it could infect many more people if left unchecked, although, young people are showing a preference for designer drugs like ecstasy.

The body is a delicate and precious machine, some would say the temple of the soul; the house of God, perhaps. It requires care and needs to be finely tuned if it is to work for us. The old adage which suggests that a healthy mind and body go together is very apt. True physical well-being is a marvellous feeling. No drug-induced state surpasses the good-to-be-alive sensation that comes when you are in tune with the life force within you. With heroin as part of your life, you can kiss goodbye to that sacred sensation of tingling and pulsing with the joy of simply being alive and well. That in itself is reason enough to steer clear of smack and take up meditation instead. Yoga brings rewards. Smack brings pain and, occasionally, physical death. Spiritual death is almost inevitable for heroin users and yet most of them simply do not notice. How can they? They are too stoned to be aware of it. Enough said. The case against heroin seems watertight already.

Why addicts see things differently

But let me change tack and play Devil's Advocate for a while in order to look back over the situation from the addict's point of view once more. We all choose to adopt certain comfortable behaviour patterns that suit us. Smack suits addicts. They have, in their own terms, found what they want and most of them actually wish to continue taking it. They know there is a price to pay but the addiction itself would present comparatively little problem for most heroin users if drugs were freely available and penalties were not imposed for possessing them. As addicts *want* to take heroin, the fact that they also *need* it is not necessarily their main concern. They would probably use heroin daily whether it was addictive or not. Their major worries stem from the knowledge that society has condemned their chosen way of life. The drugs create less direct aggravation for addicts than society's relentless efforts to protect them from themselves!

As the drugs are illegal, they are expensive. This involves users in a heavy financial commitment, so that money trouble is one of the primary reasons why other areas of their lives suffer. Addicts cannot choose between a new coat, a larger house, a fast car and heroin. For them, there is only one solution to any situation where there is a competition between drugs and something else. Such 'choices' are painful and distressing. The possibilities of arrest and imprisonment loom large. These threats are nerve-racking and hard to live with. Indeed, the whole lifestyle that addicts must inevitably adopt negates much of the satisfaction they might otherwise gain from their chemical helpmate. They are exposed to a nasty scene fraught with dishonesty and conflict; they risk health hazards from the use of dirty syringes or impure drugs; they may be tempted to commit crime and, finally, face bankruptcy and ruin. Addicts can live with their addiction but they cannot all cope so well with the social consequences of their habit. They have chosen to enter a cage but, from their angle, they could be happy in it if not constantly exposed to gaping visitors to their human zoo who prod them with sticks and expect them to perform, labelling them as a new species: homo-not-so-sapiens.

Until they give up heroin, addicts can remain unaware of some of the more subtle consequences of drug abuse. They can overlook the fact that they frequently fail to progress and often forfeit opportunities for personal growth. Yet they may have an inkling that the cosy cocoon woven by heroin provides a false security. They rarely expect a butterfly to emerge from it. However hard they work to explain or justify their position, few heroin users would want their children to follow them into the land of nod. Their reticence on this point does not seem to be based solely on the everyday disadvantages. Deep, deep down they know that heroin closes all the doors to spiritual and personal development and leans heavily against them until the hinges have rusted and the bemused addicts have quite forgotten where they are. Users sit isolated and safely alone in their private rooms. They fail to notice that the sand in the hourglass slowly solidifies and every day becomes the same day. They feel safe and they like that feeling. Whenever reality looms, they take more drugs to block it out.

Some addicts think that they need this kind of crutch before they can bear to consider the prospect of moving at all. When they do travel, they carry the room around with them. Every morning they pack up their junk in the same way that hill walkers arm themselves with waterproofs and heavy duty anoraks to keep out the cold. Their greatest fear lies in facing the world naked without smack, without heroin to cushion them from the rawness of the elements that make up daily life. Heroin is a shield for those who feel the pain of existence too acutely. Disappointment, depression and dissatisfaction never enter the heroin user's life so long as junk is there to keep them out. Users want a short-term solution to a lifelong reality. They risk everything for that. If they could feel confident of a steady supply of heroin most would spend little time reflecting on the rights and wrongs of their position. Like a comfortable but uninspiring marriage, the partnership between smack and those who use it stretches on. The die is cast, the fate accepted; addicts are more threatened by the thought of change than by their immediate circumstances. Any divorce is a harrowing experience. Addicts are usually ready to adapt to their self-inflicted routine without too much concern. Like long-term prisoners, they settle down to life inside. Most fear being released. In a way, they are rather selfish. So long as they have smack, they can forget everything else. They have discovered that they can 'switch off' and they blind themselves to the disadvantages.

The mitigating factors

Yet the 'crime' of the heroin addict resembles that of the frightened child who will not contemplate entering the darkened bedroom without his friendly ragged teddy to share the gloom. Junkies are not 'wicked'; they are often frightened people – terrified to let themselves live, scared of their own uniqueness, afraid to risk failure or rejection, unable to survive emotional pain. Some are driven towards self-destruction because of a refusal to face up to and work out the conflicts within them. Life can be difficult but junk makes it simple. Junkies can play hide and seek with themselves for years, never finding out where they really are or who they want to be. (They are not, of course, the only ones!)

The trouble is that observers seize on the physical realities of junkies' lives because the complex emotional struggle is quite simply beyond their ken. The junk experience is not one they have shared and, therefore, when they look at junkies they see a gaggle of unhealthy fools who repeatedly refuse to respond to pertinent warnings or listen to common sense. If they were only to look more closely, they would find that the situation is far more complex and the problems much more subtle than they believe.

I hope I have shared the heroin experience and made it more accessible to those who can give the time to try to understand the spurs to a life of drug dependence. I hope, too, that I have not obscured the fact that, despite the pitfalls, it remains true that drug users can lead bearable lives and some even achieve comparative success while in the grip of drugs. What makes addiction especially undesirable to me is the fact that it diminishes the life and talents of the individual user. Addicts always have many debts but they owe themselves the chance of a fulfilling life. Their greatest debt is to themselves.

Before I leave the subject, therefore, I would like to try and deal with some of the popular misconceptions about addicts and addiction and look at some of the reasons why drug abuse has become so frightening and threatening to those without personal experience of it. Given that regular drug abuse does not contribute to an ideal way of life, the methods by which the drugs are taken and the problems caused by laws against drug use are often the major barriers to the physical health and well-being of addicts. Heroin users make the mistake of wilfully limiting their options which, finally, only adds to their problems. But society has limited their options, too, often in ways that are unconstructive, unsympathetic, short-sighted and downright cruel. There is a frightened child inside most human beings and many of us have problems coping with life. The difference between junkies and some of their critics may simply be that they dared to try heroin and discovered its cosy companionship. From their experience, it must be obvious that he who dares does not always win. In this society, junkies lose out every time. A hundred years ago they could have trundled on unharried and many of them did.

The age-old partnership between humanity and drugs: new drugs for old

The relationship between people and drugs spans many centuries. Human beings have always looked to the plants and herbs around them to cure their ills, relieve their pains, relax them, induce sleep, provide stimulation or foster mystical insights. Alcoholics and people who use tranquillisers are following in this ancient tradition. They are, of course, demonstrating similar needs to many of those who use illegal drugs. The drive to alter consciousness is neither new nor abnormal. By exaggerating its significance, the twentieth century has driven a wedge between heroin users and the rest of society, labelling them as abnormal when they are, in fact, responding to age-old needs. Perhaps it is time for us to start learning wherever possible to travel forward without the assistance of chemicals. If so, the needs of drug users must be studied and understood. They may offer valuable insights into human nature. Running away from the truth is no way to deal with any problem.

In the case of drugs, we have to consider the context in which they are taken, the laws that control them and the historical background to the present situation. The effects of the drugs themselves are not the only matter that has to be taken into account by anyone who wishes to understand our current drug problem.

It is interesting to note that during the middle ages, huge numbers of women are known to have been burnt as witches. At the time, the public believed most of them to be guilty. Guilty of what? Being cleverer than their neighbours? Owning a black cat? Curing a sick child? They were still burnt and no-one intervened. With hindsight, we recognize the tragedy; we see the pointless persecution; the voices of anguished victims cry out to us across the centuries. I wonder, in another four or five hundred years, will people look back on the plight of today's drug users and puzzle over what it was that their tormentors thought was so terrible? What did they do to deserve imprisonment and punishment? – even the death penalty (23 countries execute people for drug related crimes). Are they really so wicked?

Whether or not the thought pleases us, drug taking in one form or another has been part of human experience for many thousands of years. Every culture (except for the Eskimos who acquired alcohol through visitors from outside) has had its own drugs. One writer comments on this saying, 'We must remember that every culture throughout history has made use of chemicals to alter consciousness ... It is my contention that the desire to alter consciousness is an innate psychological drive arising out of the neurological structure of the human brain' (Weil, 1979). Weil suggests that we have become embarrassed about those needs and drives to experience altered states of consciousness and that this has led in the end to our present drugs problem: 'By trying to deny young people these important experiences, we maximise the probability that they will obtain them in negative ways – that is, in ways harmful to themselves and to society.' In certain societies 'mystic raptures' and trances are ways in which these experiences can be pursued without the use of drugs. Weil goes so far as to say, 'Society labours under the same delusion as dependent users. It thinks that problems come from drugs rather than from people ... No drug is inherently good or evil ... There really is no drug problem.'

Indeed, the biggest problem with opium and opiates may be that they were sentenced without trial at the start of the twentieth century. We have been living with the consequences of this fact ever since. It is my belief that most of the obvious health problems connected with opiate abuse have come about because of two factors. The first is the invention of the hypodermic syringe and the second is that the laws against heroin have driven people to use dirty equipment, made them refuse to seek medical help and caused them to take risks that they would not otherwise have taken.

For centuries opium and human beings lived together happily. The history of opiates can, in fact, be traced to the seventh century BC. The Sumerians and Assyrians are known to have used them. In

Homer's writing, a drug which is described as being 'potent against pain' is almost certainly a preparation made from opium. The fruits of the opium poppy were well known in Ancient Greece and Rome, and the Greek goddess Aphrodite often appears with a poppy which stands as a symbol of love and fertility. India, Persia, Turkey, China and Indonesia have all at one time or another had their uses for it, and in Britain, too, opium was widely known, often in the form of a preparation called laudanum. Up until the middle of the nineteenth century there was only a hazy notion of its bad effects and addictive properties, and, despite occasional warnings, its use continued.

Opium was known in Europe from the start of the sixteenth century and towards the end of the seventeenth century the English doctor Thomas Sydenham wrote, 'Without opium there would be no medicine.' Laudanum was popular with doctors and patients alike and had many famous devotees. Clive of India, who died in 1774, took opium for the last twenty years of his life. William Wilberforce, famous humanist and campaigner against the slave trade, used it for forty-five years, right up to his death in 1833. Many well-known writers are known to have taken opium, including Byron, Crabbe, Keats, Shelley, Scott, Coleridge and De Quincey, who wrote the famous *Confessions of an Opium Eater.* During the nineteenth century all classes and types of people were liberal in their use of opium. Manchester cotton workers used it because, as a recreational drug, it was cheaper than alcohol. People gave it to babies to stop them crying. At that time there were said to be 'few Englishmen who had not taken opium for relief or stimulus' (R. Hughes, 1972, quoted in M. M. Glatt, 1980). By the middle of the nineteenth century the average Englishman was said to take over a quarter of an ounce of opium per year. It was even recommended as a cure for hangovers.

The dragon killer's charter

It seems almost incredible that opium and the opiates should fall from grace so suddenly and completely, that a drug which enjoyed immense popularity in the middle of the nineteenth century can be the cause of so much uproar in the twentieth. The practice of intravenous injection held dangers and serious consequences for injudicious and untrained persons which helped rouse public feeling against the opiates. That is not, however, the whole story. The real war on opiates began in the United States about the turn of the century. There were several reasons for this, but none seems to have been sufficient grounds for the severity of the attack.

At the time there were thought to be something like 300,000 addicts in the United States and they were mostly white, female, middle-aged and middle-class. Fashion magazines of the period even carried pictures of attire suitable for the fashion-conscious lady to wear when smoking opium. Early temperance campaigners were also known to rely for pleasure and relaxation on opium. Nevertheless, the view that excessive use of opiates was not to be desired and should be repressed began to grow. Firstly, the Food and Drug Act of 1906 called for controls on quality, purity and so on, but following pressure and concern about exploitation of 'natives' in opium-producing lands, the Americans actually decreed prohibition of the non-medical use of opium in the Philippines. This prohibition led to the setting up of large-scale clandestine drug smuggling operations, and the beginning of the problems that such activities bring. The Americans began to involve other governments in their own anti-opiate campaign and the number of meetings, conferences and laws began to escalate over the next twenty years.

I have neither the time nor space here to explore their motives and methods. Suffice it to say that in 1914 the passage of the Harrison Act meant that for the first time in the USA, opiates were to be controlled and prescribed only by physicians. They were no longer to be available on the open market. However, to quote from an essay in *The Community's Response to Drug Use,* 'the entire federal attack on drug abusers rested on no more than their failure in one way or another to pay applicable taxes or to use forms and procedures supposedly required merely to facilitate tax collection' (K. King, 1979). In other words, moral censure became the weapon of the tax collectors who used it to whip up support for their controls. King remarks, 'Within the federal structure, America's drug repression campaign owed its very existence to an unparalleled distortion.'

If that is so, much of the problem we see today has its origins in that distortion. Following the Harrison Act, physicians found large numbers of addicts clamouring for supplies of the drugs they needed. Initially, prescribing was freely permitted, but by 1923, the situation had changed dramatically. Addicts had become socially unacceptable and those who 'treated' them by prescribing drugs were punished. Doctors were threatened, and it is estimated that between 1914 and 1938, 'twenty-five thousand doctors were arrested for supplying opiates and five thousand of them actually went to jail' (*Dealing with Drug Abuse*, a report to the Ford Foundation, p. 176). After that, addicts were largely ignored. They suffered in silence or sought supplies on the black market, and as the black market spread, a new type of addict began to appear. The new addicts were often from minority groups such as the blacks and Puerto Ricans. These people, along with small-time crooks, pimps and prostitutes, found themselves living in areas where illegal drugs were available. Soon, heroin was thought to be responsible for the crimes associated with its users. This fact became further evidence for its prosecution. By 1945, the population of addicts was about 85 per cent male and only 75 per cent white. The new addict population made an easier target for attack than the original one and addiction became very unfashionable and extremely unattractive, the prerogative of the poor and the criminal classes.

In the 1950s offenders against drugs laws faced savage sentences in many American states. In Ohio, for instance, there was a prescribed minimum of twenty years for any first offence involving a sale. Maximum sentences could be increased to life, and death penalties were added in Alabama, Georgia, Louisiana, Missouri, Oklahoma and Texas. King remarks, 'The situation created by these oppressive measures has never been much alleviated by law makers.' Indeed, the United States has spent and still spends millions of dollars on attempts to control drug abuse. Their laws and their money have failed to stem the flow of narcotics into the country or to control the increasing addict population.

British drug laws have so far been less severe than those in the States, and 'the British system' was, for a time, thought to be a model of success. In 1926 the Rolleston Committee adopted the view that addiction should be seen as an illness and not as 'a mere form of vicious indulgence'. The report recommended that doctors be allowed to administer morphine and heroin as part of the treatment of addicts. It outlined certain controls on prescribing but accepted the concept of maintenance prescribing in some cases. Doctors were expected to steer patients towards withdrawal wherever possible, although their right to supply heroin was not challenged. Many of the known addicts were, in fact, found to be doctors, nurses, dentists, midwives and pharmacists who had come into contact with heroin through their professions. The numbers of people involved were comparatively small and there seemed no cause for panic.

By 1961 drug misuse in Britain was on the increase and the Brain Committee was set up to review the situation. It concluded that, in relation to narcotic drugs, no changes were required. The Committee was, however, reconvened in 1964 and its findings included the fact that a major source of supply of narcotics had been overprescribing by doctors. The committee, therefore, sought to limit prescribing by limiting the number of doctors authorised to supply dangerous drugs. Their report also recommended that National Health treatment centres should be set up. In 1971 the Misuse of Drugs Act came into being and the concept of notified or 'registered' addicts was born. Substantial penalties for traffickers in controlled drugs were also introduced. In Britain, things have remained much the same for addicts since the early 1970s, with shifts in treatment policies here and there.

The acceptable face of addiction

Law makers have clearly defined dangerous drugs as those which constitute a potential danger to society as opposed to those which are merely dangerous to the health of individuals who use them. Heroin is only one of a range of substances that have been singled out for use by human beings because of their special properties. Tea, coffee, tobacco and alcohol are all examples of drugs that come into this category, and all of them have been criticised at one time or another. It is, however, interesting to note that, while heroin is not necessarily the most dangerous of these drugs, none of the others arouses anything like the emotion that heroin provokes. James Willis, former consultant psychiatrist at the drug dependency clinic in Liverpool, remarked on the imbalance of society's attitude towards certain drugs:

> Drugs in general appear to have a moral value attached to them. It is almost as if they were classified not only according to their pharmacological properties but in an unstated way

according to their presence at some point along a moral scale with tea and coffee at the 'good' end and diamorphine [heroin] at the bad end.

Along with a number of other people who have researched into the topic, he talks about the phenomenon of a 'condoned addiction'. This term describes a situation where alcohol and tobacco, 'two of the most important health hazards in the western world', are tolerated, and advertised and promoted by people who have an interest in their sale. He concludes,

> We are left with the disquieting knowledge that certain types of addiction are selected by society in a capricious way to be regarded as either 'good' or 'bad' and thus either susceptible to encouragement or promotion or supposedly susceptible to treatment, rehabilitation or punishment.

Alcohol: a deadlier foe?

For no logical reason other than custom and precedence, alcohol has long enjoyed a protected position in our society. In 1957 Robert S. de Ropp wrote somewhat indignantly, 'Just why the alcoholic is tolerated as a sick man while the opiate addict is persecuted as a criminal is hard to understand.' De Ropp highlighted his own response to this apparent injustice, adding, 'There is, in the present attitude of society in the United States toward opiate addicts, much the same hysteria, superstition, and plain cruelty as characterized the attitude of our forefathers towards witches.' Doctors and observers have, for a long time, been fairly liberal in their condemnation of the misuse of alcohol. They have made it clear that of all the potential drugs of abuse, alcohol is one of the most damaging, since relatively light consumption clearly causes some damage to such organs as the brain and liver, and heavy consumption causes serious damage and sometimes death.

Alcohol can lead to scenes of degradation every bit as unpleasant and appalling as those associated with heroin addiction and its effects have been well known for many years. It has, indeed, been linked to the destruction and premature death of many well-known and well-loved figures. The lives of the writers Oscar Wilde, Dylan

Thomas and Brendan Behan are all said to have been ended prematurely as a result of the effects of alcoholism. There are footballers, boxers, snooker players, popstars, actors, politicians and news readers who are all known to have fallen prey to problems with drink. Despite all the casualties, alcohol remains socially acceptable. Many countries even have a national drink that has come to symbolise that place. Vodka, Guinness and whisky are all synonymous with the countries they represent. It seems a bitter irony that alcohol should be respectable while heroin is outlawed, alcoholics given sympathy, tolerance and even indulgent affection while junkies receive scorn. The effects of alcohol are easily as serious and detrimental as those of heroin.

Legal drugs: a double standard?

Despite this, alcohol is freely available while heroin is banned. Recently, there has been a big furore in Britain about the prospect of increasing the maximum length of prison sentences for dealers in drugs. But how far can we equate small, street drug dealers with murderers and violent criminals? Consider the following: a small, local drug dealer, in practical terms, fulfils the same role as a publican. In exchange for money he dispenses a dangerous drug for recreational use by others who are well aware of the risks. Publicans, however, are respectable and respected members of society. Many 18-year-olds work behind the bars of our pubs and hotels. We consider their work to be honest and respectable. We see nothing wrong in it. In our arrogance we fail to give a thought to the fact that in some countries, Saudi Arabia for instance, alcohol is considered a terrible evil. There, it is viewed with the same distaste and suspicion with which heroin is seen here. Those who make it or supply it face severe sentences. When they come up for trial westerners are outraged and shocked. Most western people mutter bitterly about those terrible Saudi Arabian laws. They feel resentment and irritation at the concept of public floggings for offenders who merely fancied a little tipple. They know that alcohol can be perfectly safe if used correctly and sensibly. Not everyone who takes a drink will end up a raving maniac, suffering the DTs and sidestepping the proverbial pink elephants. The Saudis are condemned as a brutal, backward, foolish, primitive and uneducated race.

Yet the same people who criticise the Saudis for their moral stance against alcohol call for drug 'pushers' to be hanged. Naively, they condone the use of alcohol and condemn the sale of heroin. The simple truth is that both substances can be misused, both can be lethal for those who over-indulge, but we must keep a sense of proportion. A society that is well acquainted with the evils of the 'demon drink' should not get so hysterical about the misuse of the fruits of the poppy. Hops, grapes and poppies have all shared in the history of mankind. They still do. Without ill-considered and comparatively recent laws against the use of opium we might not have the sort of heroin problem we see today.

Temazepam: another legal drug bites the dust

It is interesting to note that attempts to control addicts' behaviour by thwarting their desires often exacerbate the situation. The facts surrounding the sleeping tablet, Temazepam, demonstrate this. Considered a much milder and less dangerous drug than the barbiturates which fell from grace some years ago, Temazepam was prescribed regularly to addicts as part of a plan to help them to come off heroin. The intention was to help them to get to sleep during the long and difficult nights experienced throughout withdrawal. A capsule with a liquid centre, it seemed harmless enough – not so. Addicts quickly discovered that it could be injected. Taken this way, it had a much more dramatic and powerful effect. Some began to buy Temazepam on the black market, using them to mask the symptoms of withdrawal. Others began to seek them out as a pleasure in themselves and some, of course, became addicted.

Temazepam has unpleasant side effects, and users sometimes become disorientated or aggressive. Their behaviour makes them a risk to themselves and to others. In order to discourage the practice of injecting these drugs, the formula was changed so as to make the liquid centre into a thick jelly like substance. Their fans simply began to heat up the 'jelly' until it melted, making it easier to inject and causing even greater risks to their heath. People have had limbs amputated because of complications caused by Temazepam and one 26-year-old woman I know suffered a heart attack in the street following a Temazepam 'binge'.

Seeking the views and co-operation of drug users is far more productive and worthwhile than attempts to separate them from heroin, which frequently causes worse problems. Temazepam is still a cause for concern and new controls on its use have been introduced in Scotland where it has become an offence to possess the drug without a prescription for it. Thus, we have yet another reason to drag users before the courts despite the fact that the law has failed to control drug abuse in the past. It is tempting to suggest that the old adage 'the law's an ass' is just as true today as it ever was.

CHAPTER 10

ℭ The big bad bogey drug

Bad news is the best news

A major part of our drug problem seems to lie in the myths and attitudes perpetuated by a news-hungry media, for whom bad news is always good news. The manner in which certain newspapers set out to hound drug users who are unlucky enough to be famous is a callous and disgusting spectacle. When a junkie dies the papers have a field day giving details of his appalling, debauched lifestyle and speculating on the role of the parasitic pushers. When an alcoholic dies no one rushes off to interview representatives of major breweries about his 'unlawful killing'. He has been lawfully killed in a manner which is apparently acceptable to journalists and public alike. The papers thunder out the consensual view of drugs and drug users, and no one dares contradict their pronouncements. The media paint a melodramatic picture of addicts. On the whole they are seen as wicked rather than ill. Frequently punishment, not compassion, is called for. They are usually thought to have forfeited their rights to jobs, respect, and sometimes liberty. It is commonly assumed that all will steal, lie, cheat, even sell their own mothers into bondage for a 'fix'. Self-indulgence and lack of willpower are thought to be the very least of their failings. It may be some time before the general public sees drug addiction as an illness similar to alcoholism, an illness whose victims require tolerance, understanding, medical help and support from the community.

What have we learnt about heroin users?

Physicians and other medical professionals have recognized that narcotic addiction and alcoholism are serious, chronic, relapsing diseases that need prompt diagnosis and long term treatment.

Millman, Cushman and Lowinson, 1981

There are two major conclusions that must come out of an honest study of the world of the heroin addict. Firstly, the state of addiction and all that it implies should arouse pity rather than scorn. We should lay aside any initial urge to condemn those who use the drug and try to understand their predicament. Once a habit is established, unless they are prepared to be ill, addicts have virtually forfeited the power of choice. Junkies need smack just as cars need petrol. When they run out, they cannot function again until further supplies are obtained. You may say they have been foolish and pigheaded to get themselves into such a mess. They have and they would probably be the first to agree with you, but there are few people who cannot admit to having been wrong or having made an error of judgement at some time. Knowing what is wrong does not, necessarily, make problems disappear. Like cigarette smokers who live with the threat of bronchitis, emphysema and lung cancer, junkies are painfully aware that their addiction is undesirable but many of them repeatedly lose their battle against the habit. When the addicted seek help the door should not be closed against them. Before you slam it shut on their bony fingers, consider whether there is anything in your past that you regret. Many addicts show great courage in facing up to their position. It is not easy to admit that you have let yourself down and to ask for help. It is harder still when the attitudes of others are hardened against you.

Secondly, the state of addiction is frequently a life sentence. Even when drug-free, users often have to carry on the struggle against the powerful urge to relapse. A former addict can still be lured back again by fascination for the Pandora's box that houses the opiate family. Just one more peep under its lid can lead back into the cruel snare of addiction but the attraction is so powerful that some users repeatedly fail to resist it. The root of the problem lies not, primarily, with the effects of the drugs the addict uses but in the overriding compulsion to keep on taking them. Sometimes addicts hate themselves for giving in to the longing for heroin. The desire to punish them should be tempered by that knowledge. Sadly, however, heroin has acquired a frightening image as the big bad bogey drug and this interferes with the establishment of humane and constructive social policies.

Panic and fear of the unknown characterize the public response to heroin although most people have only a vague and exaggerated notion of its destructive power. Anything strange, unusual or beyond the experience of the average citizen has always provoked a combination of distrust and dislike, frequently culminating in attempts to drive out or destroy the alien being. Minority groups who are different have always been persecuted. Wise women were once burnt as witches. Heroin addiction arouses many of these dangerous primitive responses in even the most educated person. Thus, old-fashioned prejudice and superstition can become an enormous barrier to genuine efforts to see drug problems in perspective and formulate a sensible plan of action.

A look at the issue of drugs and parenthood will bear out the way that an over-emotional response to heroin gets in the way of wise policy making. Some people who are not heroin users have received very light sentences when convicted of wilfully starving or assaulting their children. If a heroin-addicted parent is charged with any form of neglect or misconduct, whether intentional or not, the proverbial 'book' is almost certain to be thrown at him or her. This precedent has already been set. Society has decided that heroin users are bound to make unfit parents. Despite the fact that many women carry on using the drug precisely in order to meet the demands of motherhood, addicted mothers are always under suspicion and this has led to a witch hunt where the pregnant heroin-addicted woman is the quarry. The case of the heroin-addicted mother is, in reality, a complex one. I want to examine it in some detail in order to show how the simplistic, media-encouraged popular view of her can stand in the way of an appropriate social policy.

Witch hunt in the maternity ward

A good deal of emotional response is generated when a prospective mother is found to be a heroin addict. It is, however, perfectly possible for a woman to have a successful pregnancy and produce a healthy baby despite her heroin addiction. I was surprised to learn, when I questioned a doctor who works at a well known drug dependency clinic, that the risk to the foetus from heroin is not as great as people imagine and may well be smaller than the risk from other drugs, including tobacco and alcohol. We have only to recall the problems with thalidomide to realise that some drugs can put the foetus at greater risk than heroin. Heroin does cross the placenta but not in the same quantities as some drugs.

I do not wish to mislead the reader. Clearly, any irresponsible use of drugs, and not least heroin, during pregnancy is wholly undesirable from a medical viewpoint. What surprised me, however, was the following statement from a consultant psychiatrist at a drug dependency clinic: 'Babies born to smokers have low birth weights roughly similar to those of heroin-dependent mothers but, undoubtedly, the greatest risk to the unborn child is from alcohol. One gin and tonic a day can cause brain damage in the baby' (private correspondence). It is, of course, true that babies born to heroin-dependent mothers have smaller birth weights than the average and no sensible person would advocate the use of heroin during pregnancy. But for those who are already addicted to heroin, the choice to stop on the discovery of a pregnancy is not as simple and straightforward as it might seem to an outsider. It must be recognized that sudden withdrawal of the drug is very likely to result in spontaneous abortion. This can happen because uterine contractions are a feature of severe withdrawal. Dr Susan Boobis, an advisor to the National Childbirth Trust, told me,

> Heroin should not be withdrawn during pregnancy, especially during the last three months as the increased muscular activity during withdrawal could lead to oxygen lack in the baby and possibly result in premature labour. Under medical supervision, however, the pregnant addict may be enrolled in a methadone maintenance programme, and this is considered by some to be beneficial.

Thus, the decision by a woman to stop taking heroin during pregnancy could be fatal for the baby.

Furthermore, the emotive question of the baby undergoing the anguish of withdrawal in its first days need not necessarily arise. An acquaintance of mine who has taken heroin for many years has given birth to two healthy sons during that time. She did not declare her addiction to doctors at the hospitals where she gave birth to her babies and she believes that, by breastfeeding them, she was able to wean her children safely off the drug. According to her, they showed no undue signs of distress and the truth was never suspected by doctors. The babies, both boys, are today lively, bright and apparently normal children, one of whom is already at school and doing well. It is, of course, true that babies born to addicted mothers will often withdraw and, in such a case, the baby can be treated, under medical supervision, with reducing sedatives which alleviate the symptoms.

I checked the breastfeeding theory with the National Childbirth Trust and found that studies in the United States have corroborated the instinct of addicted mothers that when they breastfeed their babies the natural process of weaning the child off mother's milk and onto solid food can also help to wean the child off drugs. It has been found that opiates from the mother's system do enter breast milk, and one study states that 'many authors felt that infants could be maintained symptom free on mother's milk provided that the mother continued to receive adequate dosage of opiates' (Good-friend, Shey and Klein, 1956). As feeding continues, the amount of milk taken by the infant decreases naturally over a period of time. Thus, the quantity of drugs reaching the baby's system decreases gradually. In effect, the baby experiences a slow and, therefore, comparatively painless withdrawal from the drug. There are doc-tors who feel that this method of 'treating' an addicted baby is preferable to the administration of sedatives because the baby suf-fers far less during the natural weaning process. Notwithstanding the happy outcome of the case described above, however, it is dan-gerous to conceal heroin addiction during pregnancy. The baby can experience withdrawal symptoms even with breastfeeding and appropriate medical treatment would be required to prevent the possible death of the baby.

There is no doubt that opiate addiction in a pregnant woman – or any woman – is not a matter for complacency. On the contrary, some research shows that such a state results in disadvantages to both mother and child. It is true that the consequences of opiate addiction during pregnancy can be comparatively bland but in high doses of drugs they can be extremely serious and one study from the New York Academy of Sciences states, 'the potential hazard to the fetus, neonate and child is overwhelming' (Millman, Cushman and Lowinson, 1981).

What does emerge from a close examination of the medical facts is that the problems associated with addicted mothers can be more a consequence of their social circumstances than a directly medical result of their physical dependence on the drug. Loretta P. Finnegan points out in her paper 'The effects of narcotics and alcohol on pregnancy and the new born' (1981), 'Breast feeding is a twenty-four hour a day, seven day a week commitment by the mother which seems impossible for the heroin addict given her chaotic life style.' She explains that in 'women carefully maintained on methadone ... breast feeding is possible', but adds that of the mothers in her study who attempted it, most did not continue for more than a matter of weeks 'due to their inability to persist with such a commitment'. The lifestyle of an opiate-addicted woman does not foster a straightforward successful pregnancy. The paper quoted above points out, referring to the addicted woman, that she 'spends her day either in a euphoric state or a sick state during which time she is seeking drugs. She has little concern for a good diet, adequate sleep, or obtaining any prenatal care, the lack of which are known to seriously affect the outcome of pregnancy.' It further states, 'the vast majority of these women neglect general health care and, therefore, are predisposed to a host of obstetrical and medical complications during pregnancy.' Thus, the addict's circumstances and lifestyle are as much a part of her problem as the drugs themselves.

To sum up, there is said to be a higher rate of miscarriage and still birth among heroin users than non-users but poor diet, self-neglect and non-attendance at an ante-natal clinic are undoubtedly factors which contribute to this situation. I have already pointed out that withdrawal of the drug can cause spontaneous abortion. Perhaps, therefore, the difficulty in keeping up a supply of drugs is one of the factors that account for the increased rate of miscarriage among heroin users. Remember, too, that many addicts keep their addiction secret so that statistics do not reflect the whole truth. A more positive approach from society as a whole might encourage more of them to admit to their problem and seek help. Certainly I believe that the solution to dealing with addicted mothers lies in giving them increased support rather than calling for their children to be snatched away from them. Treating mothers who use heroin as irresponsible, unsafe parents is bound to reduce their own self-esteem, dash their hopes for the future and leave them without the will or confidence to fight against their addiction.

As mothers, known heroin users are a group who attract considerable public censure. It is not fair, however, for people to judge them as a homogenous group who are all likely to behave in the same way. Many heroin users are successful capable parents. The few who are not arouse an emotional response which puts all mothers who use heroin in danger. That danger is that someone will decide that they are unfit to bring up their children. To say that any heroin user is an unfit parent is, however, as unfair as suggesting that all people with blue eyes will make unfit parents because you have known one who did. The key to understanding the situation is always to be open-minded and to never lose sight of the fact that addicts are individuals.

If a woman does decide to stop using drugs, she will find treatment facilities are not arranged with the needs of the family in mind. Crèche facilities are not provided at clinics and many fail to go into hospital for detoxification because of fears for the welfare of their children. A few street agencies have begun to cater for women's needs by starting women's groups, counselling services and offering childminding facilities to enable women to attend meetings. This is, at least, a step in the right direction. A very important task still needs to be undertaken, however, and that is to educate people to accept that a woman who takes heroin is not necessarily an unfit mother.

Fear and loathing in the courts of law

I have already suggested that the public views heroin with a mixture of loathing and fear. To some, it is the Devil's Powder and there are those who act as if even to succumb to the temptation to gaze upon it could turn a person to stone. People are so horrified by the terrible personal and social consequences that can befall anyone who uses it that their judgment is clouded. Doctors and others with experience of the problem have, however, had much to say over the years which does contradict a good many of the prejudices against heroin. For over thirty years physicians have been making it quite clear that the concept of what heroin addiction actually involves has become distorted. They have often pointed out that addiction to heroin or morphine does not, necessarily, lead to impaired intellectual functioning or the destruction of the lives of drug users. It has long been clear that individuals might take opiates over a period spanning twenty years or more without showing moral or intellectual deterioration. It may surprise readers to learn that when clean drugs are available the user's health need not suffer unduly.

In 1970 Ball and Urbaitis stated, 'there is insufficient scientific basis for maintaining that the long term use of opiates – in and of itself – is related to any major medical condition.' In 1972, a study by Brecher found that there was 'general agreement throughout the medical and psychiatric literature that the overall effects of opium, morphine and heroin on the addict's mind and body under conditions of low price and ready availability are on the whole amazingly bland'. Indeed, researchers and enlightened observers tend to agree that the greatest risks associated with opiates come from the use of dirty drugs and equipment or from the lifestyle that many addicts are driven to adopt.

Thus, the real truth about opiates as doctors and other researchers see it is far removed from the public version of the facts. It seems that, for a multiplicity of reasons, society is terrified of the truth. It does not want to discover that people might take heroin without physical danger. Heroin is easy to attack and, therefore, it comes under heavy fire. Sadly, only the casualties of the drug scene present themselves for public examination. Junkies are all judged by that yardstick. It is, therefore, assumed that all will degenerate to the same degree, even though members of the medical profession have offered sound evidence to the contrary. A report on drug abuse made to the Ford Foundation in the United States and published in 1972, has these comments on American laws related to drug abuse:

> We do feel, however, that current policy – which singles out particular drugs and makes their possession or use a crime – should be changed for very important empirical reasons. We believe that the individual and social harm caused by imposing criminal sanctions on drug users far outstrips the benefits of this approach. Handling drug users as criminals has created widespread disrespect for the drug laws, has resulted in selective enforcement, has possibly done more to encourage than to discourage illegal drug use, has undercut bona fide efforts to explain the important differences among various drugs ...

Despite the range of well-researched opinion that raises many questions, society as a whole continues to increase the laws against drug users and, in so doing, exacerbates the situation.

Social policy: the need for a new approach

It grieves me deeply to see our prisons filling up with young men and women whose only crimes have been linked to the abuse of drugs. Ever since the sanctions against drug users first began there have been liberal voices crying out against the 'penalties of mindless savagery' (King, 1979, page 143) that await junkies. There has been debate concerning the 'normality' of addicts, about the type of person who becomes an addict, their motives, their treatment, indeed, every aspect of the subject, although one fact is obvious: 'Byzantine cruelty remains a prominent element in America's attitudes toward her drug addicts, in a pattern that has been fairly consistent – and quite relentless – for half a century' (ibid., page 134). At the present time my concern is that attitudes are hardening towards drug users on this side of the Atlantic and that we will see similarly savage and unproductive laws over here, the beginnings of which are already in evidence. It is, for instance, interesting to note that a Home Office publication sets out the government's strategy against drug abuse as follows:

- reducing supplies from abroad
- tightening controls on drugs produced and prescribed here
- making policing even more effective
- strengthening deterrence
- improving prevention, treatment and rehabilitation

The government has clearly made aggressive sanctions a priority. Treatment and prevention are *last* on its list of objectives. At the Conservative Party conference in 1985 David Mellor outlined new proposals to increase sanctions against pushers and bring in new forms of control. He remarked that there were few better reasons for building a prison than 'filling it with drug traffickers'. 'Above all' he called for 'punitive sentences for dealers', yet these methods have failed elsewhere. There is little reason to suppose that they will work here. Like him, I believe that it would be a good idea if 'everyone in our community says "no" to drugs', but I do not believe that some of the methods he puts forward will achieve this end.

It is not surprising that daring and sincere individuals are standing up and suggesting that, instead of strengthening sanctions against users and small-time street dealers, we should consider the possibility of decriminalizing heroin altogether. At a time when there have been tragic deaths which can be directly linked to drug misuse, such a viewpoint can easily be dismissed as irresponsible and stupid. When I began writing this book I, too, believed whole-heartedly that heroin should remain a controlled drug, with penal-ties for its illegal possession, but the book has taken me nearly a year to complete and during that time my views have developed and changed. I have begun to pity the thousands of youngsters who are now criminals because they use heroin. I have watched as soci-ety's views have polarized, making addicts into pathetic, weak vic-tims and turning pushers into evil, wicked villains, forgetting that the user and the pusher is often one and the same person. My read-ing has convinced me that savage laws that condemn and punish users and small dealers will not stamp out the problem. I have become painfully aware that most victims of addiction become ill because of the fact that clean, cheap drugs are not available. The only people who really profit from the whole business are the major criminals who are behind the giant international smuggling operations.

At a local level, decriminalization of heroin would remove the health risks and bring addicts out into the open so that more would seek treatment. They would no longer need to buy overpriced drugs on the black market. This fact alone would dramatically reduce the profits of dealing in heroin, leaving major drug traffickers with less incentive to ply their trade. It would save large amounts of public money and it would mean that foolhardy youngsters would not be turned into criminals overnight. It would prevent a considerable number of petty crimes and, of course, wipe out the whole concept of heroin as a glamorous and mysterious substance.

I do not, of course, intend to imply that decriminalization of heroin should mean a 'free for all' where it would be available in supermarkets like a bag of sugar. Controls would still be needed to curtail its use, but doctors should be freed from the shackles imposed on them following abuses perpetuated some years ago by a handful of their colleagues. Junkies should also be liberated from the stigma of criminal status that follows the inevitable proceedings taken against them when they are found in possession of the drugs they need. The police could then get on with the job of tackling 'real' crime rather than being used as somewhat inept and inappro-priate social workers. At the moment they are expected to stamp

out a major social problem that has its roots not in criminal mentality but in an inability to cope with the inevitable stresses of life.

The practicalities of organizing some form of decriminalization or
widespread prescribing could, of course, be fraught with difficulties.
The Home Office asserted, 'the decision (i.e. to radically alter policies
regarding the treatment of addicts) is too big for doctors. It would
take an Act of Parliament to alter things'. Catch-22 strikes again.
Which MP is going to commit political suicide in the wake of 'war on
drugs' propaganda to raise the issue in the Commons? It would take
a concerted campaign by Saatchi and Saatchi to alter public consciousness and raise their awareness of drug issues. Furthermore,
those addicts who are plausible professionals and who might just
demonstrate to the public that heroin itself need not destroy lives are
too afraid of the consequences of 'coming out', to stand up and be
counted. Thus, the truth continues to be obscured, controls remain
stringent and penalties for those involved in drug use and supply are
likely to get worse before they get better – if they ever do.

At the end of this book, what do we have? We have the doctor
and patient struggling to meet each other across a battleground
strewn with the debris of half a century of punitive law making and
hasty, ill-considered policies; the public fleeing in ignorance and terror; drug users, half of them only in trouble because they were so
attracted by the idea of 'forbidden fruits', reeling from the shock of
society's pronouncements against them; plagues, purges, pontifica-
tions and problems, with junkies caught in the crossfire and confusion as the haters and the helpers fight it out, reeling from the
wounds inflicted by a hostile force that does not even know its
enemy. Clearly, negative critics and aggressive law makers can create as many problems as the drugs themselves. The scene need not
be so fraught. It is time for all interested parties to start working
together to find a way forward. Heroin addiction, as we see it
today, wipes the smiles from the faces of the young, ravages their
bodies, and breaks the hearts of most of its devotees. But we must
accept that the drug itself is not the sole origin of so much of the
suffering associated with it. That fact must filter through to all concerned if progress is to be made. If we fail to understand that the
problems stem not from drugs but from people, we will continue to
search unsuccessfully for a way forward.

This book has been written for ordinary people with the intention of offering a realistic insight into the drug problem. It is not an

academic study, nor does it purport to be. There is, however, much well-documented evidence that a good deal of furore about drugs is a matter of prejudice rather than fact. I felt I could not, in fairness to addicts and readers alike, complete the book without making some attempt to put the situation into perspective. All I ask is that we keep a sense of proportion. If we must kill the dragon, let us do it humanely.

CHAPTER 11

₵ *A prescription for living?*

Trisha is a friend who has used heroin for many years. She moved to Merseyside from her home in another part of the country to escape the chaos into which her life had descended because of drugs. She had a 4-year-old daughter to think of and had served three short spells in prison as a direct result of activities geared towards supplying herself with heroin. A new town, a new start, a new police force who wouldn't drag her in for questioning the second they laid eyes on her. Moreover, there was a drugs clinic in the area that reportedly supplied prescriptions for heroin. Life was looking up.

Trisha and her husband, both in their 30's, had struggled with all the negative and complex problems of heroin addiction since they were in their late teens. Their life had been a cycle of dramatic highs and lows. Shoplifting, dealing, courts and prisons were all familiar to them. Yet now, all they really wanted to do was create a stable home for their daughter, and start building a meaningful future for themselves. You don't believe it? I do. I visited their home. It was a neat house, semi-detached, well furnished, clean as a new pin. The garden flourished. Herbaceous borders spilled onto new mown lawns. A tidy car stood shining in the drive. Doubtless, the neighbours saw them as a 'nice couple'. Their daughter was a lovely little girl. Bright, pretty, smartly dressed in cute outfits that any mum would have been proud of. She was always polite and had no idea about the drug taking that shaped her parents' lives.

Trish and Tony had become clients of the local drugs' clinic and were receiving prescriptions for the heroin they needed. Their lives started to improve. Trish began studying and made it onto a University course. Things were looking good. Statistics show that most addicts will eventually age out, if they live that long(1). Doubtless, Trish and Tony could have been among them, but time was not on their side.

Reactionary critics of the clinic they attended began to work towards getting their treatment stopped. Trisha worried and fretted and worked tirelessly to convince enemies of her treatment regime that for her and Tony (and others like them) it had become an essential life-line without which their lives and possibly their health, could be destroyed. Despite her efforts – which included meeting Health Authority officials, writing endless letters, leafleting conferences, organizing addicts to make protests and speaking to the media – Trisha and her supporters lost the battle. Her consultant was replaced; the policy at the clinic she and Tony attended changed and things began to fall apart. They were told that in a matter of months they must reduce their drug intake with a view to giving up drugs altogether. Not an easy step to have forced upon you. Think of all the cigarette smokers who can't even cut down. It's not easy to change the habits of a life time, even when you want to – when it's forced upon you, the chances of success are even slimmer. Trisha argued and fought but slowly the reduction continued.

Unable to cope she and Tony began scoring on the black market again and, suddenly, Tony became ill. At first, he thought he had flu but he got worse instead of better and was admitted to hospital. By then it was too late. The bacteria present in Tony's blood as a result of injecting 'street' heroin had reached his heart valves and began to multiply. Tony died just before Christmas, leaving Trisha without a husband and their little girl without a father.

This would never have happened if he had continued to receive treatment from the clinic until he himself was ready to come off heroin. Indeed, Tony is one of 16 former clients of the local drug clinics who have died since Dr Marks was removed and prescribing policies changed. (The figures, of course, are unconfirmed at the time of writing but even sceptics must be aware that there is more than rumour behind the local outcry.) In December 1995, *The Guardian* ran an article on the fact that these deaths were so shocking that Labour had called for a public inquiry(2). Too late for Tony. Suddenly, however, the reductions in scripts were on hold. For how long? Until someone came up with an argument to explain away these needless deaths. Not so. Already the furore has died down and the reductions in prescriptions are continuing.

Heroin users find themselves at the mercy of the whims of those in charge – and don't forget, breaking any habit is not easy. Most heroin users wish they were not addicted but they are and just wanting to come off is only part of the battle. You must feel ready to do so and until then you need a clean, safe supply of drugs to help keep you alive and well. Heroin users are dying as the debates rage on, and the inquiries are planned. Attempts to force them off do not work. Tea and sympathy is no good. They need realistic options. Now.

Notes

1 The point is made in the following work that addicts will age out – but only if they remain alive and well long enough to do so: 'From Stimson and Oppenheimer's findings there would appear to be a spontaneous rate of remission from addiction of 3 per cent per annum, provided the patient lives.' Taken from a paper presented to the Royal College of Psychiatrists, entitled, *Addicts, who cares? What has psychiatry to offer as part of a wider strategy for substance misuse prevention?*, Glasgow, 1995.

2 Pilkington, Edward, 'Labour Seeks Inquiry as more Heroin Addicts Die', *The Guardian*, 16 December 1995.

CHAPTER 12

ℭ *There is a bus out of Rock Bottom*

As things stand, junkies live on the front line. They dodge through a war zone, caught between jack-in-the-box dealers and pop-up policemen. Some can, and do, sink very low. But anyone who really wants to can still find a way out. Last week I met Keith again. I could not believe it. Twelve months ago he looked as if it was all over. He was basically dead, aside from the formalities. He was thin, ill, literally half-starved, a wraith, a walking ghost, cranking marzine in his groin, overdosing all over town, being scooped up from public toilets, doorways, park benches and trundled off to hospital to stumble out and do it all again. Keith was just about finished. Then he had a bit of luck. He overdosed and came to in hospital, strapped to a bed. They pumped him full of vitamins and put him through a straight cold turkey that made him wish he had the strength to murder them all. For two weeks, he lay on that bed plotting vengeance so violent that the visions of the hell he invented for his tormentors made Hieronymous Bosch look like a playground. He yelled and sobbed, cursed and pleaded, but in the end he came through. He started to feel better; he began to get well. It was only then that the truth hit him. As he lay there feeling about as good as a hedgehog that had been flattened by a lorry, he began to be grateful. He was off drugs. Once he realised that he hung on grimly and, for the first time in weeks, he began to smile. He lived, he got well; he grew strong and fit. His gaolers became his saviours.

Back on the scene everyone thought he was dead. They continued to waft back and forth like mist between dealers' houses and their cheerless bedsits, thinking little and doing less. When Keith turned up hale and hearty, clean and cheerful, shock waves crashed across town. Keith got a job. Twelve months later, he still has it. Keith looks so well and happy that a stranger would never guess the truth. Keith is perfectly sane and healthy but he will never stop being grateful to the doctors who took responsibility for his life.

Pete had a similar experience. He died twice in hospital and woke up with a huge bruise on his chest. He had passed through the doorway into death but his doctors had thumped on that door until they brought him back. They won the battle for his life that he had lost. They shamed him into making a stand. Pete is well now. He looks great: chubby, grinning, bouncy, full of witty one-liners and cheeky repartee. Pete is good fun. The grave he dug for himself is empty. He threw his works into it and walked away. He did have a hit six months later, just to see what he was missing. It made him throw up. He was sorry he had wasted the money. He does not want to die and he does not miss drugs. Pete is going to make it. What about you?

CHAPTER 13

ℭ *The shape of things to come? – a postscript*

At first glance it is hard for heroin users to find cause for optimism in the current climate. For one thing, attempts to supply themselves with drugs offer little cause for satisfaction. Increasing pressure on dealers has meant that street drug prices have soared while quality has slumped. Ten years ago street heroin taken from a local Liverpool dealer was described by the police as 70 per cent pure. Today, it is likely to weigh in at 30 per cent or even 20 per cent pure. In cash terms you are paying up to twice as much for drugs that may be a quarter of the strength they were ten years ago. The decline in purity is, of course, matched by a rise in unknown adulterants. Not a comforting thought. On the other hand, the only sizeable experiment in offering a maintenance prescription of pure heroin to British addicts has been run to ground and effectively closed down. It is virtually impossible for most heroin users to obtain pure heroin legally via a clinic or from a doctor.

At the same time, the courts have, on the whole, become less sympathetic to pleas of drug addiction as mitigation. If you aspire to buying larger amounts to keep costs down, (ounces or quarter ounces work out a lot cheaper than buying small 'bags' at £20 a time) you may be open to a charge of supplying. If so, penalties for that offence have increased with additional unpleasant consequences of being found guilty, such as the seizure of assets. A nasty prospect for anyone. I did actually hear of a book shop owner who, while said by his friends to be innocent, was convicted of having the intention to supply heroin and, subsequently, lost his business which had, in fact, been built up over many years of sheer hard work and owed nothing at all to any illegal activities – drug related or otherwise. The man was simply a heroin user with a little more hard cash available than most.

On the brighter side there is now much more interest in the real issues surrounding heroin users. Of course, articles such as, 'Junkies sell deadly Hitler drug to children for £1.' (*News of the World*, 15 October 1995) do, inevitably, still appear but there is also a trend towards much more sincere in-depth reporting of serious issues. *The Independent* and *The Guardian* both regularly deal with developments in treatment strategies and the like in a fair and rational way. Recently, both television and radio have contributed to the more meaningful aspects of the drugs debate. The truth about users and the problems they face is beginning to filter through. Credible individuals from politicians to pop stars have been numbered among those putting their weight behind calls for more sensitive and sensible responses towards the 'drugs problem'.

Ten years ago, when this book was first waiting in the wings for publication I was soundly taken to task for much of what I had written. Two separate firms of lawyers suggested that charges of 'offences against the Obscene Publications Act' and/or 'incitement to criminal acts' could be levelled against me. Cuts were duly made and dark mutterings about the wisdom of the whole project were heard. Indeed, I suspect that only the sums of money already committed to the project spared me from the anguish of seeing my book and my dreams of becoming an author consigned to the nearest bin. Even the line, 'heroin is nice' was selected as a target for the censor's pen. This was likely to send thousands of youngsters rushing headlong to perdition like so many adolescent lemmings. At this stage I put my foot down. I have never been a political zealot but felt that this line helped to make sense of the whole experience of drug addiction. Without it, observers might think heroin users were completely mad; if it was so awful why should anyone take it? I, at least, hoped to tell the truth. Finally, common sense prevailed, the crisis passed and the book crept into print.

Such a conflict would seem ridiculous today. Much of what was considered unthinkable a decade ago is now common knowledge. That, surely, implies progress of a sort. People realise that addicts can and do lead useful lives and hold down even quite demanding jobs. Indeed, some firms are testing hair for traces of drugs before (and after) taking on an employee. Not a nice prospect for the addicted member of staff but undeniable proof that people no longer believe in the once popular image of the scrawny, scruffy, skid-row junkie. They know junkies can use soap like anyone else.

In fact, a social worker I know is now engaged in placing known heroin addicts in full-time jobs with the full knowledge and co-operation of prospective employers. This, surely, represents a potentially major shift in attitudes on the part of some people. Clearly, heroin is no longer quite the big bad 'Bogey Drug' it once was – not for everyone, at least.

Indeed, attitudes seem to be polarizing. On one hand, prohibitionists and scaremongers shout as loudly as ever; lock up your daughters (and sons); life imprisonment for suppliers; abstinence for all. On the other hand, their more liberal counterparts call for greater understanding, more flexible treatment options and even decriminalisation. The heroin user is stuck in the middle, hoping that the smoke raised by the war on drugs will clear and a way forward will come into view. But careers have been based on condemning or supporting drug users. All the foot soldiers and generals will not pack up and go home just like that. There are signs of hope but the armistice is a long way off yet. This is civil war, the most painful and damaging form of conflict; it will not be over until we can find some common ground – or until one side batters the other into submission.

Perhaps, ironically, the very range of drugs available now will work to the advantage of the heroin user. Heroin has become just one problem drug among many. Ecstasy is the current 'Bogey Drug', attracting the most attention with the same extreme views being aired as we have witnessed in the case of heroin: legalize it; control it; make it safe versus ban it; hang suppliers; terrify youngsters with shock horror anti-drug campaigns. The middle ground lies in accepting the fact that most of us do hanker after 'artificial paradises', that the pain, monotony and limitations of life foster an urge to escape, that, as Huxley said, 'the longing to transcend ourselves has always been one of the principal appetites of the soul'. That appetite is shared by users of alcohol, ecstasy and heroin alike. It is the appetite and not the drug which needs to be understood. Perhaps we are beginning to realize that.

ℭ *Services for drug users*

Services available to drug users can be divided under the following headings.

Day projects, voluntary and volunteer organisations

A number of organisations exist to provide help for drug users. Some are well-established projects that receive financial help from the Department of Health and Social Security. Others depend on voluntary workers who give their time without receiving payment. These organisations offer a range of services that may include some or all of the following:

> giving practical help;
> providing support for drug users, their families and friends;
> offering assistance with legal problems;
> assessing medical needs and advising on referral for
>   rehabilitation;
> running counselling services including telephone counselling;
> giving advice in an emergency;
> advising on the formation of self-help groups;
> arranging prison visits;
> providing support and assistance for ex-offenders;
> helping with accommodation problems;
> providing advice, education and training for professionals
>   working in the drugs field.

Some groups also offer help to solvent abusers, those with alcohol or tranquilliser problems and multi-drug abusers. Most of these centres operate on a drop-in basis although appointments may be needed for special help such as individual counselling.

Hospital treatment under the National Health Service

A number of hospitals throughout the country provide treatment for drug users. Most operate a strict catchment area and there is usually a waiting list for hospital beds. Some hospitals provide only in-patient detoxification while others operate only out-patient clinics. Some do not prescribe drugs. In most cases, patients have to be referred for treatment by a general practitioner.

Residential houses

1 *General*
   Throughout the country a number of projects offer residential accommodation to drug users. Some houses exist merely to offer much-needed short-term help for drug users in crisis, while others aim to help with long-term rehabilitation. Some take residents on court conditions or directions and some only accept voluntary referrals. Most of them require patients to be drug-free on entry although a few can arrange medical withdrawal.

2 *Concept houses*
   These organisations usually offer a long-term rehabilitation programme. This often includes intensive group sessions, and houses are likely to operate a hierarchical structure where residents work their way up to positions of greater responsibility. Some provide places for as few as four people, while others can house up to fifty residents at a time. Better-known examples of the concept house are Phoenix House, Alpha House and Inward House. Details of their programmes can be obtained through information centres or from SCODA. Concept houses can usually take people on court conditions.

3 *Christian houses*
   A number of houses are run by Christian staff and operate according to Christian philosophy.

Key addresses

SCODA (Standing Conference on Drug Abuse)
Waterbridge House
32–36 Loman Street
London SE1 0EE
Tel. 0171 928 9500

Provides general information and contact addresses for appropriate specialists, whatever your enquiry. Always a good place to start. Also has a 'dial and listen' service for details of drug agencies. Dial 100 and ask for FREEPHONE DRUG PROBLEMS.

ISDD (The Institute for the Study of Drug Dependence)
Tel. 0171 928 1211

Housed at the same address as SCODA, above. Provides information on research into all types of drug abuse.

Re-Solv (The Society for the Prevention of Solvent and Volatile Substance Abuse)
30A High Street
Stone
Staffs ST15 8AW
Tel. 01785 817885

Only deals with the misuse of solvents, glue sniffing etc. Provides assorted leaflets and educational materials plus useful addresses of agencies who can help abusers and their families.

There are many local day projects, information centres and advisory services. They may offer advice, counselling and referral services. They usually advertise locally or can be traced via SCODA or your GP.

Release
Day time Tel. 0171 729 9904
Night time Tel. 0171 603 8654

Runs a national 24-hour emergency service for anyone who has been arrested or needs legal advice. There are also day and night time telephone services offering advice on general matters related to drugs.

ADFAM National – Charity offering help to families and friends of drug users.

Confidential telephone Helpline on 0171 498 4680

Families Anonymous
Tel. 0171 498 4680

Self-help support group for families of drug users. Branches in many areas of the country.

Hospital Clinics, Community Drug Teams and Residential Services can be found either via a GP or by contacting SCODA for details of local services in your area.

In Scotland, contact Scottish Drugs Forum, 5 Oswald Street, Glasgow G1 4QR (0141 221 1175)
In Wales contact Welsh Office Drugs Unit, Welsh Office, Cathays Park, Cardiff CF1 3NQ (01222 825111)

NA UK Helpline 0171 498 9055
UK Service Office PO Box 1980, London, N19 3LS –
Tel. 0171 272 9040
UK Literature Line (Sale & Distribution of Literature)
0171 281 6123

Narcotics Anonymous (NA) is a nonprofit Fellowship or society of people for whom drugs has become a major problem. (Similar to Alcoholics Anonymous.) Meetings are held regularly in most areas. The only prerequisite for attendance is a genuine desire to stop taking drugs.

TACADE (The Advisory Council on Alcohol and Drug Education), 1 Hulme Place
The Crescent
Salford
Greater Manchester M5 4QA
Tel. 0161 745 8925

Non-government organisation that provides and distributes educational material and training aids.

BAPS
Health Publications Unit
DSS Distribution Centre
Heywood Stores
Manchester Road
Heywood
Lancs OL10 2PZ

Freephone 0800 555 777. Copies of free Dept. of Health Publications available.

❡ Bibliography

Ball, J.C. and Urbaitis, J.C., 'Absence of major medical complications among chronic opiate addicts', *British Journal of Addiction*, vol. 65, no. 2, pp. 109–12, 1970.

Brecher, E.M. and the Editors of Consumer Reports, *Licit and Illicit Drugs*, Boston and Toronto, Little Brown & Co., 1972.

Brill, L., *The Clinical Treatment of Substance Abusers*, Glencoe, Ill., Free Press, 1981.

Courtwright, David T., *Dark Paradise*, Cambridge, Mass., Harvard University Press, 1982.

De Ropp, Robert S., *Drugs and the Mind*, Scientific Book Club, 1957.

DHSS, *Guide to the Misuse of Drugs Act 1971 and to Certain Regulations Made Under the Act*, London, HMSO, 1977.

'Drug Misuser and Social Cost', *British Journal of Hospital Medicine*, vol. 52, no. 2/3, 1994.

Einstein, Stanley (ed.), *The Community's Response to Drug Use*, Oxford, Pergamon Press, 1979.

ERIT 'Towards a Federation of European Professionals working in the Field of Drug Abuse', Platform Position Paper, March 1993, outlining philosophy on drug users agreed by European countries including Belgium, France, Portugal, Switzerland, UK, Italy, Spain and Republic of San Marino.

Finnegan, L.P., 'The effects of narcotics and alcohol on pregnancy and the new born', *The Annals of the New York Academy of Sciences*, vol. 362, pp. 136–57, 1981.

Ford Foundation, A Report to, *Dealing with Drug Abuse*, London, Macmillan Press, 1972.

Garfoot, Dr A., Letter to *The Guardian*.

Glatt, M.M., 'United Kingdom: opiates: use and control measures over the years', in S. Einstein (ed.), *The Community's Response to Drug Use*, Oxford, Pergamon Press, 1980.

Goodfriend, M.J., Shey, I.A. and Klein, M.D., 'The effects of maternal narcotic addiction on the new born', *American Journal of Obstetrics and Gynecology*, vol. 71, pp. 29–36, 1956.

Gray, Mike, 'Liverpool Clinic to Lose Funding on April', Los Angeles, 1995.

Halton Drug Dependency Service, *Estimates of the Prevalence of Use of Illicit Drugs in Mersey Region in 1989*.

Hellawell, Keith, '90% of Kids will be Druggies in 10 Years Time', *The Sun*, 2 November 1995.

Henman, A., *Harm Reduction on Merseyside: The rise and fall of a radical paradigm of health care for illicit drug users*, Liverpool John Moore's University, 29/30 June 1995.

Home Office, *Tackling Drug Misuse: A Summary of the Government's Strategy*, London, Home Office, 1985.

ISDD, 'Major US Studies agree: treatment pays for itself 7 times over', *Druglink*, November/December 1994.

Jamieson, Anne, Glanz, Alan and Macgregor, Suzanne, *Dealing with Drug Misuse*, London, Tavistock, 1984.

'Junkies sell Deadly Hitler Drug to Children for £1', *News of the World*, 15 October 1995.

King, R., essay in S. Einstein (ed.), *The Community's Response to Drug Use*, Oxford, Pergamon Press, 1979.

Kolb, L., 'Pleasure and deterioration from narcotic addiction', *Mental Hygiene*, pp. 699–724, 1925.

Le Dain, G. (n.d.), *Final Report of the Commission of Inquiry into the Non-Medical Use of Drugs*, Ottawa.

Marks, John, 'Addicts, who Cares? What has psychiatry to offer as part of a wider strategy for substance misuse prevention?', Royal College of Psychiatrists, Glasgow, 1995.

Marks, John, 'The Paradox of Prohibition', *Mersey Drugs Journal*. Dr Marks was Director of Mersey Drug Dependency Service at the time.

Marks, John, 'Proceedings of the Royal College of Physicians of Edinburgh', *The North Wind and the Sun*, vol. 21, no. 1, July 1991.

Marks, John, 'Wanted for Murder'.

Marks, John, 'Who Killed the British System?'

Medical Working Group, Department of Health, Scottish Office Home and Health Dept., Welsh Office, 'Drug Misuse and Dependence – Guidelines on Clinical Management.

Millman, Robert B., Cushman, Paul, Jr and Lowinson, Joyce H., *Research Developments in Drug and Alcohol Use*, New York Academy of Science, 1981.

Newcombe, R., 'Methadone Morality', March 1994.

Neuberg, Roger, 'Drug dependence and pregnancy: a review of the problems and their management', *Journal of Obstetrics and Gynaecology of the British Commonwealth*, vol. 77, pp. 117–22, 1970.

North Cheshire Health District, *Annual Report of the Director of Public Health*, 1993.

O'Donohue, Noreen and Richardson, Sue, *Pure Murder*, Dublin, Women's Community Press, 1984.

Palombella, A., *Philosophy Widnes Drug Dependency Unit*, 1991.

Payne-James, Jason J., Dean, Peter J., Keys, Derek W., 'Drug Misusers in Police Custody: a Prospective Survey', *Journal of the Royal Society of Medicine*, vol. 87, January 1994.

Stevenson, Richard, 'Legalisation an Economist's View', *Mersey Drugs Journal*, vol. 2, no. 3.

Toynbee, Polly, 'Ecstasy and the Agony', *The Independent*, 15 November 1995.

Weil, Andrew T., essay in S. Einstein (ed.), *The Community's Response to Drug Use*, Oxford, Pergamon Press, 1979.

Widnes D.D.U. and Halton N.H.S. Trust, private correspondence.

Widnes D.D.U., 'The English System in Widnes, Merseyside'.

Willis, J.H., 'What we don't know about drug addiction', *Speculations in Science and Technology*, vol. 1, no. 5, 1978.

Willis, J.H. and Osbourne, A.B., 'What happens to heroin addicts? A follow-up study', *British Journal of Addiction*, no. 73, pp. 189–98, 1978.

Young, Elizabeth, 'Methadone and Madness', *The Guardian*, 20 August 1994.

❡ Index